Belief, Agency, and Knowledge

Matthew Chrisman is professor of ethics and epistemology at the University of Edinburgh.

His research is focused on epistemology, metaethics, philosophy of language, and political philosophy. He has published widely in these areas, including articles in *Noûs*, *Philosophical Studies*, *Philosophy and Phenomenological Research*, *Philosophy & Public Affairs*, and *The Journal of Philosophy*. He is author of *The Meaning of 'Ought'* and *What Is This Thing Called Metaethics?* He was elected a member of the Young Academy of Scotland in 2016, where he led in creation of the Young Academy of Scotland's Charter for Responsible Debate. He completed his PhD and MA at the University of North Carolina, and his BA at Rice University.

Belief, Agency, and Knowledge

Essays on Epistemic Normativity

MATTHEW CHRISMAN

OXFORD
UNIVERSITY PRESS

Great Clarendon Street, Oxford, OX2 6DP,
United Kingdom

Oxford University Press is a department of the University of Oxford.
It furthers the University's objective of excellence in research, scholarship,
and education by publishing worldwide. Oxford is a registered trade mark of
Oxford University Press in the UK and in certain other countries.

© Matthew Chrisman 2022
© 2021 Publication or dissemination of this manuscript
without written permission of the author is expressly prohibited.

The moral rights of the author have been asserted

First Edition published in 2022
First published in paperback in 2025

All rights reserved. No part of this publication may be reproduced, stored in a retrieval
system, transmitted, used for text and data mining, or used for training artificial intelligence,
in any form or by any means, without the prior permission in writing of Oxford University Press,
or as expressly permitted by law, by licence or under terms agreed with the appropriate
reprographics rights organization. Enquiries concerning reproduction outside the scope of the
above should be sent to the Rights Department, Oxford University Press, at the address above.

You must not circulate this work in any other form
and you must impose this same condition on any acquirer.

Links to third party websites are provided by Oxford in good faith and
for information only. Oxford disclaims any responsibility for the materials
contained in any third party website referenced in this work.

Published in the United States of America by Oxford University Press
198 Madison Avenue, New York, NY 10016, United States of America

British Library Cataloguing in Publication Data
Data available

Library of Congress Control Number: 2022932392

ISBN 978–0–19–289885–2 (Hbk.)
ISBN 978–0–19–899342–1 (Pbk.)

DOI: 10.1093/oso/9780192898852.001.0001

The manufacturer's authorized representative in the EU for product safety is
Oxford University Press España S.A. of Parque Empresarial San Fernando de Henares,
Avenida de Castilla, 2 – 28830 Madrid (www.oup.es/en or product.safety@oup.com).
OUP España S.A. also acts as importer into Spain of products made by the manufacturer.

For Dylan and Meryl

Preface

When I asked my father to paint a picture for the cover of this book—and hasn't he done it beautifully!—he considered the title and said, "Well, I know what belief and knowledge are, but what are agency and normativity?" His insightful question captures the central puzzle of this book.

We all intuitively understand what it is to believe something, and it's easy to recognize differences between merely or even truly believing something, and genuinely knowing it. But knowledge is not just different from other kinds of belief—it's *better*. It is something we *should*, at least sometimes, pursue. And when we have a knowledgeable belief, we *should* normally maintain it and stand prepared to share it with others. Insofar as these 'should's pertain to our understanding of knowledge, they are a species of what most philosophers would recognize as "epistemic" rules or (more vaguely) norms. (The intended contrast is with ethical normsativity, though as we will see there may be an ethical dimension to epistemic normativity.)

Having identified some epistemic norms, we might say that activities such as inquiring, investigating, observing, recalling, reasoning, integrating, discussing, and debating are amongst the various ways that people exercise their "doxastic" (i.e., belief-involving) agency in accordance with epistemic norms. That is to say, we don't focus on bodily action with effects outside of a person's mind but rather on the various intellectual activities that pertain to their beliefs (though we needn't insist on a sharp line between what's in the mind and what's outside the mind). Then, I want to say that exercising one's doxastic agency is a central part of what it is to be not only a fully human person, but also a lover of wisdom, i.e., a philosopher.

To a first approximation, then, this book is about how, in the abstract, all of these epistemic norms and doxastic activities work to generate and expand knowledgeable belief amongst lovers of wisdom.

People's intellectual interests vary, of course. Some of us are interested in abstract theoretical topics, others in the political history of modern states, others in the mating patterns of hermaphroditic flatworms, others in the evolution of NBA defenses, and others still in the plight of Britney Spears. Personally, I love it all, including knowing about *how* knowing works across these various domains. Maybe that's why I chose a career in philosophy, but I think most people are philosophers to an extent. And this book pertains to all of us philosophers. In it, I investigate the nature of human belief in its relation to our exercise of doxastic agency, the content and force of epistemic norms, and the deeply human practice of keeping track of how well each other's beliefs live up to these norms.

When I began to study philosophy academically, I was impressed by the model of the individual intellect: thinking hard and mostly in solitude about a topic, ultimately expressing a novel and insightful vision for how to understand the world, and then offering it to the rest of us, fully polished. I spent a lot of my time in college in the library! Whether reading Plato, Aquinas, Descartes, Hume, Kant, Wittgenstein, Sartre, Sellars, or Rawls, one can easily get wrapped up in their unique mode of argumentation, imagining that the goal of being a philosopher is to create something like what each of them created, apparently from scratch and in relative isolation. I have come to think, however, that this is *not* generally how human knowledge is created and spread—be it knowledge about the meaning of life or the location of the nearest shop selling wine.

Humans live in deeply interconnected and interdependent ways, and our intellectual pursuits are no exception. Furthermore, in the normal course of life, we form a great many of our beliefs so fast and automatically that it would be more than a bit strained to say that most of our belief-forming cognitive activity is something we individually choose or control. Moreover, the evolutionary and social forces shaping the intuitive ways we naturally think and process information seem to operate in a mostly subterranean way that bypasses anything traditional philosophers would recognize as a faculty of reason.

These observations reveal cracks in the "Great Man" theory of the history of philosophy, but they also challenge the very assumption that belief and knowledge have much to do with the exercise of some kind of agency, or even that there are valid epistemic norms. How can there be things people really should or should not believe, if belief formation is mostly automatic? Why would we ever think someone constrained by arational evolutionary and social pressures is responsible for what they believe? But, if we really value knowledge in the way we seem to do, how could there *not* be true epistemic normative evaluations pertaining to intellectual activity for which people are responsible? This book represents my attempt to address the challenge expressed in these questions.

For decades if not centuries, analytically-minded epistemologists have sought to explain the difference between true belief and knowledge by investigating the concepts of 'belief' and 'knowledge', and the way they are mediated by concepts such as 'justification', 'reliability', 'warrant', 'evidence', and 'reasonableness'. This project has often taken the form of an analysis of what it means to say that an individual S knows that *p*. But it has also taken other forms, such as genealogical, bio-functional, or pragmatic explications of the concepts involved in attributing knowledge to an individual. I think this project has taught us many interesting things about belief and knowledge, but I don't think it has taught us very much about the connection between these and doxastic agency and epistemic normativity.

Because of this, as I see things now, the most interesting epistemological questions are not (mainly) about what it means for an individual to know something, but about how people relate intellectually to other members of their epistemic communities, and how in turn those communities are maintained, expanded, and diversified by people related intellectually to each other. Accordingly, in this book, I often address specific debates within what might be called "individualistic" epistemology, but I always do so with the underlying aim of showing how examining the relevant issues through the lens of a resolutely *social* epistemology has significant promise for enriching our understanding of these issues.

Just to give one example I touch on briefly in Chapter 7, but hope to pursue in more detail in future work: Many people are interested in what it takes for people's beliefs to be free. To answer this question, the traditional approach would investigate the conditions of individual cognitive control and rational self-determination of particular beliefs: What does it take for an individual to have or lack the ability to make up their own mind about whether some proposition is true? In contrast, a more social-epistemological approach encourages investigation into the social and political conditions leading to or protecting against the dominating influence of *other people* on interconnected people's systems of beliefs. Propaganda, indoctrination, epistemic bubbles, advertising, adaptive preferences, and class interests can all detract from freedom of belief, whereas good education, well-organized distribution of and reliance on expertise, open and transparent channels of communication, and political norms of free speech can all enhance freedom of belief—how can we explain that? The metaphysics and politics of doxastic freedom are both valid projects, but they can't be done in isolation, and I think epistemologists have spent a lot of effort on the former, without doing enough to explore the latter.

The role of our social interconnectedness has been all the more salient to me over the past two years. I completed this book during the global Covid-19 pandemic, which has upended the ways we live together, both epistemically and medically. Daily bulletins with public health knowledge have become the norm, and now it isn't only the epidemiologists who regularly worry about the role of shared appreciation of scientific expertise and collective knowledge in keeping people safe and alive. From the political role of the anti-vax movement to the markedly different responses various governments have taken towards their own scientific experts, from the statistical basis of r-numbers to the imperfect state of scientific knowledge about the effectiveness of facemasks—recent conversations amongst friends and family have taken a distinctively social-epistemological turn.

More personally, it has been an tough couple of years. For months and months, seeing extended family and gathering in-person with groups of friends was prohibited, and my wife Jean and I were trying to continue working while being primary school teachers for our young children with limited support. Plus, I was supposed to be writing a book!

Nevertheless, the past two years have also had their blessings. My daughter Meryl, who wasn't even born when I wrote my previous book, has gone from being a relatively unformed preschooler to reading me books at night, having definite opinions about how to deejay the car stereo, and shooting a mean fade-away jumper. And my son Dylan continues to amaze me with his perseverance in the face of dyslexia, his ability to remember detailed plot twists in *Lord of the Rings*, and his extremely detailed knowledge and love of the natural world. Furthermore, I have been extremely proud to be married to a dedicated frontline medical worker in Britain's NHS, and grateful to have a partner who keeps things real.

So, although I've probably said (and definitely thought) a bit too much that I wish they could leave me alone while I'm working on this book, the intensifying interconnectedness amongst Jean, Meryl, Dylan, and me as a family unit has been a positive by-product of the pandemic. And, while that was facilitated by my seeing friends and colleagues both in Edinburgh and around the world much less, I've been extremely grateful to those who have remained in contact through email, group messages, and online talks. These things have surely fed my inclination to see all sorts of philosophical questions through more social lenses.

This book was written while I enjoyed a sabbatical from the University of Edinburgh and a British Academy Mid-Career Fellowship. Without the support of these organizations, and their flexibility in the face of homelife challenges during the pandemic, I would not have been able to complete it. I appreciate this support and flexibility. I'm also grateful to Peter Momtchiloff and anonymous reviewers for Oxford University Press for encouraging me to organize the book as a series of three parts that are individually accessible but also related in a way whose unity is hopefully apparent. These readers also helpfully pressed me to address a number of objections and to make various chapters more reader-friendly. So you should be thankful to them too!

While I was writing the book, I had the pleasure of working with the Young Academy of Scotland on a project to create a charter for responsible public debate. This fed into my participation in the Royal Society of Edinburgh's Post-Covid 19 Futures Commission. I was previously skeptical of the buzzword "knowledge-exchange" sometimes thrown around contemporary academia to refer to the two-way interaction between theoretical knowledge created in universities and practical knowledge created outside of universities. But these opportunities have been great cases of knowledge exchange with the project of this book. I am especially grateful for what I have learned in this context with Alice König, Peter McColl, and John O'Connor.

Much of the material in this book derives from papers published previously, which I have updated, expanded, and integrated. I am grateful to the publishers for permission to re-use the previously published material. I hope readers who have encountered any of the papers in the past will want to see how they have changed and now form a package, but for convenience, here is a description of the genesis of this package:

- Chapter 2 derives from "The Normative Evaluation of Belief and the Aspectual Classification of Belief and Knowledge Attributions." *Journal of Philosophy* 109 (10) (2012): pp. 588–612.
- Chapter 3 derives from and significantly expands on "Performance Normativity and Here-and-Now Doxastic Agency." *Synthese* (2017): pp. 1–9.
- Chapter 4 derives from and significantly expands on "Epistemic Normativity and Doxastic Agency." *Noûs* 52 (3) (2018): pp. 508–529.
- Chapter 5 derives from "The Aim of Belief and the Goal of Truth." In *Self, Language, and World: Problems from Kant, Sellars, and Rosenberg*, edited by Jim O'Shea and Eric Rubenstein, pp. 188–208. Atascadero, CA: Ridgeview Press (2010).
- Chapter 6 derives from "Ought to Believe." *Journal of Philosophy*, 105 (7) (2008): pp. 346–370.
- Chapter 7 is almost entirely new material, but jumps off from some ideas sketched in "Believing as We Ought and the Democratic Route to Knowledge." In *The Ethics of Belief and Beyond: Understanding Mental Normativity*, edited by Sebastian Schmidt and Gerhard Ernst, pp. 47–70. New York: Routledge (2020).
- Chapter 8 derives from "From Epistemic Contextualism to Epistemic Expressivism", originally published in *Philosophical Studies* 135 (2) (2007): pp. 225–254.
- Chapter 9 is also almost entirely new material, but draws on ideas sketched initially in "From Epistemic Expressivism to Epistemic Inferentialism." In *Social Epistemology*, edited by Adrian Haddock, Duncan Pritchard, and Alan Millar, pp. 112–128. Oxford: Oxford University Press (2010).

I also want to acknowledge my truly inspirational intellectual community in the Philosophy Department at the University of Edinburgh. There are so many great colleagues and students here pursuing fascinating projects, and there is an amazing willingness of people to trade papers or have pick-up philosophy chat. I feel an embarrassment of intellectual riches, and am saddened by the way the Covid-19 pandemic has kept us out of the halls of the Dugald Stewart Building. Many people have given me helpful feedback, not only on the original papers but also on the development of them into this book. I am very grateful for this, especially for the feedback from James L. D. Brown, J. Adam Carter, Michelle Dyke, Sandford Goldberg, Graham Hubbs, Sophie Keeling, Aleks Knoks, Lilith Lee, Arturs Logins, Michael Lynch, Barry Maguire, Berislav Marušić, Anne Meylan, Miriam Schleifer McCormick, Ram Neta, Makan Nojoumian, Angie O'Sullivan, Franziska

Poprawe, Andrés Soria Ruiz, Sebastian Schmidt, Melanie Sarzano, Mona Simion, Tillmann Vierkant, Sam Wilkinson, Silvan Wittwer and surely a few others who I am forgetting. Grace Garland swooped in at the last minute and gave the book a full read, making many helpful editing suggestions.

When I wrote my PhD thesis at the University of North Carolina from 2003 to 2006, I saw myself as working in ethics and epistemology, mining interesting comparisons and contrasts between these normative domains. In doing this, my principal guides were Geoffrey Sayre-McCord and Jay Rosenberg. My first book, *The Meaning of 'Ought'* might be seen as an expression of the meta-ethical side of this stellar education, and as such it was heavily influenced by ideas I learned with Geoff. The present book could then be seen as an expression of its meta-epistemology side, and so I see it as heavily influenced by the ideas I learned with Jay. Jay used to say that the most important property for a dissertation to have is being done. But I'm still sad that Jay died before I got a chance to hear if he thinks my dissertation is finally not just done but also good. My memory of him lives strong in several of the following chapters.

Matthew Chrisman

October 2021

Contents

1. Introduction ... 1
   1.1 Epistemology as a Normative Discipline ... 1
   1.2 The Axiological and Deontological Dimensions of Epistemic Normativity ... 2
   1.3 Overview and Preview ... 7
   1.4 Inspiration ... 12

PART I. DOXASTIC AGENCY

2. Beliefs Are States Not Performances ... 21
   2.1 Introduction ... 21
   2.2 A Brief Introduction to Verbal Aspect ... 24
   2.3 Belief Attributions Aren't Performance Descriptions ... 26
   2.4 Two Responses to the Objection ... 30
   2.5 Conclusion ... 34

3. Belief Formation Doesn't Exhaust Doxastic Agency ... 38
   3.1 Introduction ... 38
   3.2 Inquiry and Deliberation in the Age of Involuntarism ... 39
   3.3 Reliabilist Virtue Epistemology Renewed ... 43
   3.4 Conclusion ... 49

4. The Activity of Maintaining Beliefs ... 55
   4.1 Introduction ... 55
   4.2 Belief as Active Self-Determination ... 56
   4.3 Challenges for Beliefs as Active States ... 59
   4.4 What Is Belief Anyway? ... 63
   4.5 Doxastic Agency in the Maintenance of Systems of Belief ... 67
   4.6 Conclusion ... 70

PART II. EPISTEMIC NORMS

5. The Aim of Belief and the Goal of Truth ... 81
   5.1 Introduction ... 81
   5.2 The Radical Argument Outlined ... 82
   5.3 The Radical Argument Explained and Defended ... 85
   5.4 Constitutive Aims and Evaluative Norms ... 92
   5.5 Social Epistemic Goals ... 95
   5.6 Conclusion ... 97

6. Doxastic Involuntarism and 'Ought to Believe' 101
   6.1 Introduction 101
   6.2 Rejecting "Ought Implies Can" 102
   6.3 Sellars on State Norms 105
   6.4 Ought to Believe as a State Norm 108
   6.5 Conclusion 113

7. Social Foundations for Epistemic Normativity 119
   7.1 Introduction 119
   7.2 Epistemic Norms and Individual Interests 122
   7.3 Hobbesian Epistemic Normativity 126
   7.4 Rousseauian Epistemic Normativity 130
   7.5 Responses to Two Objections to the Rousseauian Account 135
   7.6 Two Clarifications about the Scope of Social Foundations for Epistemic Normativity 137
   7.7 Conclusion: Speculation on Doxastic Freedom and Responsibility 139

PART III. EPISTEMIC DISCOURSE

8. From Epistemic Contextualism to Epistemic Expressivism 149
   8.1 Introduction 149
   8.2 Two Problems for Epistemic Contextualism 151
   8.3 Ethical Speaker-Relativism and the Two Problems 156
   8.4 Ethical Expressivism and the Two Problems 158
   8.5 Epistemic Expressivism Solves the Two Problems 161
   8.6 Conclusion 164

9. From Epistemic Expressivism to Epistemic Inferentialism 172
   9.1 Introduction 172
   9.2 What Is Epistemic Inferentialism? 173
   9.3 Epistemic Inferentialism Is Better than Epistemic Expressivism, Part 1 176
   9.4 Epistemic Inferentialism Is Better than Epistemic Expressivism, Part 2 180
   9.5 Epistemic Inferentialism Fits Well with Social Accounts of Epistemic Normativity 183
   9.6 Conclusion 186

Bibliography 191
Index 215

1
Introduction

1.1 Epistemology as a Normative Discipline

Do we really have knowledge of ordinary facts, the nature of reality, the existence of other minds, or even our own mind? Assuming we do, how exactly do we acquire such knowledge through processes such as perception, reasoning, testimony, and introspection? What is knowledge, anyway? These questions lead to questions about epistemic concepts. How is the concept of knowledge related to the concepts of truth, belief, and justification? What about the concepts of cognition, certainty, understanding, and wisdom? Developing fully satisfactory answers to these core questions of epistemology requires a better understanding of epistemic normativity and, more precisely, of the normative character of epistemic concepts. That is the topic of this book.

One might propose to understand epistemic normativity simply as those standards one's belief must meet in order to count as knowing something. Typically, these standards are thought to relate to, but exceed, truth, and to involve things such as justification, reliability, competence, warrant, and reason. One might then study epistemic normativity by seeking to better understand these concepts.

Unsurprisingly, then, these concepts have been at the core of epistemology for centuries, and philosophers have often regarded them as normative concepts. However, that way of thinking about the normative character of epistemic concepts is too thin to capture what I aim to discuss in this book, and it doesn't seem to warrant calling epistemology a normative discipline. After all, though there *are* standards for the correct application of every concept, we don't always think of those standards as rules or norms constituting a distinctive *normative* topic for investigation, or conceive of those concepts as normative in any distinctive or interesting sense. To be a football, for instance, something must be a ball, be inflatable, and satisfy other standards. But that doesn't mean that we recognize a distinctive category of football normativity, or treat the concept of a football as normative in some interesting sense meriting philosophical investigation.

Moreover, epistemologists ask normative questions that don't have clear analogs in other areas—questions such as: Are there constitutive norms of belief? Does assertion have an epistemic aim? How do epistemic and non-epistemic values figure in scientific inquiry? What distinguishes epistemic from practical reasons? Why do we prize knowledge over true belief? Do the rules of theoretical rationality have categorically binding normative force? How should a subject's credence update diachronically in light of new evidence? What are the intellectual virtues? When are we allowed to bootstrap into justifications for our beliefs? Is testimony a *sui generis* source of knowledge? How does epistemic credit distribute across a community of knowers? When and how are people blameworthy for believing falsehoods? Is there a distinctively epistemic form of injustice? Are there specifically epistemic reasons to prefer democracy over other forms of governance?

It is these sorts of questions that lead me to think that epistemic concepts are distinctively normative in a way that merits further philosophical investigation into the topic of epistemic normativity. I will touch on the issues involved in many of these questions throughout this book, yet my interest is not in fully answering them here, but rather in better understanding the broader topic of epistemic normativity. To that end, and by way of specifying further the topic of this book, in the next section I distinguish two dimensions of recent discussions of normativity in epistemology.

1.2 The Axiological and Deontological Dimensions of Epistemic Normativity

When discussing normative issues in epistemology, some epistemologists are concerned with *axiological* questions. They note an ancient and persistent intuition that knowledge is valuable. Of course, when the truth value of p matters to one's practical purposes, knowledge is better than ignorance about whether p. However, the intuition is not (mainly) about instrumental value. In many cases, knowledge that p and unknowledgeable true belief that p would seem to have the same instrumental value, but we're still inclined to think that knowledge is a worthier aim.[1] Moreover, it's not just that *some* people happen to care non-instrumentally about knowing certain truths; it's rather that knowledge is something we *all* should sometimes want, over and above any value it may carry for satisfying our particular desires or interests. Further still, when someone knows something, they seem praiseworthy in a non-moral and non-instrumental way; we evaluate them positively in attributing knowledge to them, crediting them with achieving something that is good in a distinctively epistemic sense. If that's right, then knowledge seems to have a mysterious normative pull on us beyond any instrumental or moral value it may carry. How does that work?

Another area of inquiry into normative issues in epistemology concerns broadly *deontological* questions. Epistemologists note that when we know that p, we can be said to believe what we ought to believe with respect to p, in some ostensibly special "epistemic" sense of 'ought'. This idea is supported by the observation that, when we believe what we epistemically ought to believe, we may nonetheless believe something we don't want to believe, something that thwarts our interests in other ways, or even something that manifests a morally dubious character. Indeed, many epistemologists would say that endeavoring to believe what we ought to believe is not some derivative or secondary part of our lives; this activity is a crucial part of having a self-conscious take on what is the case, and it structures how members of epistemic and moral communities relate to each other. Accordingly, one might say that we ought to believe in certain ways investigated by epistemology, much like we ought to act in certain ways investigated by ethics. It is for this reason that we sometimes blame each other for believing badly, and we sometimes praise each other for believing in warranted, justified, or reasonable ways. These ought-related ideas are not about what is statistically normal, but are rather about what is required or favored by various distinctively epistemic norms, which we appeal to in blaming and praising each other's beliefs. This raises important deontological questions, such as: What are the contents of the "robust" norms relevant to whether we count as knowing something, how do they get their normative grip on us, and what do they presuppose about our capacity to live up to them?

The axiological and deontological dimensions of the topic of epistemic normativity are interesting in their own right, but, as I understand it, much of the epistemological literature addressing them is motivated by two vague but attractive ideas: philosophical naturalism and doxastic involuntarism. So, I next want to explain how these ideas structure the project of this book.

Philosophical naturalism is the idea that we should seek to answer philosophical questions in a way that takes seriously a broadly scientific understanding of what reality is like, which includes conceiving of ourselves as part of nature and subject to the same sorts of forces as other animals. This approach to philosophy has its roots in Aristotle, Spinoza, Hume, and Nietzsche, and it became dominant in the wake of the scientific revolution, and especially in the last seventy-five years. Of course, almost no contemporary philosopher would reject a commitment to taking science seriously in thinking about philosophical questions, but I have two more specific ideas in mind when I speak about philosophical naturalism here.

First, I think we should embrace a form of *object naturalism*, according to which the only stuff that is real is natural stuff, i.e., the sorts of things that are subject to natural forces that are studied by the natural sciences. This means that we should reject explanations that appeal to non-natural or supernatural entities, properties, or forces. So, it is an obvious nonstarter to claim that knowledge has some special non-natural property, whose possession simply makes it the case that we ought to pursue it. Moreover, there is pressure from object naturalism to assimilate the kind of value that we think knowledge has, to other sorts of value that are more easily recognizable in a scientific picture of reality.

However, commitment to object naturalism is consistent with recognizing that not *all* truths can be articulated only in terms of scientific concepts, or concepts reducible to scientific concepts. In my view, there are truths not only about how things are (in reality), but also about what people ought to do, think, and feel. And I think the latter kinds of truths don't have to be reducible to the former kinds in order to help make sense of the value of knowledge within philosophical naturalism. To this end, in Part II of the book, I will argue that knowledge is valuable in large part because of the stabilizing role it plays in social cooperation that is comprehensible only from within the perspective of various normative commitments we have toward each other as members of a community.

Second, I think we should also embrace a form of *subject naturalism*, according to which the natural sciences have a lot to teach us about ourselves, and in particular about the operation of our minds.[2] Accordingly, where theories in epistemology or philosophy of mind imply or presuppose some claim that is in tension with dominant scientific views, we should take that as a reason to rethink those theories. More specifically, as we will see, some prominent theories about the value of knowledge seem to be inconsistent with dominant views in linguistics about the meaning of the word 'believes', and I think that is an important problem for those views.

Of course, philosophical questions and theories can stretch and challenge various kinds of scientific understandings of reality, which are often highly provisional and subject to further experimentation. But the subject naturalist contends that we should seek to answer philosophical questions in ways that integrate the best science, in pursuit of a synoptic and intersubjectively defensible account of humans and the reality in which we live.

However, a commitment to subject naturalism is importantly weaker than the idea that philosophy should aim to be *scientific*, or to offer a fully third-personal perspective on the world that strives for a "view from nowhere". Our understanding of subjectivity, intersubjectivity, and normative issues about what people ought to do, think, and feel are all central concerns of philosophical inquiry that seem to me to be outside the scope of describing and explaining reality. So, although our philosophical accounts of these things need to cohere with our best scientific understanding of what humans are like, I don't think philosophy should strive for a view from nowhere on these issues.

Turning next to doxastic involuntarism. Descartes's reference in *Meditation IV* to "the freedom to give or withhold...assent"[3] to a belief and his idea that judgment requires the cooperation of the intellect and the will, are sometimes interpreted by epistemologists as placing a form of *voluntarism* at the heart of what is involved in believing as we epistemically ought to believe.[4] However, pushback comes already with Spinoza and Hume; and I think *in*voluntarism about belief is now rightly regarded as the dominant view in contemporary epistemology, despite some opposition.[5] Put simply, this is the idea that we don't typically voluntarily choose what we believe, like we usually voluntarily choose how we act. I will discuss this idea more in Part I of the book, but let me register two comments here in order to specify a version of this doctrine that I take as orientation for what follows.

First, involuntarists shouldn't deny that we have the capacity to choose to *do* things, even to engage in purely "intellectual" actions, that affect what we believe. We can obviously voluntarily change the world in ways that we know will change what we believe (open a book, turn on the news, flip a light switch). It's also plain that we can voluntarily think about a question and reflect on topics that we know will cause us to form new beliefs, though we don't know in advance which ones. It also seems that we can voluntarily subject ourselves to various forms of indoctrination or mindfulness that might be reasonably expected to alter our belief systems in predictable ways. None of that, however, impugns the idea that belief is importantly different from action in its interaction with the will.

Second, although belief is not *chosen*, I think it is wrong to equate this with the idea that belief just *happens* to us, somewhat like a headache. So, I disagree with the sentiment Heil expresses, writing, "our beliefs seem mostly forced on us.... they come to us unanticipated and unbidden" (1983, 357). It may be right that we find ourselves believing certain things rather than choosing what to believe, and I certainly recognize the category of pathological beliefs that remain with us unbidden. However, it seems wrong to me to think of belief on analogy to a headache, as some merely empirical condition of our minds which we passively host. Unlike our headaches, our beliefs typically reflect our subjective take on what is the case, which is something we participate in, at least partly as agents, and not wholly as patients. We can often cite reasons *for which* we believe things, and these are not merely facts that cause us to believe things—they are *our* reasons for believing what we believe. And even when someone cannot easily cite their reason for believing something, or we suspect what they say isn't the real reason, there are still usually reasons that could be cited to rationalize what they believe. This distinguishes beliefs from mental conditions that are forced upon us like headaches.

I have already indicated in passing some ways that doxastic involuntarism and philosophical naturalism bear on the axiological and deontological questions about epistemic normativity, but let me spell this out in more detail. From a naturalistic orientation, I suspect it is relatively easy to accept that people value certain things for their own sake, and that other things are derivatively valuable for the way they relate instrumentally to things people value for their own sake. However, making sense of a robust form of epistemic value that transcends what people *happen* to value and pertains to what people *should* value is more challenging. For one thing, such categorical value looks "queer", in the meta-ethical sense that its features seem quite different from everything else we know about through observation and broadly scientific investigations of reality. For another thing, it can seem rather strained to maintain that knowledge has a kind of categorical normative pull, thus making it the case that we ought to pursue knowledge, if one also thinks that we don't choose what we believe. Sure, maybe we can influence what we believe by engaging in various actions, but if our beliefs aren't generally a reflection of our choices, then why would achieving knowledgeable belief be something for which we might merit a distinctive kind of non-moral and non-instrumental epistemic praise? Why would we think people ought to pursue it?

Related to this, a lot of recent cognitive psychology suggests that our thought processes are heavily influenced by evolved biases and heuristics that are pretty good at keeping us alive, but insensitive to various kinds of epistemic reasons for belief, and easily manipulated by advertising, framing, and wishful thinking.[6] Similarly, social psychology and political science suggest that large swaths of our conceptual repertoire are heavily influenced by in-group socialization and class interests. These forces are good at making social groups cohesive and cooperative, but they are often insensitive to various kinds of epistemic reasons for belief and are easily manipulated by group dynamics that have nothing to do with increasing knowledge.[7] And, more generally, many psychologists and sociologists think we are highly unreliable in even knowing what we believe. Although simple and obvious beliefs might easily be brought to occurrent consciousness, these scientists insist that our cognition is typically much more dominated by tacit beliefs, cultural presuppositions, partial credences, vaguely appreciated inferential dispositions, and belief-like implicit biases—none of which are easy to bring to consciousness.[8]

In light of these observations from the science of human cognition, I am skeptical of the practice in much current epistemology of focusing on simple and obvious cases of belief, and asking whether the subject has adequate enough grounds for the belief to count as knowledge (assuming it is true). While most epistemologists will grant that we don't choose to have these beliefs, it is usually assumed that we are in a position to know what we believe and why we believe it (both the proximate cause and the rational basis). But the picture in psychology, sociology, and political science is of credal states that look much messier and opaquer than that. Maybe these states are not properly regarded as beliefs, but even if they merely shape our beliefs subconsciously, it seems strange to evaluate what we believe with the sort of robust normative 'ought's mentioned earlier. How can we be properly praised and blamed for the opaque subterranean operations of unconscious biases, ingrained heuristics, socially inculcated credal tendencies, and so on?[9]

In sum, the basic puzzle is this: If knowledge ascriptions entail that someone believes as they normatively ought to believe, and this is viewed as a distinctively valuable and praiseworthy way for one's mind to be, then believing must normally be within the scope of our immediate agency; but involuntarism and naturalism commit us to the idea that our agency touches our beliefs only atypically and indirectly.

In light of this puzzle, my overarching project in this book is to develop a better understanding of the axiological and deontological dimensions of epistemic normativity from within the perspectives of philosophical naturalism and doxastic involuntarism. I think there is a pervasive temptation amongst naturalists and involuntarists to adopt deflationary attitudes toward these dimensions of epistemic normativity, by arguing either that they are based on a misunderstanding of the science of human nature, or that they can be easily assimilated into other normative phenomena that don't appear mysterious from a naturalistic point of view. For example, Quine famously argues that epistemic normativity is just instrumental normativity with the end of truth.[10] And many philosophers claim in one way or another that epistemic 'ought's are just the standards deriving from the evolved functions of our cognitive systems.[11] However, if knowledge is something we all should sometimes want over and above any instrumental value it carries, and if endeavoring to believe as we ought is an importantly central part of how we think of ourselves as human, then it doesn't seem to me that epistemic value can be (simply) instrumental value for the end of truth, or (merely) derivative of evolved functions.

Throughout the book, then, doxastic involuntarism and philosophical naturalism operate as orientating assumptions, but not—at least as I see things—as motivation to adopt a deflationary attitude toward epistemic normativity. Doxastic involuntarism and philosophical naturalism make the robustness of epistemic normativity something that needs to be explained rather than explained away.[12] More specifically, I take seriously the idea that knowledge is distinctively valuable and that there are distinctively epistemic and agency-implicating norms for belief. I seek to advance our understanding of how this could be the case, given commitments to the involuntarist distinction between action and belief and to a broadly naturalistic understanding of human beings and our place in nature.

1.3 Overview and Preview

The book is organized around three related topics: doxastic agency and the objects of epistemic normative evaluation (Part I), the content and nature of epistemic norms (Part II), and the meaning and communicative role of epistemic normative statements (Part III). The axiological and deontological dimensions of epistemic normativity run throughout the book, with a somewhat heavier focus on the latter. Subject and object naturalism and doxastic involuntarism serve as orientating assumptions mostly in the background. I will make cross-references between the book's sections, but the idea behind my organization is to provide three more-or-less self-contained treatments of different topics in meta-epistemology.

My aim is not to provide a comprehensive theory of epistemic normativity. I'm not even sure what that would look like, but I'm pretty sure it would require integrating answers to various meta-normative questions in epistemology with answers to similar questions in other normative domains, and this is not my aim here. That being said, in many cases, the three sections of this book represent the expansion, repackaging, and integration of ideas that I have previously defended or floated in standalone papers over the past fifteen years, in which I have often profited from comparing and contrasting various meta-normative issues in epistemology with parallel issues in ethics. My intention in expanding, repackaging, and integrating this material here is to try to show how I see the core claims defended in many of these papers not as a merely opportunistic crossover from ethics to epistemology, but as contributing to a distinctive and valuable approach to core issues in epistemology.

Part I is anchored around the concept of doxastic agency. If we assume that action is teleological in that it always involves pursuit of an end, and that all genuinely robust norms relate to how agents ought to pursue ends, then belief seems like it's going to have to be action-like for there to be genuine norms of belief.[13] Accordingly, some philosophers have sought to assimilate epistemic value and 'ought's to other apparently less mysterious kinds of normativity by arguing that, even if belief is not, strictly speaking, an action, it is still rightly seen as a way agents pursue the end of truth. (I consider this view in Chapter 2.) Alternatively, even if we don't assume that belief itself is a pursuit of the end of truth, there remains a pervasive tendency amongst many epistemologists to think that epistemic norms must really apply to something conceptually nearby that *is* action-like in this way, such as inquiry or deliberation or belief-formation. (I consider this view in Chapter 3.)

I want to motivate a more complex picture of the nature of doxastic agency and epistemic normativity, which turns on taking seriously various conceptual distinctions between *states* of belief, *processes* of belief-formation, and *activities* of belief-system maintenance. More specifically, I think it's important that we recognize that, as states, beliefs are unchanging through time, and so believing something is not itself a way of pursuing some end. This might encourage a focus on belief-formation, which I think is rightly viewed as a dynamic cognitive performance that can be evaluated for how well it results in the end of someone's having a true belief. However, we'd be mistaken to assume that the etiological issue of a belief's formation exhausts or even captures the main way we exercise agency in and over belief. The always ongoing atelic activity of belief-system maintenance is, in my view, more central to doxastic agency and more important for understanding epistemic normativity. This is a key idea driving many of the arguments in this book.

I understand belief here as the mental state we are normatively evaluating when we evaluate whether someone has knowledge. And, in my view, such evaluations turn on how well the belief manifests epistemically optimal integration with other aspects of our cognition, via the activity of belief-system maintenance. Dispositions to engage in various cognitive performances of belief-formation, whether intellectual actions such as inquiry and deliberation, or cognitive performances such as processing perception, testimony, or memory, will often be important aspects of our evaluation of this integration, even if they are not specifically what we are evaluating when we evaluate whether someone knows something.

Part of my motivation for that idea is to develop a picture that makes space for various kinds of interpersonal distribution of epistemic responsibilities in our epistemic communities, which requires others to contribute to maintaining a believer's system of belief. This picture offers a new, more social way to think about the axiological dimension of epistemic normativity, whereby the value of an individual knowing that p sits not within the individual, but at the level of the epistemic community which is in part responsible for the pursuit, maintenance, and transmission of knowledge. I think this kind of distribution of epistemic responsibilities provides an attractive way to make sense of children and nonhuman animals believing as they ought to believe, even when we are reluctant to think that they have much capacity to exercise their own doxastic agency in or over their beliefs. Additionally, I think this kind of distribution helps to make sense of the socially externalist nature of many of our concepts, whose warranted application often depends on the intellectual activity of experts and institutionalized practices of intellectual deference.

Part II of the book turns the focus to epistemic norms, asking what they have to be like in order to be genuinely normative yet still apply to our doxastic states rather than to things we actively do. In my way of thinking about the content of epistemic norms, the normative evaluation of belief is central, but normative evaluation of other aspects of cognition remains important. For me, the reason belief remains central has to do with the more specific content of epistemic norms and their relation to importantly social activities that depend upon and expand knowledge shared amongst groups of people.

Since knowledge production and belief-system maintenance are largely social affairs, at least in us humans, we should focus more of our theoretical efforts on understanding how these interpersonal phenomena work. Not only do we learn most of what we know from other people, and work together to expand our common knowledge of issues of mutual interest, the very conceptual resources necessary to know most things depend on a complex system of recognition of, and deference to, other people as potential sources of knowledge on specific topics.

A common barrier to this more social way of thinking about epistemic normativity is the idea that we should comply with epistemic norms, to the extent that we should, not because this promotes cooperative social integration, but because *beliefs aim at the truth*; thus, complying with these norms is how one pursues the truth in forming and maintaining a belief. In Chapter 5, I consider this popular though quixotic idea. Many epistemologists will insist that, even if belief doesn't have truth as a literal aim, truth is still the epistemic telos of doxastic activity, and that we can separate epistemic evaluations of doxastic activity and belief from non-epistemic activities in terms of their relation to truth. I suspect this line of thought is guilty of tacit reliance on the assumption that all genuine norms evaluate something action-like and so telic, and I want to resist this assumption in developing a more complex picture of epistemic normativity. But to do so, I think it is helpful to see what we can salvage from the idea that truth is the distinctively epistemic telos. So, in the chapter, I respond to some arguments from philosophers who reject the idea that truth has normative significance in epistemology. This discussion provides a context for showing how one can embrace the thought that truth functions as a constitutive norm for belief, even while rejecting the thought that doxastic activity and belief literally aim at truth. The function of truth, in my view, is not in determining means to an end, but rather in determining the sorts of evaluations of each other's beliefs that matter *epistemically*.

When the operation of epistemic normative evaluations is understood in relation to this conception of the normative significance of truth, I think we can begin to make sense of the way in which implicit reference to epistemic norms is used in training each other in forming beliefs and maintaining belief systems, such that the activity is largely automatic and unreflective. On my view, then, epistemic norms function somewhat like syntactic rules of a language, which are orientated toward communication. These "rules" are not typically followed directly by the person forming a belief or saying a sentence; rather, they are implicitly referenced and sometimes explicitly deployed by others who teach someone how to think and speak, and by others who regulate whether someone thinks and speaks appropriately. However, the analogy goes only so far. Syntactic rules of a particular language are conventional and have merely hypothetical normative force, which derives from the usefulness of coordination for the purposes of communication, whereas I tend to think of epistemic norms as nonconventional and, as I indicated earlier, having categorical normative force.

Accordingly, in Chapters 6 and 7, I seek to develop an account of how this might work. In Chapter 6, I argue that we should think of claims about what someone epistemically ought to believe as adverting to norms which are not "action norms" that believers follow in the formation of belief, but rather "state norms" that are relevant to the evaluations others make of a believer, to keep track of who is or isn't a good source of knowledge on various issues. By reflecting on the role that various state norms play in guiding the action of those responsible for the states, and by recognizing that epistemic communities are partly constituted by relationships of epistemic dependence (e.g., teacher–student, expert–policymaker, someone with a particular experience–someone making generalizations), I think we can make space for normative claims about someone's belief that imply (in various ways) normative claims about the behavior of others rather than about the believer in question. We may of course refer to norms of belief in trying to influence someone's beliefs, but I deny that claims about what someone ought to *believe* normally have the same prescriptive or recommendatory function as claims about what someone ought to *do*.

This is because I view belief-system maintenance as a more socially distributed practice than the traditional Cartesian picture would allow. Moreover, I see this social practice as sitting on top of evolved cognitive dispositions, often exploited as cognitive hacks, that our evolutionary past has baked into our ways of processing of information about the world. Because these hacks are fallible, however, the interpersonal practice of belief-system maintenance must also function to systematically correct the ways we are naturally inclined to process information about the world, which this practice has done and will continue to do to expand drastically our knowledge and understanding about specific topics.

In light of this idea, in Chapter 7, I consider several accounts of the source of epistemic normativity. How do epistemic norms, conceived as state norms applying primarily to states of mind, get a grip on us? Why do we care in the ways that we manifestly do about whether people's beliefs meet the epistemic standards necessary for knowledge? To explain how epistemic norms could be nonconventional and have categorical normative force, I develop two ways of grounding epistemic normativity in our essential sociality. The thought common to both is that epistemic norms have their grip on us because of our membership in a community of information-sharers and because of our joint participation with others in the epistemic practices of this community. On these views the force of epistemic norms is still explicable in terms of our individual interests, but the relevant interests are ones we have only as essentially social beings. I use this idea to explain the categoricity of epistemic norms by appeal to the way this membership and participation in an epistemic community is inescapable, unlike membership and participation in particular linguistic communities.

This takes me into Part III of the book. Many naturalistically inclined philosophers have worried about the ontological commitments of normative language that implicitly recognizes categorical normative force. I hope that seeking to ground epistemic normativity in our essential sociality goes some way to addressing this worry. But the main thing I want to argue in response to this worry is that we don't need to view epistemic discourse as committing us *ontologically* to categorically normative properties as features of reality. This is because there are attractive nondescriptivist accounts of normative language that can and should be extended to epistemic normative language. These hold that epistemic normative claims are not descriptions of features of reality.

This idea is based in a more general idea, which I defend in other work, that there is an important difference between thought and talk about how reality is, and thought and talk about how someone ought to act, think, or feel.[14] In light of this distinction, I see the normative as distinct from the descriptive. (This ties into the perennial idea that there is a conceptual divide between 'ought' and 'is'.) I have no illusions that these aspects of our thought and discourse can be analytically separated into something like a nondescriptivist semantics for normative words and a descriptivist semantics for non-normative words. Indeed, I doubt that there are any words that are used only normatively. Nevertheless, I think it is a pervasively mistaken assumption in much of epistemology that our epistemic normative claims are purely descriptive of reality. Overcoming this assumption is the key to squaring my view of epistemic normativity with object naturalism. As a result, I argue in Chapter 8 that knowledge claims embed a normative component, and that we should explain the meaning of this normative component in nondescriptivist terms.

The idea that normative claims are not descriptions of reality is most commonly associated with expressivist views in meta-ethics. And I explain how it is pretty easy to get from a relatively popular contextualist view about knowledge attributions, to an expressivist view that parallels one recently prominent way of developing ethical expressivism. However, I have long thought that expressivism is not the best way to develop a nondescriptivist account of an area of discourse. So, in Chapter 9, I go on to articulate and motivate the kind of nondescriptivist, but also non-expressivist, approach to explaining the purpose and meaning of epistemic discourse that I favor. In other work, I have defended the idea that ought-claims should be treated along inferentialist lines recognizing their distinctive normative-modal semantic potential, which generates a view of normative discourse according to which normative concepts function as something like "inference-tickets", rather than descriptions of reality or expressions of noncognitive attitudes.[15] So the view of epistemic discourse ultimately defended here is an application of that idea to the specific case of epistemic claims.

Because I don't think of the book as presenting a complete and unified account of epistemic normativity, but rather as investigating three important topics relevant to understanding epistemic normativity, I expect readers can profitably read individual sections without reading the whole book, or in a different order to how they are presented. Moreover, many of the chapters were originally written as standalone papers, and I have tried to retain some of their legibility as such (at the minor cost of repetitiveness at the beginning of each chapter). Nevertheless, I intend for a unified picture to emerge from the book. To amplify this and come at the unifying themes from a more historical perspective, I want to conclude this introductory chapter by discussing two philosophers whose ideas and approaches to the normative character of epistemic concepts have inspired a lot of my work in epistemology, though they have figured in my previously published papers only occasionally.

1.4 Inspiration

One of my inspirations throughout this book is E. J. Craig, whose well-known book *Knowledge and the State of Nature* (1990) is famous for effectively challenging the project of articulating non-circular necessary and sufficient conditions for the correct application of 'know' in ordinary language. To challenge this methodology,

Craig proposes an alternative. He suggests we should first attempt to explain the purpose of the concept of knowledge and then use this as a guide to its correct application. Furthermore, because he supposes that the concept of knowledge is universal in human communities, he suggests that hypotheses about what that concept does for us should proceed from naturalistically plausible but relatively limited conceptions of the social and biological ecosystems in which this concept might have emerged. This is the "state of nature" he refers to in his title, and it is a version of what I called subject naturalism earlier. Craig then seeks to tell a "just-so" story, arguing that a concept functioning very much like our concept of knowledge could have originated out of a primitive situation of keeping track of good informants in a cooperative social arrangement, where each individual's stock of useful information was limited, and different community members could be expected to have access to different pieces of useful information.

One might suppose this means Craig thinks that one counts as knowing that p only if one would be a good informant about whether p, which is of course going to vary quite dramatically from situation to situation, depending on why someone needs the information and what would happen if they were mistaken. However, an important lesson Craig teaches is that an account of the purpose of the concept of knowledge needn't be an account of a necessary (or sufficient) condition for the application of the concept.

Craig's account of why this is the case turns on the idea (part of his just-so story) that there was a proto-concept of knowledge that individuals used for keeping track of good informants, and that this developed over time through a process of "objectification" as it became more and more important to keep track of good sources of information without having to depend on the individual needs of particular people. I'm deeply influenced by Craig's suggestion that the concept of knowledge has its core application in interpersonal interactions occurring in mostly cooperative social circumstances of limited individual access to important information that is diversely distributed.[16] Because of this, my methodological tendency in what follows is to give primacy neither to the purely first-personal and subjective view from within one's mind, nor to the third-personal and objective view from outside of human practices, but rather to the first-personal-plural/second-personal and intersubjective perspective of social practices that involve attributing belief and knowledge to one another.

Although Craig doesn't present it in this way, I see this as part of a broadly constructivist methodology in philosophy.[17] Rather than imagining that we have a full grasp of what justice or knowledge or numbers are, such that enough careful reflection on these things would allow us to understand their nature, constructivists seek to deploy our partial understanding of such things to provisionally identify the sorts of socio-ecological circumstances where using the relevant concept will advance our shared interests. They then work from an account of the circumstances of use to further illuminate the target concept via more detailed conceptions. But they also work from these more detailed conceptions to further specify the circumstances, where using the target concepts is useful.

Throughout this book, I apply this holistic methodology to various concepts that are relevant for understanding epistemic normativity. It's a version of the familiar reflective equilibrium methodology but, crucially, it takes as inputs not just intuitions about when a concept applies but also ideas about the collective practical purposes toward which a concept is used. A major upshot for epistemology, I think, is that knowledge is not best studied as some pre-theoretically delineable phenomenon or fixed substance whose nature we can investigate while being sure that the investigation itself isn't changing the object of investigation. This is what I think Craig means when he writes, "Knowledge is not a given phenomenon, but something we delineate by operating with a concept which we create in answer to certain needs, or in pursuit of certain ideals" (1990, 3).

This insight is also present in the other major inspiration for this book. Wilfrid Sellars is perhaps best known amongst epistemologists for his groundbreaking essay *Empiricism and the Philosophy of Mind*, in which he famously mounts a sustained and multi-fronted critique of the "myth of the given." Related to this, he provocatively suggests that, "in characterizing an episode or state as that of knowing, we are not giving an empirical description of that episode or state; we are placing it in the logical space of reasons, of justifying and being able to justify what one says" (1956, sec. 36). On the face of things, this suggestion might be interpreted as expressing a commitment to a fairly stark form of normative non-naturalism and rationalistic internalism. This is a view that conceives of knowledge as something in an irreducibly normative realm of reality—"the space of reasons"—that only beings with the conceptual and linguistic wherewithal to justify what they say can have.

This is not the way I think this passage or Sellars's overall epistemology should be understood. In my view, Sellars means instead that it is a mistake to think of the study of knowledge on analogy to the study of natural kinds, such as water, or natural phenomena, such as gravity. With regards to these topics, we often engage in "empirical descriptions" of reality which aim to answer, ultimately, to the way things are, independently of our thoughts about reality or our various purposes when living in it. By contrast, Sellars's idea is that knowledge attributions shouldn't be seen as attempting to describe some empirically discoverable fact, but rather as attempting to ascribe a status to someone's belief within a particular normative framework the tacit commitment to which is partially constitutive of a human practice.

Accordingly, I don't think Sellars's talk of the "space of reasons" should be understood as reference to an independent realm of reality which is somehow irreducibly normative in its character, but rather as an evaluative stance we take up toward ourselves and others when thinking about what we ought to believe. This is a form of what I called object naturalism earlier. It inspires me to follow Sellars in thinking that knowledge attributions are not (primarily) descriptions of a person, but rather evaluations of someone's belief as having a particular epistemic status: roughly, being what a person ought to believe *epistemically speaking*.

Although I will stress the role of knowledge and belief attributions in interpersonal cooperative situations in order to make sense of the normative aspect of epistemic discourse, I think we can also find ourselves in those situations with young children and family pets. And once we have the concepts of knowledge and belief on the table, we can use these tools for purposes that are slightly different from the ones most prominent in interpersonal circumstances (e.g., for talking about what a computer or an institution knows). Because of this, I think we shouldn't interpret the famous passage from Sellars as proposing to exclude these beings from the scope of normative epistemic evaluations. We should instead interpret him as proposing to locate knowledge attributions on the "ought" side of the divide delineating claims about how reality is from claims about what various kinds of beings ought to do, think, and feel.[18]

Beyond epistemology, Sellars is well known for his meta-philosophical idea that a central task of philosophy is to integrate the "manifest" and "scientific" images of humans in the world. As he understands these, both are evolving, culturally distributed pictures of how we humans fit into, think about, and act on reality, but they seem to be in stark tension.

In the manifest image, reality contains all of the ordinary things of commonsense, such as tables, sunsets, money, countries, obligations, and, of course, people. Furthermore, we humans are assumed to be typically reflectively intelligent beings who deploy mostly reliable perceptual and reasoning capacities in our acquisition of knowledge about reality. And our actions are understood as intentionally chosen based on our understanding of reasons, values, and norms. In the scientific image, in contrast, everything in reality is constituted by subatomic particles interacting according to mostly deterministic laws that it is the task of science to discover. This means that we humans are, variously, collections of atoms subject to the laws of physics, complexes of biochemical reactions selected for by evolution, and social animals whose ways of interacting are mostly determined by our particular ecological niche. In this picture, human action is constituted by movements that are ultimately explicable in causal rather than normative terms, and ordinary "knowledge" is treated as, at best, conditioned approximations that can serve as the springboard for developing better scientific understanding of what nature is really like. These are, of course, just "pictures". But I think Sellars is right that one of the core projects of post-enlightenment philosophy is to reconcile them.

In this context, a commitment to naturalism is sometimes understood as the view that the scientific image is progressing toward an objectively true account of what nature is really like, and the manifest image is irreparably false and ultimately eliminable, even if initially inevitable and often useful for our everyday lives.[19] However, I don't think this is his view, and in any case, the kind of philosophical naturalism that orientates this book is not one which treats the scientific image as developing toward an ultimate replacement of the manifest image, and not one that would eschew manifest concepts or truths simply because they cannot be reduced to scientific concepts and truths. This is inspired by Sellars's metaphor of a "stereoscopic" (1963, 10) fusion between images, rather than a gradual replacement of one by the other.

In this regard, what is important for my purposes here is the way he proposes to distinguish the material content of reality from the conceptual forms of thought that might be exercised in reference to it. Regarding the material stuff, he's a reductivist: what exists and the way it behaves are ultimately explicable in terms of the (material) entities and (natural) forces posited by the best science. However, regarding the conceptual content of thought, he's a non-reductivist: the content of the concepts we think with and the ways we think with them contain important and ineliminable ideas that are not reducible to scientific ideas. This is what I think he means when he writes, "When I talk about the in principle replaceability of the manifest image by the scientific image, I do so with respect to the content of the world, its material and not with respect to those forms which concern the normative, the obligatory, the correct, the incorrect, the valuable" (2009, 221–22).

In epistemology, I think we can see the tension between these images reflected in the tension between first-personal and third-personal approaches toward understanding doxastic agency and epistemic normativity. So, my attempts at a more first-personal-plural/second-personal and intersubjective approach could be seen as contributing to the pursuit of a stereoscopic vision. I don't see the subjective form of understanding as reducible to the objective form of understanding, or vice versa; but, in pursuing an intersubjective form of understanding, I think both can be brought into the sort of fuller three-dimensional understanding that is exemplified by stereoscopic vision.

In the following chapter, I begin Part I, which is about the objects of epistemic normative evaluation and the role of cognitive agency in these objects. More specifically, I shall argue that beliefs are the primary objects of epistemic normative evaluation, despite the fact that we don't generally exercise our cognitive agency in choosing belief like we exercise our practical agency in choosing action. This will also provide a context to consider various theories of what belief is. In my view, belief is potentially a lot of different things, but importantly it is always a *state* of mind.

Notes

1. The question, of course, traces back to Plato's *Meno*. It was revived in contemporary theories of knowledge, especially by Kvanvig (2003a), Zagzebski (2003), and Percival (2003). See also the helpful discussions of the various value problems in epistemology in Pritchard (2007, 2010). Further useful discussion in Riggs (2007), Greco (2009b), Kappel (2010), Hazlett (2013), and Meylan (2013).

2. For discussion of the difference between object naturalism and subject naturalism, see Price (2004).
3. Descartes (1641/2006, 34).
4. See Della Rocca (2006) for useful discussion of subtleties in Descartes's position on the voluntariness of belief and the freedom we have in believing.
5. For statements and defenses of involuntarism, see especially Price (1954), B. Williams (1973), Kornblith (1982), Heil (1983), Clarke (1986), Alston (1988), Plantinga (1993b), Audi (2001), Adler (2002), Levy (2007), and Nottelmann (2007 and 2017). I say earlier that this is the dominant position, but it depends of course on how exactly it is stated, and there are many epistemologists who defend some kind of voluntarism. See especially, O'Hear (1972), Grovier (1976), BonJour (1980, 55), Holyer (1983), Ginet (1985), Chisholm (1991), Heller (2000), Steup (2000, 2017), Weatherson (2008), McCormick (2011, 2014), Coady (2012, 12–15), Chakravartty (2017), Lockie (2018, chs 3–4), and Rinard (2018) for various defenses of qualified forms of voluntarism about belief.
6. I have in mind especially dual-systems or -processes views which hold that, although some cognitive processing is slow, deliberate, and effortful, most cognitive processing is fast, automatic, and effortless. For discussion, see especially, Evans and Over (1996), Sloman (1996), Stanovich (1999, 2011), Kahneman and Frederick (2002), Barbey and Sloman (2007), Evans (2008), Carruthers (2009), Kahneman (2011), and Stanovich and West (2000). See also Vierkant (2022) for argument that this view is incompatible with doxastic involuntarism. But the idea that most cognition is quick and automatic is not limited to dual-systems or -processes views. Gilbert, Krull, and Malone (1990) discuss apparent blocks to rejecting false information. Mercier and Sperber (2017) defend and discuss other views that fall outside of the dual-systems or -processes view.
7. See, for illustration, the various examples discussed in Hardwig (1985), Coady (2012, chs 5–6), and Cassam (2019).
8. For discussion, see Bem (1970), Lycan (1986), Gopnik and Meltzoff (1994), Carruthers (2009), and Mandelbaum (2014).
9. Some epistemologists suggest that we should distinguish between two kinds of belief. So-called "basic" or "animal" belief is treated as the product of automatic cognitive systems, such as perception, whereas "higher-order" or "reflective" belief is treated as within the purview of human reasoning, deliberative rationality, and sometimes even voluntary choice. Although I accept that there are differences between these levels, I demur at the suggestion that we can treat them separately, or that normative epistemology should be primarily concerned with reflective belief. Even basic perceptual beliefs constitute part of a subject's take on the world, and they are arguably held for reasons in a way that headaches are not held for reasons. And, often, when we attribute knowledge, we imply that an agent has a variety of beliefs sitting at various levels of any supposed cognitive hierarchy. So, as long as we assume that knowledge requires belief that meets certain epistemic standards, we are going to need to make sense of the way in which even the most basic perceptual beliefs are normatively evaluated.
10. See Quine (1969, 1986) and Maffie (1990). See Kornblith (1995, 2002, ch. 5) and Wrenn (2006) for discussion of some problems and attempts to address them.

11. See Plantinga (1993b), Kornblith (2002, ch. 5), and Bird (2007, 94). For related discussion, see Burge (2010), Graham (2010, 2012, 2014), Simion, Kelp, and Ghijsen (2016), and Simion (2019, 2025).
12. For a contrasting viewpoint, see Côté-Bouchard (2017), who argues that epistemic facts merely imply some norms rather than involve any sort of robust or categorical normativity. As evidence, he suggests that, in contrast to moral facts, epistemic facts lack five features that might be thought to be characteristic of genuinely normative facts: necessary connection with value, necessary connection with desire, necessary autonomy from non-normative facts, necessary connection with motivation, and necessary connection with control. I won't respond in detail to Côté-Bouchard here, but I think there is a conflation between a putatively necessary connection between some fact and one of these features, and a putatively necessary feature of some concept and one of these features. I think we can agree, e.g., that not all knowledge is valuable, while still insisting that our concept of knowledge is a concept some of whose application marks out something as distinctively valuable. And similarly, I think we can agree, e.g., that not all claims about what someone ought to believe presuppose that the believer has control over their beliefs, while still insisting that the concept of what someone ought to believe is a concept whose application depends on the idea that somebody has control over what some people believe.
13. In introducing a recent volume of collected essays from leading epistemologists on epistemic normativity, Littlejohn writes, "The chapters in this collection are concerned with epistemic norms.... What must we do to conform to the norms that govern belief, deliberation, assertion, and action?... In offering an account of epistemic norms, we have to specify the relevant norm act (e.g., asserting p, believing p, treating p as a reason for believing q, etc.)" (2014, 1). This is an example of the assimilation of norms of belief to norms of other sorts of doings, which runs throughout that volume and many others like it.
14. For an overview of my inferentialist development of this idea, see Chrisman (2023).
15. See especially Chrisman (2016a, ch. 6), Chrisman (2018b), and Chrisman (2023).
16. For further developments of the Craigian idea, especially in a more social direction with which I am sympathetic, see Kusch (2009), Henderson (2009 and 2011), Kappel (2010b, 72–73), Greco (2010, ch. 5), Graham (2015, 268), Henderson and Greco (2015, 5), Hannon (2019, ch. 5), and Queloz (2021, ch. 6).
17. Compare Korsgaard (2003) and Street (2010). Unlike many Kantian constructivists in ethics, I do not think of Craig as pursuing a constitutivist version of the constructivist project, whereby the relevant concept is thought to be somehow necessary for any agent or thinker. For Craig, the concept of knowledge may be universal amongst humans, but that is because of our particular ecological-social niche and contingent cognitive limitations.
18. Compare O'Shea (2007, ch. 7), DeVries (2005, ch. 5), and Rosenberg (2007, ch. 1).
19. Granted sometimes Sellars seems to embrace this view. See Sellars (1971, 396–397), where he describes himself as "an extreme scientific realist." There is also his famous claim that "in the dimension of describing and explaining the world, science is the measure of all things, of what is that it is, and of what is not that it is not" (1956, sec. 42).

PART I
DOXASTIC AGENCY

2
Beliefs Are States Not Performances

2.1 Introduction

Perhaps this is a caricature, but a lot of traditional epistemology seems to be implicitly Cartesian in the way it assumes that belief is analogous to action.[1] Both belief and action are treated as possible objects of reasons-responsive choice (though different kinds of reasons), and both are understood as possibly resulting in something valuable (though different kinds of values). Traditionally, epistemologists then debate what is reasonable or rational to believe, much like ethicists might debate what is reasonable or rational to do. In this vein, we could blame people for not believing as they epistemically ought to believe, much like we blame people for not acting as they ethically ought to act. Moreover, this Cartesian assumption provides a tidy way to think about axiological and deontological dimensions of epistemic normativity. Knowledge can be understood as a species of belief chosen for reasons to do with what is epistemically important (truth, justification), such that we can understand its value in terms of what is achieved through such choices. And it makes sense to subject our beliefs to deontological evaluations because they fall within the ambit of our voluntarily exercised agency.

Now, however, most naturalistically inclined philosophers of mind hold that beliefs are the automatic results of cognitive systems evolved to process information quickly for the purposes of survival, rather than anything that we explicitly choose in pursuit of values.[2] For this and other reasons, most epistemologists now (rightly) regard Cartesian voluntarism as mistaken. We can make sense of evaluating cognitive systems, like other physiological systems, for how reliably they perform their function. But it becomes challenging to explain why knowledge is more valuable than true belief in a distinctively epistemic and seemingly categorical way, and the deontological evaluation of what people believe becomes similarly puzzling.

These kinds of puzzles have motivated many reliabilist epistemologists, whose theory of justification is based on the reliability of belief-forming methods, to try to beef up their conception of epistemic normativity. In this vein, in decades of influential work, Ernest Sosa has combined traditional forms of reliabilism with ideas from virtue theory in ways that promise an attractive and integrated response to the axiological and deontological puzzles about epistemic normativity. One of his key ideas is to grant naturalists and involuntarists that belief is not an action, and that belief is mainly formed automatically, while still insisting that belief fits alongside action in a broader category of performances to which the categories of what he calls "performance normativity" can be fruitfully applied.[3] Ultimately, I think this won't work, and it is the project of this chapter to explain why—along the way we will learn several important lessons about belief and epistemic normativity.

Although there are many subtle and fascinating details I will have to gloss over, here is Sosa's main idea in his own words: "Beliefs are a special case of performances, epistemic performances. When a belief is correctly attributable to a competence exercised in its appropriate conditions, it counts as apt and as knowledge of a sort" (Sosa 2007, 93). Similarly, he begins a later book writing:

> Belief is a kind of performance, which attains one level of success if it is true (or accurate), a second level if it is competent (or adroit), and a third if its truth manifests the believer's competence (i.e., if it is apt). Knowledge on one level (the animal level) is apt belief. (2011b, 1)

Importantly, Sosa thinks that all performances can be evaluated along the three different dimensions: whether they are successful (which he sometimes calls "accurate"), whether they are skillful (which he sometimes calls "adroit"), and whether the success is because of (in the sense of "manifests") the skill, rendering the belief "apt". Further, he thinks of these performances as manifestations of person-level cognitive virtues. They are not the mere reliable execution of subpersonal processes, but rather are traits *of* a person. These traits, when virtuous, can result in knowledge that is rightly understood as something valuable: an achievement of the cognitive agent.

To explain this, Sosa uses an analogy to an archery shot. An archery shot may succeed or not at hitting a target. Hence, accuracy is one way to evaluate an archery shot. But skill is a different way to evaluate an archery shot, since some successful shots are unskillful but lucky, and some failures are skillful but unlucky. So, skillfulness, i.e., adroitness is a second way to evaluate an archery shot. Moreover, when an archery shot is both skillful and successful, this success may or may not be because of the skill. Sometimes, success is due to luck even though the shot was skillful. For example, Sosa considers a skillful shot blown off target by an unlucky wind but blown back on target by a lucky wind. Thus, a third way to evaluate an archery shot that is both accurate and adroit is in terms of whether it is apt, in the sense that its success is because of its skill.

The important point is that a performance that is good in the first way may fail to be good in the second way, and vice versa; but a performance that is good in the third way is good in the first way *because* it is good in the second way. Intuitively, being good in the third way—that is, in his terminology, being "apt"—is better than being good in the first and second ways, even when these are concurrent but not related.

Then, Sosa's core strategy is to apply this framework to belief. If he is right that belief is a kind of performance, his virtue-epistemological framework has the potential to address both the axiological and deontological puzzles in ways that are sensitive to some of the motivations for more traditional reliabilist approaches as well as competing evidentialist approaches, but better than both of them. For the axiological question, Sosa suggests that we think of belief as a subject-level performance that is successful when it is true and skillful when it is justified. By being a subject-level performance, belief is treated as a central part of our subjective take on reality, and not some merely empirical condition of our subjectivity (in contrast with headaches).

Next, to accommodate and diagnose Gettier (1963) cases, where a person's justified true belief is luckily correct and so not typically thought to be knowledge, Sosa argues that a belief does not amount to knowledge unless it is true *because* it is justified—that is, successful because skillful (as opposed to successful because lucky). Assuming that apt performances are better qua performance than merely successful and skillful performances, Sosa's view correctly predicts that knowledge is better than belief that falls short of knowledge, even Gettierized true and justified belief.[4] He writes,

> it would always, necessarily be proper for one to prefer one's knowing to one's merely believing correctly. This is just a special case of the fact that, for any endeavor that one might undertake, it is always, necessarily proper for one to prefer that one succeed in that endeavor, and indeed succeed aptly, not just by luck. (2010, 189)

Crucially for making progress on our understanding of epistemic normativity from a broadly naturalistic point of view, this way of addressing axiological issues in epistemology does not require the assumption that beliefs are actively chosen, like actions are often thought to be. After all, many person-level performances, cognitive or otherwise, are automatic, unchosen, and even outside the domain of conscious control. For example, a person successfully does something when they exercise their linguistic competence to understand a sentence in their native language; however, this is not (typically) something they choose to do or something they can consciously control. It makes sense, nonetheless, to talk about whether and when someone *ought* to understand some sentence. Similarly, Sosa thinks it makes sense to talk about whether and when someone *ought* to engage in the performance of believing something. Hence, conceiving of beliefs as performances also promises to remove much of the mystery surrounding our practice of deontologically evaluating beliefs.

So, it initially appears that Sosa's virtue epistemology provides impressive traction against both of axiological and deontological puzzles about epistemic normativity, while avoiding the assumption implicit in the Cartesian picture that belief is chosen like action, and improving on what was already attractive about the reliabilist picture. The idea that beliefs are performances promises to put virtue epistemology à la Sosa on very attractive middle ground in contemporary epistemology. Moreover, Sosa and others have gone on to develop this framework in various ways that provide nuanced and robust accounts of all sorts of epistemic phenomena, such as the relationship between animal knowledge and reflective knowledge, the role of perception and higher-order judgments about perception in knowledge, the place for interpersonal evaluations in fostering a society of knowers, and so on.[5] Nevertheless, there is an important problem at the very heart of the program, and I think understanding it will put us on a better course for getting at both the axiological and deontological dimensions of epistemic normativity.

2.2 A Brief Introduction to Verbal Aspect

The problem is that belief simply cannot be a performance, and by extension knowledge cannot be properly understood as an apt performance of believing.[6] This is a corollary of the piece of philosophical common sense that belief and knowledge are *states*. And states and performances are fundamentally different kinds of things; one is by its nature stative and unchanging, whereas the other is by its nature active and changing. Virtue epistemologists inspired by Sosa may be inclined to reject this thesis as nothing better than philosophical dogma standing in the way of important progress on the axiological and deontological puzzles. But I think the thesis is not only philosophical common sense, it is also enshrined in ordinary common sense via the meanings of the words we use to talk about belief and knowledge. In what follows, I want to demonstrate this by taking a detour through a bit of linguistic theory, which turns out to be relevant not only for appreciating what I see as a systemic problem in virtue epistemology, but also for motivating my proposed alternative framework for working toward better accounts of the axiological and deontological dimensions of epistemic normativity.

It is common in linguistics to characterize the occurrence of verbs in various phrases and sentences in terms of tense (e.g., past, present, future), mood (e.g., indicative, subjunctive), and voice (e.g., active, passive). Linguists also characterize the occurrence of verbs in terms of *aspectual* categories. Here, the terrain is more complex and less familiar, and there is not as much agreement about what to call the aspectual categories, or how they are linguistically marked in languages such as English. However, it is widely agreed amongst linguists that there are interesting interactions between grammatical categories, such as the simple, perfect, and progressive forms of verbs, and semantic features of verb phrases, such as the way they include ideas of change, duration, or telicity.[7] Linguistic theories of aspect seek to explain this syntactic-semantic interaction.

The classic typology of English verb phrases is due to Kenny (1963, 171–186), who distinguishes between "statives" and "nonstatives"—that is, verb phrases referring to states, such as "He owns the house," and verb phrases referring not to states but rather to something that happens or occurs. Then, harking back to Aristotle (1924, 1048b),[8] Kenny distinguishes within the latter category between "activities" and "performances"—that is, between verb phrases referring to occurrences that have no necessary endpoint, such as "He is tinkering on the house," and verb phrases referring to occurrences that have some necessary endpoint, such as "He is building the house," Vendler (1957) argues that we should divide the latter category into what is sometimes called "accomplishments" and "achievements", based on whether the verb phrase refers to something nonpunctual but telic, such as "He is building the house," or punctual and telic, such as "He is (just now) completing the house."[9]

Don't worry about Kenny's and Vendler's specific terminology. Their philosophical interests were in the philosophy of agency, but the types of linguistic tests we can use to aspectually classify a verb phrase in one of these categories apply to verbs other than verbs of agency. This is why it is now common to use more neutral terminology.[10]

In any case, the general idea behind aspectual typology is that verb phrases falling into one or another of the categories can be distinguished in terms of a number of semantic features, such as whether their referents are conceived to be dynamic, durative, or telic.[11] Moreover, we can use various linguistic tests, which turn on the interaction between syntactic and semantic features of a sentence, to determine which of these features are possessed by the relevant verb phrase. I've outlined these with my preferred terminology and some illustrative examples in Figure 2.1. But the precise names of the various categories are somewhat arbitrary; what's important is not the names but how features such as dynamism,

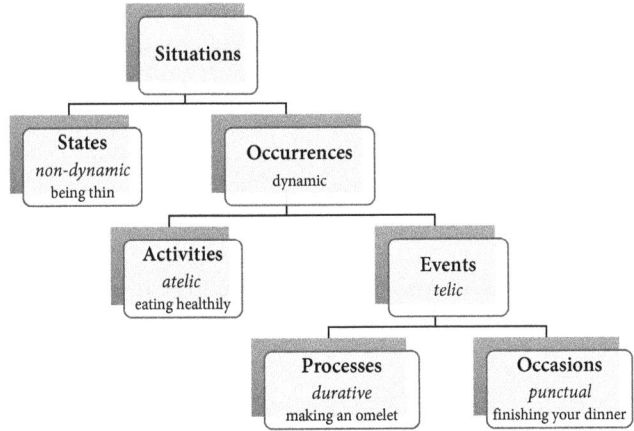

Figure 2.1 Verb phrase aspect typology

telicity, and durativity divide up the terrain of possible situations. What is dynamic involves change over or at a time. What is telic involves direction toward an endpoint or aim. What is durative takes time.[12]

The important point about this typology for my purposes is that it allows us to devise linguistic tests to aspectually classify arbitrary sentences of our language (at least the logically atomic ones) as descriptions of states, activities, processes, and occasions.[13] It is probably easiest to appreciate how this works by applying some tests to specific examples. Doing so will also provide several points at which we can call into question Sosa's claim that belief is a kind of performance. (My basic contention will be that descriptions of paradigmatic performances always fall under a different aspectual category, usually *processes*, than that of belief and knowledge attributions.)

One might worry that an argument based on linguistic tests for English is too parochial, as epistemology is concerned with phenomena that have nothing specifically to do with this particular language. However, I treat these linguistic tests as providing clues about the concept expressed by the English word 'belief', which can of course be expressed in other languages. Different tests would be needed to find similar clues from other languages, but they would still be clues about the underlying conceptual structure.

2.3 Belief Attributions Aren't Performance Descriptions

With these tools from semantics to hand, let's next consider belief attributions. According to the typology illustrated in Figure 2.1, states differ from occurrences in that they are nondynamic. And we can test for whether a verb phrase refers to something dynamic by considering the semantic contrast between simple and progressive uses of the verb. Some of the literature on aspectual classification suggests that the mere availability of the progressive (*-ing*) form in English is a marker of occurrences as opposed to states. This is encouraged by the fact that the progressive is available in sentences such as

(1) a. He is jogging. (activity)
     b. He is making an omelet. (process)
     c. He is (just now) finishing his dinner. (occasion)

which convey something happening or occurring, that is, something dynamic, while the progressive is not available in paradigmatic state descriptions, such as

(2) a. He is owning the house. (?)
     b. He is desiring something to drink. (?)
     c. He is being thin. (?)

However, although the unavailability of the progressive seems to be a sufficient condition for a verb phrase to be nondynamic[14] and so aspectually classified as a state description, we should recognize that there are also intuitive state descriptions deploying the English progressive, for example:

(3) a. Currently, we are living in Sydney.
    b. The statue is standing in the parking lot.
    c. A photograph of Grandma is sitting on the back of the toilet.

The traditional explanation of state descriptions deploying the English progressive is that these sentences refer to states that are considered somehow temporary. Goldsmith and Woisetschlaeger (1982, 84–85) argue (convincingly in my view) that a deeper analysis is needed.[15] But whatever analysis that is, we already have some linguistic evidence against Sosa's idea that beliefs are analogous to archery shots. To appreciate this, contrast

(4) a. He is shooting the arrow.
    b. It is hitting the target because of his skill.
(5) a. He is believing that p. (?)
    b. He is knowing that p. (?)

Sentences with the form of (5a) and (5b) are generally anomalous. There may be contexts where one could say, for example, "He is believing that the story is true, but as soon as Sally appears he will know it is a lie." However, if these are legitimate sentences of English, they clearly occur in contexts where the belief is temporary or otherwise not part of the structure of the situation. This means that they are like the sentences in (3), and we should not let marginal uses of the progressive 'is believing' dissuade us from the view that belief attributions are state descriptions. Moreover, it does not seem to me that (5b) can ever be a grammatical sentence of English. (I find it telling that linguists often use knowledge attributions as a paradigm example of a state description). This means that belief and knowledge attributions should be aspectually classified as statives. Importantly, that contrasts with the correct aspectual classification of paradigmatic descriptions of performances and achievements such as those in (4). In the typology outlined in Figure 2.1, these are *process* and *occasion* descriptions, not state descriptions. This suggests strongly, against the core idea of Sosa's account of epistemic normativity, that belief and knowledge ascriptions are about states rather than performances.[16]

This result can be confirmed by a related test for whether a verb phrase refers to something conceived of as dynamic or involving change. With nonstatives, we typically use the simple present form of the relevant verb only if repetitiveness, seriality, or habitualness is suggested. For example, contrast

(6) a. He is jogging.
    b. He is writing a book.
    c. He is (just now) winning the race.
(7) a. He jogs.
    b. He writes a book.
    c. He wins the race.

The sentences in (6) are naturally interpreted as referring to a single occurrence, whereas the sentences in (7) are typically used in contexts suggesting repetitiveness, seriality, or habitualness, such as: "He jogs every day," "He writes a book whenever he has a sabbatical," or "He wins the race every year."[17] The opposite is true for statives:

(8) a. We are living in Sydney.
    b. The statue is standing in the parking lot.
    c. A photograph of Grandma is sitting on the back of the toilet.
(9) a. We live in Sydney.
    b. The statue stands in the parking lot.
    c. A photograph of Grandma sits on the back of the toilet.

To be sure, the sentences in (9) can be expanded to convey some form of repetitiveness, seriality, or habitualness, but they do not sound strange absent such context.

Next, consider sentences which should be analogous from the point of view of Sosa's virtue epistemology:

(10) a. He shoots the arrow.
     b. It hits the target (because of his skill).
(11) a. He believes that *p*.
     b. He knows that *p*.

Sentences (10a) and (10b) are analogous to sentences (7b) and (7c). To describe a one-off occurrence, one would not normally use these sentences, which are in the simple present, but another form of words involving the progressive, such as, "He is shooting the arrow" and, "It is hitting the target (at this precise moment)." The same is not true of sentences (11a) and (11b). These are instead analogous to the sentences in (9). So, again, we get the result that paradigmatic descriptions of performances refer to something dynamic and so should be aspectually classified with nonstatives, whereas belief and knowledge attributions refer to something nondynamic and so should, *pace* Sosa, be aspectually classified with statives.

The basic result is that belief and knowledge attributions seem to be about something nondynamic, whereas paradigmatic performance descriptions (for example, of arrow shootings) seem to be about something dynamic and so nonstative. I think this shows that Sosa's suggestion that belief is a performance—which when successful (true) because skillful (justified) is apt (knowledge)—involves him in a sort of category mistake in the way he uses these words.[18]

Later, I will consider some responses to this objection and some other possible ways a virtue epistemologist might try to deploy the categories of performance normativity, but it is both independently interesting and relevant for what follows to return to the semantics of aspect in order to distinguish among different kinds of nonstatives. In the verb phrase typology in Figure 2.1, tests for telicity and duration can be used to distinguish among the three kinds of nonstatives—activities, processes, and occurrences. That is, we can separate three categories based on two features:

(a) activities (e.g., jogging): durative and atelic
(b) processes (e.g., writing a book): durative and telic
(c) occurrences (e.g., winning the race): nondurative and telic.

The basic thought is that a verb phrase such as 'is running' allows us to talk about something that takes time but does not imply a specific endpoint, whereas a verb phrase such as 'is writing a book' allows us to talk about something that takes time and implies a specific endpoint, and a verb phrase such as 'is winning the race' allows us to talk about the point in time at which some implied endpoint is reached. Of course, we may say, "He is running," when we know that he plans to run precisely a mile, but the endpoint is not incorporated into the meaning of the verb phrase we use. Similarly, we may say, "He is winning the race," when we know that winning the race takes a small but not infinitesimal amount of time, but, as far as the meaning of the phrase goes, the occurrence is conceived of as point-like.

The most widely used test for determining whether an English verb phrase is durative/nondurative or telic/atelic has to do with the interaction between the past progressive and the perfect tenses. For some verb phrases, the past progressive implies the perfect, but for others it does not. For example, notice the following contrasts:

(12) a. He was running (then), so he has run (at some point in the past).
　　　b. He was writing a book (then), so he has written a book (at some point in the past). (?)
　　　c. He was winning the race (then), so he has won the race (at some point in the past).

The reason (12a) sounds fine is that as soon as someone is engaging in the activity of running, it is true to say of him that he has engaged in that activity. We can conclude then that the phrase 'is running' refers to something durative but atelic. By contrast, (12b) sounds odd because someone who was writing a book could be interrupted and never finish. Hence, the phrase 'is writing a book' refers to something durative and telic. The sentence (12c) is more difficult to evaluate (and doing so is not crucial to my purposes here). The thought behind classifying this differently from (12a) and (12b) is that, although there is an implied endpoint to 'is winning the race', this phrase refers not to the progression toward that endpoint but only the moment of achieving it.

I have already explained why belief and knowledge attributions should be aspectually classified as state descriptions, while descriptions of paradigmatic performances should be classified in the opposite node of the typology as event descriptions. But it is interesting to ask: Where, as we move lower in the typology outlined in Figure 2.1, should we classify descriptions of paradigmatic performances? Consider the following:

(13) a. He was shooting the arrow (then), so he has shot the arrow (at some point in the past).
      b. He was skillfully hitting the target (then), so he has skillfully hit the target (at some point in the past).

Linguistic intuitions about these sentences might reasonably differ, but it seems to me that (13a) is anomalous like (12b) is anomalous. Shooting an arrow does not take long, but it could surely be interrupted, such that one could be in the midst of shooting an arrow but not yet have shot the arrow. If that is right, it indicates that the phrase 'is shooting the arrow' refers to a process (and partially vindicates Kenny's original term "performances" for this node of the typology). By contrast, it seems to me that (13b) is like (12c). That's because hitting the target with skill refers not to the progression toward the implied endpoint but the point of time when one achieves it. And if that's right, it indicates that the phrase 'is skillfully hitting the target' refers to an occasion.

2.4 Two Responses to the Objection

So far, I have argued against Sosa's key idea that belief is a performance, but the objections I've pressed arise for any view that treats belief itself as action-like in progressing toward an end (telicity). My insistence that belief is stative, and so not telic, is not based on some dogma about beliefs being states; it is based on the semantics of the words 'believe' and 'know'. Using tools from the linguistics of verb-phrase aspect, I have argued that our ordinary conception of belief is of something stative and not dynamic. All of the epistemology and philosophy of mind that assumes beliefs are states is simply building on that ordinary conception. (In Chapter 4, I will provide a further explanation of why it is useful for folk psychology to deploy a concept of belief as a state.)

Someone defending Sosa might argue that the stative aspect of the meaning of the ordinary word 'believe' stands in the way of philosophical progress on understanding epistemic normativity. But there is a significant risk in this move that the resulting epistemological theory ends up being about something other than what ordinary people are talking about when they talk about belief and knowledge, and what most epistemologists are concerned with when they wonder what it takes for someone's belief that *p* to be such that they count as knowing that *p*.[19] For this reason, I propose to account for the axiological dimension of epistemic normativity by building on the idea that the distinctive value of knowledge depends in part precisely on the durative and nonchanging character of states. I suspect it is so natural to use stative verbs to refer to belief and knowledge because we value knowledge, at least in part, because of how it, as a kind of belief, is maintained stably "in waiting" across time. Performances simply do not have these characteristics.

I will come back to this idea in Part II, but in the meantime, let me anticipate how it might be thought to point the way to a reply to my argument from the previous section. One might think I'm being overly pedantic about aspectual categories. After all, we move fairly easily from the idea that someone believes that *p* to the idea that they *maintain* the belief that *p*; and maintaining a belief that *p* seems like something one might be said to do. So, maybe the performance relevant to the distinctive value of knowledge is *maintaining* a belief. I think this is what Sosa has in mind when, in response to the objection that belief does not require conscious activity like most paradigmatic performances, he encourages us to consider "those live motionless statues that one sees at tourist sites" (2007, 23). He suggests that these provide a nice analogy for his view, since, as he puts it, "Such performances can linger, and need not be constantly sustained through renewed conscious intentions. The performer's mind could wander, with little effect on the continuation or quality of the performance" (2007, 23). Could the virtue epistemologist escape my argument earlier by transposing the idea of performance normativity from belief states to belief maintenance over time?

There is surely something right about stressing the importance of belief maintenance when it comes to addressing the deontological and axiological dimensions of epistemic normativity. This incorporates what I will call the "here-and-now" element of epistemic normative evaluations that causes problems for the views I consider in the next chapter. However, the problem with this as a response to my initial objection to Sosa is that maintaining a belief is not a performance. At least, the verb phrase 'is maintaining a belief' would be aspectually classified with verb phrases used to talk about activities (because it is atelic, like 'is running'), and—as we saw earlier—paradigmatic performances are referred to by verb phrases aspectually classified with process descriptions (which are telic, like 'is writing a book').

This is not some mere accident of grammar. The telic aspect of performances seems to be part of why we can distinguish among the three dimensions of performance normativity: success, skill, and aptness. Hence, something atelic, such as maintaining a belief, will never be the right sort of thing to which to apply these evaluative distinctions. So, I think virtue epistemology à la Sosa would not be rescued by transposing the categories of performance normativity from belief to *maintaining a belief*, however easy it is to move between the two ideas.

What about those live motionless statues? Their performance, in my view, is maintaining a pose for some period of time. It requires no great skill to stand still for ten seconds, but doing so for ten minutes is a pretty impressive performance. By contrast, one can maintain a belief for ten seconds or ten minutes or for any length of time, and the belief might count as knowledge, no matter how long one maintains it. So, if our ordinary ways of talking about these things are indicative of our ordinary conception (which I think they are), then maintaining a belief is an activity rather than a process. But, since we use process descriptions rather than activity descriptions to talk about paradigmatic performances, the bare idea of maintaining a belief is not plausibly thought of as a performance. Again, this means that the structures of performance normativity do not apply to it.

I think Sosa's more considered response to my objection is to claim that he is just using the term "performance" in a technical sense having to do with things that constitutively have aims. He writes, "in our sense a 'performance' is just any state or action or process that has a constitutive aim" (2015, 67). But how could a belief conceived of as state, which therefore involves no dynamicity or telicity, have a constitutive aim and so therefore also be a "performance" in some technical sense?

I don't want to pick a fight about the word 'performance' (well, at least not any more than I already have), and it is not unreasonable for Sosa to suggest that, although performances such as archery shots might be the easiest example to appreciate, there are other things which admit of the distinction between success, skill, and success because of skill. Perhaps anything with an aim could be said to admit of this distinction by something like analogical extension from the core case of archery shots. If so, then even if some pedantic philosopher like me insists that beliefs are states rather than performances, it may still be cogent to think that beliefs admit of the normative distinctions that are characteristic of performances because they "aim at the truth". If this is right, then could we perhaps hold onto Sosa's basic analysis of epistemic normativity in terms of performance normativity?

I remain unsure whether the idea that belief aims at the truth is cogent (more on this in Chapter 5) and what that means for the applicability of the categories of performance normativity. But, in light of the popularity of this idea amongst philosophers, let me outline two rejoinders here. (I'll make a more concessive observation about this debate at the end of the next chapter.)

The first rejoinder is that this move is ad hoc. Unless there are other states that plausibly admit of the distinctions that are characteristic of performance normativity, it will be entirely theory-driven to think that the state of belief fits into a normative structure derived from thinking about performances. Recall that the main attraction of applying the categories of performance normativity to belief was that we already have a fairly good and naturalistically respectable understanding of this kind of normativity; so, assimilation of epistemic normativity to this kind of normativity will illuminate something that was otherwise mysterious. Now, however, it looks as if there's still going to be a mystery about how a kind of normativity, derived from the durative and telic nature of performances, crosses over to apply to states, which can have "aims" only metaphorically or stipulatively.

Of course, there are examples of other states that some philosophers claim to have constitutive aims. For example, desires are sometimes said to aim at the good like belief aims at the truth. However, even if this highly controversial claim is true, it seems strange to me to try to evaluate desires for their success, skill, and aptness vis-à-vis this putative aim. So, what I think we really need in order to be comfortable with this second response to my objection is a general way to identify states with constitutive aims, as well as reasons independent of epistemology to think that applying categories such as successful, skillful, and apt to these states would make sense. Moreover, it's important to be careful here not to conflate application of these categories to the states themselves, with application to the *formation* or *acquisition* of these states. (That's the topic of the next chapter.)

The second rejoinder is that, although the idea that belief aims at the truth is a popular metaphor in philosophy, if we ground the virtue epistemologist's idea that belief can be normatively evaluated like performances on this metaphor, then we risk understanding epistemic normativity only as well as we understand this metaphor. And I suspect that we do not understand this metaphor very well. Or, maybe more precisely, I suspect there are a lot of importantly but subtly different things different philosophers understand by this metaphor. So, I worry that founding an account of epistemic normativity on the idea that belief is a state that constitutively aims at the truth again risks confounding rather than advancing our understanding of the deontological and axiological dimensions of epistemic normativity.

Even if we concede that belief has truth as its aim (whatever exactly that means) and are careful not to conflate belief itself with the formation of belief, this concession doesn't affect the observation that belief itself is not something dynamic. It is a way of being, rather than something someone does. So, trivially, the state of belief itself is not something one can *do* skillfully, which of course means that believing, itself, cannot involve a change from merely aiming at the target to achieving the target. Yet, leaving aside the metaphor of aiming at the truth, this is precisely the assumption that virtue epistemologists such as Sosa seem to need to be true in order to make sense of an account of epistemic normativity as a species of performance normativity.

Compare: the answer to a crossword puzzle—i.e., the ink on the page—might be said to be correct iff it matches the canonical solution, and that normative biconditional might be part of what constitutes one's answer as an answer to a crossword puzzle. However, that doesn't make the ink on the page something someone is *doing* in any intuitive sense. Rather the *act* of filling in the crossword— i.e., *putting* the ink on the page—is the relevant performance in this case. This is what we evaluate in terms of concepts such as *skillful* and *apt*. Similarly, I doubt that belief states themselves can be skillful or apt, even if they are sometimes accurate or correct, such that someone forming them achieves the "aim" of belief.[20]

2.5 Conclusion

If norms of action in consideration of what's morally important are treated as the primary concern of ethics, then maybe norms of belief in consideration of what's epistemically important should be treated as the primary concern of epistemology. This leads to the idea that a central part of epistemology is the "ethics of belief". On the other hand, one who is moved as I am by doxastic involuntarism and/or philosophical naturalism might jump to the opposite conclusion, namely that epistemic norms are not "genuine" or "robust" like ethical norms, not even indirectly or implicitly so. I think such a deflationary approach is inappropriate. In my view, a more robust commitment to epistemic normativity can animate epistemological research into deontological and axiological phenomena. However, I argued in this chapter that it is important not to be tempted, in this effort, to think that believing is a kind of doing rather than a kind of being. This is basically how I interpret Sosa's program, and where I locate his error.[21]

The idea that beliefs are a kind of performance offends against our normal philosophical ways of thinking about belief and linguistic facts about our ordinary ways of talking about beliefs in everyday life. This point applies not just to Sosa's performance-based view but to any view that assimilates beliefs to performances done in pursuit of an end. Furthermore, the stative nature of belief provides an important clue for developing a better account of the axiological and deontological dimensions of epistemic normativity. Perhaps we value knowledge in the way we do precisely *because* it is unchanging, in a way only a state could be. And perhaps the deontological evaluations of actions (in their presumption of voluntariness or control) are different from the deontological evaluations of beliefs precisely *because* they are evaluations of something unchanging, in a way that only a state could be.

I'll pick up these clues in later chapters (especially Chapters 6 and 7) and add a social spin to them. But first it will prove instructive to consider some other ways in which epistemologists have sought to use the normative categories applying to various actions and performances to develop accounts of epistemic normativity. More specifically, in the next chapter, I turn to the idea that belief-*formation* is the proper target of epistemic normativity.

Notes

1. See Nelson (1997) and Newman and Nelson (1999) for what I take to be a more accurate take on Descartes's actual views on some of these issues.
2. See especially, Stanovich (1999, 2011), Carruthers (2009), Kahneman (2011), Stanovich and West (2000), Mercier and Sperber (2017), and Mandelbaum (2014).
3. See Sosa (2003, 2007, 2010, 2011b). Here, I focus on Sosa's recent works because they develop one of the clearest and most sophisticated versions of the basic idea. Similar ideas have been pursued by others broadly sympathetic to virtue epistemology, for example, Zagzebski (1996) and Pritchard (2012). I'll discuss a view of epistemic normativity closely related to Sosa's in the next chapter, where I consider Greco's (2004, 2010) version of virtue epistemology. Throughout these chapters, I will be assuming with Sosa and these other virtue epistemologists that knowledge is a subspecies of belief. This may be wrong, but it is such a widespread assumption in epistemology that I will not take the space to consider how the debate over the normativity of belief looks from the point of view of someone who denies it.
4. There are putative counterexamples to this explanation of the value of knowledge in the literature, which I will not discuss here, except to note that the objection I want to develop is more general. For example, Lackey (2007, sec. 2) has stressed that we get at least some knowledge from testimony, where the success is more because of the cognitive skill of the informant than the knower, which calls into question whether knowledge requires manifesting epistemic skill. And Pritchard (2010) has argued on the basis of Ginet-Goldman-style barn-façade cases (see Goldman (1976)) that not all instances of successful-because-skillful belief are instances of knowledge.
5. See especially, Pritchard (2012), Sosa (2015), essays collected in the first part of Fernandez (2016), Kelp (2018), Sosa (2019), Carter (2022), Phillips (2020), and essays in Kelp and Greco (2020).
6. In some ways, this is an updated version of a point made by Heil and Audi when they argue that beliefs are not events, whereas actions are, so the norms we apply to action don't apply to belief. Heil writes, "S's believing that *p* seems not to be a special kind of *event*, but a *state* of a certain sort" (1983, 356). Audi writes, "Actions are events, in the ordinary sense in which the occurrence of an event entails that of a change. Beliefs are not events (though their formation is). To believe is not to do something or to change anything; nor does having a belief over time entail changing over the time in question in any way related to the belief. Beliefs, then, are not actions" (2001, 101).

7. Brinton (2009, ch. 1) distinguishes usefully between the grammatical category "verbal aspect" and the semantic classification of a verb phrase in terms of what is known as an "*aktionsart*". Her argument is that these are intimately related but that only confusion comes from running them together. The classical typology of English verb phrases that I discuss later is a semantic (*aktionsart*) classification, which can be explained and motivated by some linguistic tests picking up on grammatical categories such as the progressive.
8. However, it is doubtful whether the distinction between *enérgeiai* ("activities") and *kinéseis* ("movements") plays exactly the same role for Aristotle as it does for Kenny or linguists who follow his classification of verb phrases.
9. There are other possible typologies than the one I am going to use here. Brinton (2009, 33–36), canvasses three others and compares these usefully to the ones derived from Kenny and Vendler. See Boyd and Boyd (1977) and Dowty (1979, 180–186). Brinton also discusses and refines the refinements suggested by Comrie (1976, ch. 1). The optimal typology will to some extent depend on the purposes for which it is designed. All of these typologies make a distinction between statives and nonstatives, which is all that really matters for my argument later. I have adopted the Vendler–Kenny approach because it is most familiar to philosophers and because it makes the stative/nonstative distinction at the highest level.
10. Mourelatos (1978, 423) helpfully proposes some topic-neutral terminology to use in place of Kenny's and Vendler's terminology, but he uses 'process' in a way that means that processes are atelic. It is now more common to use the term 'activity' for this and save 'process' for movements toward an endpoint. However, as Mourelatos (1993) later recognizes, even this is potentially misleading for the way it suggests a sequence of discrete steps. I have retained the term 'process' in spite of this potential to mislead.
11. Compare Comrie (1976, ch. 2) for more extensive discussion of each of these categories.
12. Compare also Rothstein (2004, 6) for a very similar articulation of the typology, though she uses slightly different terminology.
13. See Dowty (1979, 51–55) for useful discussion of this typology, its history, and a compendium of many more linguistic tests than I will discuss here. Mittwoch (1988) contains helpful criticism and refinement of several of these tests involving durational phrases and the adverb 'already'. Also van Voorst (1992) contains a helpful discussion in a linguistic context of specifically psychological verbs such as 'to believe'.
14. All significant proposals for articulating the semantics of the progressive in English predict this. See especially Parsons (1989), Landman (1992), and Higginbotham (2004).
15. Sentences (3b) and (3c) are adapted from Goldsmith and Woisetschlaeger (1982, 84–85). Their argument consists of cases where such sentences are expanded with clauses indicating that the state is not temporary. Their deeper analysis has to do with the distinction between features of a situation presented as "structural", in the sense that they structure experience of the situation, as opposed to features presented as "phenomenal", in that they are experienced.
16. Could a sentence deploying a stative verb phrase be about the same thing as another sentence deploying a nonstative verb phrase? Perhaps. This is a difficult question at the interface of metaphysics and the philosophy of language which I do not hope to settle

here. But two points are relevant: First, there do not seem to be intuitive alternatives for attributing belief (and knowledge) that deploy nonstative verb phrases. Second, the important issue here is the implications of the conception of belief and knowledge reflected in the meaning of the sentences we use to talk about these things. One could engage in error theory with respect to these concepts, but that does not seem to be the way Sosa or other epistemologists want to go.

17. Exception: we sometimes use the simple present to refer to one-off occurrences when we use a rhetorical device called the "historical present". This involves projecting our narrative into the present moment of some unfolding series of events, for example, "He dribbles, he shoots, he scores!" But I think we can recognize the historical present when we see it and modulate for it. In any case, most of the belief and knowledge attributions that are at issue in epistemology are obviously not in the historical present.

18. See also Meylan (2020) for further argument supporting this conclusion.

19. Could the ordinary concept of belief change, such that it becomes about performances rather than states? This is a difficult question requiring a view about when a concept changing becomes a different concept. But what is important here is that the (current) folk psychological concept of belief is of a state of mind, which is evidenced by the fact that we use a stative verb to talk about it. Moreover, many of the intuitions driving epistemological questions are articulated with the current folk psychological concept of belief. So, unless and until that concept changes, I think we need to develop responses to the axiological and deontological puzzles that respect the idea that beliefs are states.

20. For related reasons, it's wrong to think of knowledge as an apt performance. As I argue in Chrisman (2012a), *knowledge* is also a state. So, as long as states are different from performances, knowledge could only be the *result* of an apt performance, not the performance itself.

21. Although he still presents belief as a performance, in Sosa (2015, ch. 9) he focuses on the freedom exercised in *judgment*. And one theoretical option to consider is certainly whether epistemology should give up its focus on norms of belief and focus instead on norms of judgment. A lot will depend on how we think about the relationship between judging and believing. Maybe judgment is a way of forming a belief, or maybe it's the event which begins an episode of having a belief. If the former, some of what I say in this chapter is relevant, but if the latter, the situation is less clear. These are complex issues that would take me too far afield of the main line of argument I want to develop here. I discuss the idea of focusing epistemic norms on judgments rather than beliefs in the next chapter, drawing on Boyle's (2011) criticism of this idea; see also Chrisman (2018a).

3
Belief Formation Doesn't Exhaust Doxastic Agency

3.1 Introduction

In the previous chapter, I argued that belief attributions are state attributions (nondynamic and atelic), and that descriptions of paradigmatic performances all fall under the aspectual category of processes (dynamic and telic). This makes it impossible to apply the categories of performance normativity directly to beliefs themselves when trying to understand the fact that we do make seemingly robust normative evaluations of beliefs. It also means that analyzing knowledge as identical to successful-because-skillful belief is the wrong way to understand the apparently distinctive way we value knowledge. Because of this, I think one prominent form of virtue epistemology fails in its explanation of the deontological and axiological dimensions of epistemic normativity. And, more generally, I suggested that any view that treats beliefs as telic, action-like events is going to face similar problems.

In light of this result, in this chapter, I consider two families of views that might be thought to save the idea that performance normativity is at the heart of epistemic normativity, without embracing the idea that beliefs themselves are performances or action-like events. The common strategy in these views is to shift focus from belief itself to the *formation* of belief. Belief-formation appears to be dynamic and telic in a way that belief states are not, which makes belief-formation a suitable target for normative evaluations of it as a performance. However, I think the reasons why one holds a belief here-and-now can pull apart from the reasons why one formed the belief in the past, and this undermines views that attempt to locate doxastic agency primarily in the formation of belief. In my view, knowledge attributions turn on the quality of the here-and-now exercise of doxastic agency in maintaining our beliefs, and the etiology of the acquisition of beliefs is at best contingent evidence of contemporary grounds. This encourages a focus on the agency involved in maintaining beliefs; however, I will argue that this is an atelic activity, and atelic activity is *not* a suitable target for normative evaluations of a performance, e.g., as successful because skillful.

To develop this argument in more detail, I first consider views that focus on the actions of inquiry and deliberation conceived as distinctively agential ways of forming beliefs. Then I go on to consider a version of virtue reliabilism that is similar to the view considered in the previous chapter, but focused on belief-formation instead of belief itself. In both cases, I think these views have something important to teach us about doxastic agency, but I argue that neither finds a suitable target for the epistemic normative evaluations implied by knowledge attributions. This conclusion generates adequacy constraints on a viable theory of doxastic agency, which I use to develop a positive account in the following chapter.

3.2 Inquiry and Deliberation in the Age of Involuntarism

Since at least Spinoza, many philosophers have been skeptical of the idea that belief and action are analogous in their susceptibility to deliberative choice; and at least since Hume, a picture of cognition as operating more or less automatically (and thankfully so) has been popular amongst naturalistically inclined philosophers.[1] Moreover, in recent epistemology, doxastic involuntarism has become the dominant position about the question of whether we can choose our beliefs.[2]

Alston's (1988) argument for involuntarism is perhaps best known amongst contemporary epistemologists. This argument consists mainly of noting an intuitive contrast between belief-formation and voluntary action. He observes that one can normally perform a basic action, such as moving one's finger, simply *at will*; and one can normally also perform nonbasic actions, such as turning on a light (by moving one's finger), *voluntarily*. When it comes to belief, however, it doesn't seem that one can normally form a belief at will or voluntarily. His evidence for this claim is that, even with the prospect of a very large reward, we cannot normally bring ourselves to form a particular belief at will or even voluntarily (e.g., that the number of stars in the Milky Way is even).[3]

On this basis, Alston suggests that beliefs come upon us more or less unwilled whenever our perceptual and cognitive faculties are engaged. He recognizes, of course, that we sometimes voluntarily perform actions that have predictable effects on our beliefs. For example, we choose what we look at, who we listen to, and so forth.[4] But these actions only cause us to have some doxastic attitude or other; they are not instances of forming a specific belief. Also, the sort of case Pascal imagined, where someone is imagined to choose to perform an action with the aim of eventually acquiring some specific belief, is clearly not the normal case of belief-formation.[5]

As I understand Alston, none of his observations are meant to imply that our mental lives are entirely passive.[6] People can actively choose to do things such as reflect on their last birthday, imagine a beach, mentally formulate a to-do list, and so on. These mental acts are at least as voluntary as moving one's finger or turning on a light. However, forming a specific belief is not normally up to the believer,[7] which is why Alston doubts we exercise any kind of agential control over what we believe.[8] Hence, insofar as epistemic normative evaluations presuppose agency over what we believe, he thinks we should stop making those evaluations, as they presuppose something false.

However, this way of thinking of belief-formation seems to be in tension with the obvious fact that we sometimes engage in explicit inquiry and deliberation with the aim of forming a true belief about some topic. In this vein, Lockie implores us not to ignore "our role as inquirers, as active *seekers after truth*" (2018, 55). As he sees things, we surely have some kind of normatively assessable rational influence over our beliefs when we do things, such as directing our attention at some topic we are interested in learning more about, setting ourselves the goals of figuring out what's true about it, sequencing our cognitive tasks in pursuit of those goals, monitoring the performance of those tasks, inhibiting other cognitive processes that might interrupt that performance, attending to possible conflicts between things we believe, reflecting on possible revisions of our belief systems, stopping a cognitive task, and even switching cognitive goals when something isn't working (Lockie 2018, 62–65). In a similar vein, Meylan claims that we are responsible for more than just our actions and omissions: "we are also sometimes responsible for the external consequences of these actions and omissions" (2017, 7). And she appeals to this idea to argue that, although belief-formation is not intentional action, people are responsible for their beliefs much like they are responsible for the unintentional but foreseeable consequences of their actions. In both cases, she thinks one is responsible insofar as one can exercise *indirect* control over what happens.

Moreover, even if we admit that we don't normally choose our beliefs, I think many philosophers and ordinary people would attest to a phenomenology of "making up one's mind" about difficult and important issues. Much like we might weigh reasons for and against some action, seeking to do what we rationally ought to do, at least sometimes it seems that we weigh reasons for and against believing some proposition, and make a judgment, seeking to believe what we rationally ought to believe.[9]

So, what should we think about doxastic involuntarism in light of the actions of inquiry and deliberation? It may be tempting to adopt a kind of doxastic dualism.[10] Alongside the mostly automatic belief-formation involved in normal perceptual and testimonial knowledge, perhaps we should also recognize "inquiry and deliberation" as a distinctive category of belief-formation which comprises the diverse range of mostly voluntary cognitive actions and associated performances described earlier. Both pictures of how beliefs are formed could be correct, just about different epistemically relevant aspects of our cognition. Such a détente would let us continue to recognize a robust form of doxastic agency, while conceding to Alston that not all belief-formation is properly regarded as an object of epistemic normative evaluation.[11]

There are two problems with this ecumenical theory of doxastic performances. The first problem has to do with the temporal relations between an event of belief-formation and the ongoing status of being a belief that one ought to have. I think this problem is common to both of the main ideas I discuss in this chapter, but it will be helpful to go ahead and work through an example of it before turning to the second problem.

Consider a case of someone who is curious about the idea that structural racism explains the racial wealth gap in the United States. Motivated by this curiosity, she engages in some inquiry and deliberation. She might read some prominent books and articles discussing structural racism, and while doing so, she might deliberate about considerations on either side of the argument. Imagine that she does all of this virtuously and thereby becomes convinced that structural racism does explain the wealth gap between races in the United States. Now, fast-forward many years, and imagine that our subject still has this belief formed long ago, but now she has completely forgotten most of the reasons for and against it. Let's imagine additionally that she has actually come to implicitly doubt many of the reasons for the belief that she originally regarded as its strongest support. It's not that she has reconsidered the question, but she has gone on to accept other things as true that are inconsistent with those original reasons in a way that she might notice if she were to reflect on the issue. But she hasn't actually engaged in such reflection, and she continues to hold the original belief despite the now forgotten and implicitly doubted reasons for which it was originally formed.

In this kind of case, we can grant that the subject formed the belief as she ought to have formed the belief, but I think it is far from clear that she now believes what she ought to believe about the issue. Of course, forgotten or doubted evidence doesn't always undermine our positive evaluation of a belief that was originally formed well, but my point is that it can.[12] When a subject's grasp of the evidence weakens enough and she seems completely unable to explain the basis of her belief, or when a subject would, with just a little reflection, come to seriously doubt a belief because it is inconsistent with other things she believes, I think we would be rightly inclined to revise our positive evaluation of the belief.

To be clear, I don't mean to defend a definitive verdict on this under-described case. My point is only that even when a belief is formed through the most robustly rational sorts of inquiry and deliberation, its normative status as a belief that one ought to have might still pull apart from how well it was formed via these actions. Because of this, I think there must be some other kind of agency involved in maintaining beliefs over time, even beliefs that were formed through the purportedly voluntary actions of inquiry and deliberation. And it is this *ongoing* exercise of agency that I think is more relevant to the sorts of epistemic normative evaluations implied by knowledge attributions.

Later I will discuss the idea that it's not just the formation of a belief but the sustaining of a belief that matters to epistemic normative evaluation, and I think some reliabilists have rightly included the idea of *sustaining* in their accounts of what must be reliable for someone to have knowledge. However, the actions of inquiry and deliberation are not plausibly thought to exhaust whatever is involved in sustaining a belief. Indeed, we can imagine a version of the case where the believer never re-engages in inquiry and deliberation about the belief after it is initially formed. So, this response will not avoid the objection to the account of doxastic agency considered in this section.

The second problem I want to discuss is more specific to the idea that doxastic agency is exercised mainly in belief-formation via inquiry and deliberation. As noted earlier, we form many beliefs through quick and dirty perception, memory, and testimony. But I don't think it will do to say that these are all "merely" sub-agential automatic processes, whereas "genuine" doxastic agency comes onto the scene only with inquiry and deliberation. For one thing, inquiry and deliberation depend in complex ways on the operation of these quick and dirty processes, which makes it doubtful that there are very many beliefs formed *only* by inquiry and deliberation. For another thing, even without the help of inquiry and deliberation, quick and dirty cognitive processes often result in *knowledge*. I have been assuming throughout this book that the normative epistemic evaluations implied by knowledge attributions presuppose doxastic agency. One can reject that assumption, of course, but then I think the scope of doxastic agency will look too limited to make progress on the deontological and axiological puzzles at the heart of debates about epistemic normativity (see Chapter 1). So, the problem is that the actions of inquiry and deliberation seem to be too limited in their scope to make sense of the sort of agency presupposed by our ordinary normative epistemic evaluations.

Would it help to retreat to the idea that (almost) every belief is *potentially* the product of inquiry and deliberation?[13] For some suitably strong sense of "potentially", this idea is probably correct, but I don't think it can revive the thesis that the primary locus of doxastic agency is in the formation of belief through inquiry and deliberation. For, recall that the account I am considering in this section is that doxastic agency is exercised in the formation of belief via inquiry and deliberation, which is supposed to explain how beliefs could be subject to normative evaluations which presuppose that the believer exercises some kind of agency with respect to those beliefs. The mere fact that a belief *could* have been formed through inquiry and deliberation doesn't change the fact that the actual performance we would evaluate in applying to it the categories of performance normativity would be those processes involved in quick and dirty perception, memory, or testimony.

Furthermore, there are reasons to be skeptical of the claim that (almost) every belief is *potentially* the product of inquiry and deliberation. We should grant a proponent of this idea that, for any proposition p, one can ask whether p is true, and then go on to look for reasons for and against believing p. However, I doubt that engaging in this kind of inquiry and deliberation is always (or even often) a way of *forming* a belief about whether p. The impression that we can inquire and deliberate about potentially anything comes, I conjecture, from the fact that one can engage in post hoc inquiry and deliberation for almost anything one believes. This is a cognitive action (which philosophers perhaps especially enjoy) whereby one seeks to justify a belief explicitly without ever ceasing to believe it.[14] In performing this action, however, one does not form or re-form the belief; rather, one seeks a better understanding of the reasons one has for the belief.

I think such post hoc inquiry and deliberation are important aspects of the way we maintain an overall system of beliefs, and these actions sometimes lead one to stop believing one proposition and to start believing another. (I'll discuss the activity of maintaining a system of beliefs in much more detail in the next chapter.) These actions are, however, importantly different from ones through which a person forms a *new* belief via inquiry and deliberation, or even when a person suspends a previously held belief in order to inquire anew with the aim of forming a new belief about the issue in question.[15] So the fact that we can imagine engaging in inquiry and deliberation about almost any proposition doesn't vindicate the idea that (almost) every belief is potentially *formed* by inquiry and deliberation. Thus, a retreat to the idea of *potential* inquiry and deliberation doesn't do any better to revive the thesis that the sort of doxastic agency presupposed by epistemic normative evaluations is exercised primarily in the actions of inquiry and deliberation.[16]

3.3 Reliabilist Virtue Epistemology Renewed

We're searching for the idea of a doxastic *performance* capable of grounding the thesis that epistemic normativity is a kind of performance normativity. The actions of inquiry and deliberation are performances, but we've seen that they're not suitable for our purpose because of at least two problems. The second problem would be easily avoided by broadening our understanding of doxastic performances to include other ways in which beliefs are formed besides inquiry and deliberation. Indeed, although we may not fully understand the inner workings of cognition, it seems almost trivial to say that every belief must have been formed somehow. So, the other main family of views I want to consider in this chapter is one that locates doxastic agency and the target of genuine epistemic normative evaluations in the performance of belief-formation writ large.

This is effectively the strategy of John Greco (2003, 2009a, 2010) who, beside Sosa, provides one of the most worked-out versions of the idea that epistemic normativity should be assimilated to performance normativity.[17] So in this section I want to consider his modified version of virtue epistemology, based in the idea of performance normativity.

Recall the attractions of this idea. First, although a person's performances seem to be normatively evaluable in robust ways, such evaluations do not presuppose that the person can voluntarily choose to engage in the performance. So, this approach to explaining epistemic normativity is consistent with involuntarism. Second, there is an intuitive difference between the way we value performances that are successful because skillful, and the way we value performances that are successful but not because of the person's skill. This intuitive difference provides a powerful way to explain the ancient and persistent intuition that knowledge is categorically worthier than unknowledgeable true belief.

Unlike Sosa, however, Greco does not hold that belief itself is a performance. Rather, he argues that knowledge is true belief for which the subject "deserves credit" for *forming* the belief; and "S deserves intellectual credit for believing the truth regarding p only if S's reliable cognitive character is an important necessary part of the total set of causal factors that *give rise* to S's believing the truth regarding p" (2003, 221, emphasis added). He uses this to generate an analysis of knowledge, writing, "S knows that p if and only if S believes the truth (with respect to p) because S's belief that p is *produced* by intellectual ability" (2010, 71, emphasis altered).

It is key for my discussion later to note that Greco thinks that, by focusing on the production of belief, his "virtue-theoretic account...nicely explains why etiology matters in cases of knowledge" (2010, 11). More specifically, he argues that knowledge should be conceived as a kind of success due to ability. Then, the exercise of cognitive ability in forming beliefs can be plausibly viewed as a performance, where the result of such performance is a belief. On this view, it is not belief itself but the formation of the belief that gets evaluated for its competence, and because of this, normative epistemic 'ought's can be said to be about what someone ought to do (form beliefs), rather than about how they ought to be (believe that p). So, if there is something strange about making robust normative evaluations of ways people are rather than of things people do, then Greco shows how we might switch relatively seamlessly from states of belief to performances of belief-formation in our understanding of the target of epistemic normative evaluations.

This is surely an attractive picture when we are thinking of cases where someone doesn't (yet) have a belief about p and we have views about what they ought to believe concerning p. In these cases, the question of what someone ought to believe seems to be nearly identical to the question of what belief they ought to form. This way of looking at things is also attractive when we are thinking of cases where someone has recently come to believe p through an easily identifiable cognitive process, such as simple unimodal perception or explicit reasoning, and we want to claim that they do or do not know that p. Insofar as these knowledge claims seem to entail some normative evaluation about the person's believing or not believing as they ought, it is easy to hear these evaluations as nearly identical to claims about whether the person ought or ought not *to have formed* the relevant belief.

The problem generalizing this picture, however, is that most of the things we know pertain not to beliefs that we have recently formed through discrete and identifiable cognitive processes, but rather to beliefs that were formed long ago or via complex cognitive processes that mix together various modes of perception, different kinds of memory, and some implicit reasoning. Moreover, I'm inclined to think we have lots of knowledge that doesn't come in individual propositional units, but which comes as a sort of "entailment dump" from other things we know. Similarly, much of what we know might consist in emerging "doxastic presuppositions" wrapped up in increasing fluency with particular concepts and in increasing skill at various cognitive tasks. In all of these sorts of cases, it is unclear and perhaps indeterminate when or how any one of the individual beliefs was formed, but I still think it's often correct to attribute the relevant beliefs and knowledge. These phenomena generate problems for any view which would treat the truth of knowledge attributions as dependent on the quality of the initial formation of the relevant beliefs.[18] To make this point more concrete, let's consider some cases.

I already gave one example in section 3.2 of a belief formed long ago (about the cause of the racial wealth gap in the United States) through inquiry and deliberation; that belief has been retained over time, even though the original reasons for it have been forgotten or are now implicitly doubted. This is a case where high-quality belief-formation (in the past) doesn't entail that the subject ought (now) to hold the relevant belief. I think we can also imagine cases where low-quality belief-formation (in the past) is followed by a process of improving one's evidence for the belief, such that later it comes to be the case that the subject ought (now) to believe what they believe (and have believed for a long time).

For instance, in Ginet's (Goldman 1976) famous fake barn case, Henry sees the one real barn in a district full of convincing barn façades, and he points the barn out to his young son, saying, "That's a barn." We can assume that Henry forms the belief that the object he is pointing to is a barn, that he is in full normal control of his perceptual faculties, and knows full well what a barn looks like. However, in the original presentation, we are invited to deny that he knows that the object is a barn because he could have so easily formed exactly the same belief on the basis of looking at one of the many convincing barn façades. Henry's original belief was not reliably formed (in the environment where he formed it), which is why it is usually regarded as a case of unknowledgeable true belief.[19]

Now, however, let's imagine that Henry drives up to the barn to get a closer look (maybe he wants to show his son how big a barn seems up close), and this confirms his original belief, without his ever considering the many nearby barn façades. As he gets a closer look at the barn, I think our intuitions about his belief that the object is a barn should switch. By driving closer to the barn, Henry improves the evidence for his belief, so that it is no longer the case that he could have had exactly the same visual experiences and yet still been duped into thinking a barn façade was a real barn.

In this kind of case, the original formation of the belief was epistemically suboptimal in a way that means Henry plausibly doesn't count as knowing, but he goes on to improve the grounds for this belief in a way that means he does (later) count as knowing.[20] One way to flesh out this case is as one in which Henry forms two discrete beliefs—one when he initially looks at the barn and another after he drives up to get a closer look—and it is only the second that makes him a knower. But I think there is a more ordinary version of the case in which he forms only one belief but goes on to improve his grounds for it. In this version of the case, it's not the formation of the belief, but the way the belief is contemporaneously grounded in his evidence, that matters to whether he knows.[21]

The lesson I think we should draw from these cases is that there is no necessary connection between the normative quality of the formation of a belief and whether one ought (later) to have it. The original etiology of a belief doesn't always matter to whether it counts as knowledge. Well-formed beliefs can stick around while the subject's evidence for them deteriorates, undermining the subject's status as a knower; and poorly-formed beliefs can stick around while the subject's evidence for them is improved, making the subject come to count as a knower, even when they didn't upon initial formation. To be sure, the quality of a belief's formation is often some indication of how good the subject's grounds are for holding it, but I doubt that normative evaluation of a subject's formation of a belief can be substituted for normative evaluation of the subject's continuing to hold the belief in the future. This is a big problem for the idea that the primary target of epistemic normative evaluations is in the performance of belief-formation.

To bolster this objection, let's also consider *tacit* belief and knowledge. Much of one's knowledge can, it seems, be tacit in the strong sense that not only is one not *currently* considering the proposition believed to be true, but one has *never* considered the proposition known to be true.[22] For example, although I admit that it will be controversial amongst some epistemologists, I think we should be quite happy to say that my mother knows that the rain in Spain is not purple, even though she has never considered the color of the rain in Spain. And if she knows this, then she must believe it; after all, we can rationalize various potential actions she might engage in by reference to this belief. For the same reason, moreover, I think we should say that she believes that the rain in Spain isn't mauve or the invented color International Klein Blue, or... Maybe some of this should count as her having a disposition to know, rather than as knowledge she actually has, since she would have to acquire new concepts to bring the relevant belief to consciousness. All we need for the argument, however, is that *some* dispositional belief counts as tacit knowledge, and if one doesn't like the example so far, try this instead: Think of a number above ten and then consider whether a random friend knows that she has fewer fingers than that number. Or think of a four-digit positive integer and a five-digit positive integer and consider whether that friend knows that the latter is a bigger number than the former.[23]

I'll stick with the rain in Spain example. When and how exactly did my mother form the beliefs that the rain in Spain isn't purple, or mauve, or International Klein Blue? We might say that she acquired these beliefs as she learned what rain is and what its normal color is, but it was only later that she learned what Spain is, and still later that she acquired the concept of mauve, and still later that she learned by direct acquaintance what International Klein Blue is (though she may not even have that term in her lexicon). So, it is at best very unclear *when* she acquired these beliefs, which should make us uneasy about the idea that she was active (in some kind of agency-implying sense) in forming them. Of course, we often do things habitually that we think of as exercises of our agency, either because we exercised agency in acquiring the habits or because we stand, in some sense, ready to actively intervene in them. But my point here is not that tacit beliefs are formed with the automaticity of habitual action; it's that it is not at all clear when the cognitive processes that form such beliefs are in operation.

Moreover, even if we could date the formation of these beliefs, it doesn't seem to me that we should count someone as exercising competence in forming a belief in a proposition that they have never even considered, or one involving concepts that they only minimally grasp. And, if it is unclear when tacit beliefs were formed, and it is doubtful that the someone exercised skill or competence in forming them, then the epistemological views we have been considering in this chapter are going to have to deny that my mother knows that the rain in Spain isn't purple.[24] That seems like a bad result.

The objection behind these examples is not based on the complaint that the two families of views I have been discussing are missing details about how the psychology of belief-formation works over long timescales. These details are somewhat hazy and difficult to pin down for any epistemological theory. Rather, the objection is that the quality of a performance of forming a belief does not seem to be always, or even usually, centrally relevant to whether one ought to have that belief here, now.

Greco claims that it is "relatively uncontroversial" that "one's belief that *p* has k-normative status [i.e., the normative status that is required for knowledge] only if one's belief that *p* is reliably formed" (2010, 62). I submit, however, that the revised barn façade case suggests that this claim should be more controversial. And the forgotten evidence case from the previous section, along with the case of tacit knowledge from this section, together suggest that the quality of a belief's formation is often going to be grossly insufficient, and maybe even irrelevant, for evaluating whether it has the normative status required for knowledge. Hence, if the goal of appealing to doxastic performances is to explain a central part of the structure of doxastic agency and epistemic normativity, then shifting the focus from belief itself to belief-formation is going to mean that we lose a lot of what seems to be at the center of the sort of doxastic agency relevant to epistemic normativity.[25]

One might think that, in developing this objection, I have ignored a central feature of many reliabilist views in epistemology: the *processes* by which people's beliefs are sustained or maintained. For example, in his original presentation of what came to be called process reliabilism, Goldman claims that "correct principles of justified belief must be principles that make causal requirements, where 'cause' is construed broadly to include sustainers as well as initiators of belief" (1979/2012, 36).[26] And preservationists about the epistemic role of memory have long argued that memory is a cognitive faculty through which the justification for a belief can be reliably maintained through time.[27] So, a virtue reliabilist might want to respond to my argument in this section by insisting that under the "performance of belief-formation", they really meant *both* formation and sustaining or maintaining the relevant belief.

I think maintaining a belief through time as a part of one's overall system of beliefs is an important locus of doxastic agency, and there are surely various sustaining processes that contribute to this maintenance. (More on this in the next chapter.) However, this response is an unconvincing way to salvage the idea that epistemic normativity is a kind of performance normativity. This is because sustaining and maintaining beliefs are not performances.

To see why, recall that performances are dynamic *and telic*. This is crucial for making sense of the key notion in Sosa's and Greco's account of epistemic normativity: an "apt" performance is one that achieves its end because of skill rather than luck. In the previous chapter, I argued that beliefs are not the sort of thing that literally achieve ends (because they are states, and states are nondynamic), which makes them ill-suited for an account of epistemic normativity as performance normativity. However, maintaining and sustaining beliefs do not fare any better, since they too are atelic.[28] As we saw in Chapter 2.4 (in the discussion of running and live motionless statues), an activity may be done because one views it as instrumental for achieving some end, and there may be nearby performances of engaging in an activity *for a set period of time*. But the bare ideas of sustaining a belief or maintaining a belief are not constituted by their relation to an end. This is why the sentences "He maintains the belief that p" and "She sustains her belief that q" fail the aspectual tests for telicity. I take this to be a strong reason for thinking that what we're talking about with these sentences is not the right sort of thing to evaluate in terms of categories of performance normativity, such as aptness.[29]

To be clear, in my view, good forms of reliabilism will focus more on the activities of sustaining or maintaining a belief (and improving its justification) over time, than on the issue of how reliable the formation of a belief was. So, I can certainly imagine an attractive form of reliabilist virtue epistemology that gives pride of place to the activity of belief maintenance rather than focusing exclusively on performances of belief-formation. This might even be a view that overlaps significantly with the account of doxastic agency and epistemic normativity developed in the rest of this book. However, the critical upshot at this stage is that this would not be an account of epistemic normativity that tries to address deontological and axiological puzzles primarily in terms of how well doxastic performances achieve their ends.[30] As I see things, the value which we attach to knowledge does not come mainly from the success of the formation of the relevant belief, but from the reliability of our ongoing ability to hold that belief for good reasons throughout the flux and flow of normal cognition. And the deontological evaluation of beliefs implicit in knowledge attributions attaches much more to the here-and-now activity of maintaining the relevant belief than to anything to do with the reliability of its formation.

3.4 Conclusion

I suspect the problems with the views I have been discussing in this chapter stem from a subtle ambiguity in the intuitive idea that whether or not someone knows something depends on *why* they believe what they believe. In one sense, this is the question of what *caused* them to believe it, which is closely related to the question of how they formed the belief. In another sense, however, this is the question of what *grounds* their belief, which is closely related to the question of what evidence or reasons it is based on.

The issues of cause and ground are closely connected when we are considering beliefs formed through actively inquiring and deliberating, and beliefs recently formed through other relatively discrete cognitive processes such as unimodal perception. States of belief stick around, however, and interact in myriad ways with everything else going on in our minds. Indeed, when we consider beliefs that have been formed long ago or via complex processes, the issues of cause and ground can pull apart in interesting ways.

In these cases—which I have been suggesting are the vast majority of our beliefs—the cause of a belief's formation is irrelevant for assessing whether it is a belief someone ought to *now* have, and so also whether the person counts as knowing the relevant proposition to be true. The important question in these cases becomes why the subject *continues* to believe what they believe. Hence, we are interested in their grounds for believing (and whether these are appropriately involved in the causal story of why they here-and-now hold the belief), rather than the original cause of formation (or even the original grounds if these are different from the current grounds). So, although we can and do evaluate performances of belief-formation for accuracy, skillfulness, reasonableness, and aptness, those normative categories appear in the end to be special cases of epistemic normativity, rather than reflections of the general normative difference between knowledge and unknowledgeable belief.

Nevertheless, the point of this chapter has not been mainly critical. I think there is something attractive about the idea that doxastic performances are a possible object of epistemic normative evaluation, and I definitely want to keep the performance of belief-formation in view. When we think about people and what they ought to believe, of course we may sometimes be concerned (implicitly anyway) with what beliefs they ought to form. But very often, we are concerned with something more complex than the *formation* of a belief. We are concerned with what someone ought to do, cognitively, given that they have various beliefs, memories, experiences, suspicions, hunches, etc., all of which stand in various relations of epistemological support and tension with one another.

So, although the etiology of a belief may be relevant to its normative status, epistemic normativity seems to be at least as much if not more about here-and-now doxastic agency. If this is right, the topic of here-and-now cognitive *activity* should be viewed as a challenge to develop a more sophisticated and plausible account of the cognitive doings connected to believing, and then to relate these to the puzzling sorts of deontological and axiological evaluations witnessed in discussions of epistemic normativity.[31] This is the topic of the following chapter.

Notes

1. See for instance Lycan (1986), Gilbert (1991), Cohen (1992), Dretske (1995), Mandelbaum (2010), and Sperber and Mercier (2017).
2. See especially B. Williams (1973), Clarke (1986), Alston (1988), Plantinga (1993a), Audi (2001), Adler (2002), and Levy (2007).
3. One can, of course, cause oneself to believe that the light is on by flipping a switch. See Feldman (2000). So, it's important that Alston's claim is about what's normally possible. There are exceptions when the content of the relevant belief pertains to things over which one exercises the sort of control one exercises in ordinary action, but the contents of most of our beliefs aren't like this.
4. For similar points, though they ultimately draw drastically competing lessons about the role of agency in mentality, see O'Shaughnessy (2000, 28) and Strawson (2003, 235).
5. Moreover, as Feldman (2001b) argues, there are other states (e.g., wanting ice cream or being worried about the future) that might be predictable effects of thinking about particular topics (e.g., flavors of ice cream, or climate change); however, we don't think of being in such states as a manifestation of our cognitive agency. See also Nottlemann (2007, chs 10–11) for discussions of the limits of "Pascalianism" as an account of doxastic agency.
6. Also, although I am not focused here on responsibility, it is worth noting that the category of things for which we are responsible plausibly extends beyond the category of voluntary action. As Smith (2005) notes, forgetting a friend's birthday is something one could be responsible for though it is not a voluntarily chosen action. So, I think Weatherson (2008) is right to consider other cases of things we are responsible for that aren't voluntary actions as models of our responsibilities vis-à-vis belief. Here, however, my main concern is more metaphysical: Where in the vicinity of belief do we

exercise agency? Hence, I will mostly bracket vexed questions about the scope of our responsibility for our mental states.

7. This is different from the idea that we are unfree with respect to our beliefs, or that it is inappropriate to hold people responsible for their beliefs. See McCormick (2011), Steup (2012), and McHugh (2014a) for arguments that even if our agency isn't involved in forming beliefs as it is in performing actions, we nonetheless count as free with respect to, and being responsible for, what we believe in the normal case. See Booth (2014) for a response. Whatever we say about the freedom we exercise over our beliefs, we need some explanation of the way believing as we should relates to exercising our cognitive agency as we should. I will return to the topics of freedom and responsibility at the end of Chapter 7.

8. Compare also Vierkant (2022) for an account of "cognitive shepherding", whereby we use both intercranial and extracranial devices to perform various "cognitive" acts that result in beliefs, but none of which count as acts of forming beliefs.

9. For versions of the idea that doxastic agency is exercised in judgment which can lead to the formation of a belief, see McDowell (2009), Cassam (2010), and Sosa (2015). Compare Jenkins who writes, "Reasoning is a kind of ordinary action. It is also a process which can have judgments as constituents. Furthermore, such judgments can just be events of coming to believe. Reasoning can thus be action where to reason can, in part, just be to come to believe. Given this, to reason can, in part, just be to exercise doxastic agency" (2018, 16).

10. This would tie in with the popular dual-processing accounts of cognition. See especially, Evans and Over (1996), Sloman (1996), Frankish (2004), and Kahneman (2011).

11. Compare Goldman's (2011) attempted synthesis of reliabilism and evidentialism and Sosa's (2016) discussion of "bipartisan epistemology".

12. Srinivasan (2020) develops several plausible cases of knowledge where someone holds a belief despite not being able to explain its grounds and being faced with apparent defeaters. See also Chisholm (1966, 48), BonJour (1980, 59–60), Pollock (1995, 41), and Lasonen-Aarnio (2010, 1) for discussion of various cases where initially well-formed beliefs later have their justification defeated.

13. Although they don't all put it in exactly this way, I think Shah and Velleman (2005), Soteriou (2005), Peacocke (2009), Cassam (2010), and McHugh (2013, 134–135) can all be read as proposing something in this general neighborhood. Soteriou (2013, chs 14–15) develops a much richer conception of mental agency that includes both processes of belief-formation and various activities connected to thinking. Although his concern isn't specifically epistemic normativity, this conception of mental agency is congenial to the account I sketch in Chapter 4.

14. Compare the theory of reasoning developed in Sperber and Mercier (2017). They argue that the evolved purpose of the faculty of reason is to justify ourselves to others. This doesn't mean that we cannot use reason in the privacy of our own minds, and it doesn't mean that all uses of this faculty are post hoc. But they do provide a lot of evidence suggesting that reasoning is often used socially and post hoc to justify beliefs that have been arrived at in other ways.

15. This raises the question of what belief suspension is, on which I don't want to take any particular stand. However, if this requires forming the higher-order belief that the

evidence for believing that *p* is insufficient for believing that *p*, then I think it is even clearer that we cannot do this with respect to many of the things we believe. For helpful discussion of the nature of the suspension of belief, see Friedman (2013), Tang (2016), Lord (2020), and McGrath (2020).

16. Recognizing that many beliefs which have been automatically formed can nonetheless carry the potential for reconsideration through an exercise of agency, can teach us an important lesson about the ways in which we expect people to live up to norms pertaining not only to what actions they perform, but also to what states they are in, *even if they didn't get into these states by performing actions*. Compare Smith (2005). However, it doesn't vindicate the idea that such agency is located in the mere potential to perform actions which would have put them into these states.

17. See also Riggs (2002b, 93–94) for a similar account that also stresses the importance of a person's abilities and skills causing the outcome that they believe the truth. See also Prichard (2009, 2012) for other views that shift the focus to the formation of belief rather than on belief itself for a form of reliabilist virtue epistemology. In a different way, Burge conceives of epistemic norms in terms of "standards for the formation of representational states" (2003, 513). Kelp (2018) focuses on exercises of the ability to know, but knowledge is still treated as an achievement, conceived as a success because of the exercise of an ability to form beliefs. Turri criticizes virtue epistemology on several grounds regarding the necessity of full belief and reliability, but he also develops a position according to which "knowledge is an accurate representation produced by cognitive ability" (2016, 330). For further discussion, see Chrisman (2017b).

18. I don't mean to suggest here that current time-slice views of epistemic justification or rationality are correct. See Kelly (2016) for helpful discussion of the distinction; and see Moss (2015) and Hedden (2015) for defenses of current time-slice views, at least for some kinds of epistemic evaluation, and Carr (2015) for opposition. For my purposes here, however, I only need the idea that views depending mainly on the historical event of belief-formation are problematic.

19. Greco (2010, 76–81) has interesting and, to my mind, quite plausible things to say about how this case is underspecified, and how different ways of fleshing out the practical context of attributing knowledge to Henry could give us different verdicts about whether he knows. For what follows, we can imagine a fleshing out of (along the lines of) Greco's bad case, where Henry doesn't know because in the environment where he forms the belief, and relative to the practical context of attributing knowledge, the salient cause of Henry's true belief is not his cognitive skill. Nonetheless, I think this bad case can be continued in a way that changes the normative status of the original belief formed.

20. This is different from some of the cases Jennifer Lackey (2008, 253–268) discusses, where nondoxastic memory of something like visual images is used to generate new beliefs about what happened in the past.

21. Miracchi (2015) argues on other grounds that Gettier-type cases generate problems for virtue epistemological reliabilism. Sosa (2010) accepts the counterintuitive conclusion that Henry knows in the original Ginet fake barn case. See also Turri (2011) for a virtue epistemological treatment of Gettier problems. Dogramaci (2015) considers a similar kind of case where someone forms a belief irrationally through wishful thinking but forgets her reasons for forming the belief and comes to have better reasons for its truth.

22. In Sosa (2011a, 168), he explicitly restricts himself to cases where the subject consciously considers the proposition, but he does so without comment or justification. Tacit knowledge is better than tacit belief falling short of knowledge. And when one tacitly knows something, one tacitly believes as one epistemically ought to believe. So, if Sosa's or Greco's accounts do not extend to tacit knowledge and belief, then they do not provide a satisfactory basis for addressing the axiological and deontological puzzles that I have been focusing on in this book.
23. The reason this will be controversial amongst some epistemologists is that they will want to insist that none of these examples are examples of belief, but only examples of a disposition to come to believe. But that seems to commit them to saying that my mother doesn't know that the rain in Spain isn't purple, which strikes me as far-fetched. And, in any case, I think we can distinguish between dispositional (tacit) beliefs and dispositions to believe, and recognize that most normal people have lots of both. For helpful discussion, compare Audi (1994), who draws a distinction between dispositional beliefs and dispositions to believe. He treats the former as dispositions to judge that are, so to speak, fully present in one's cognitive economy (e.g., one already has all of the composite concepts, and one's behavior can be straightforwardly rationalized by appeal to these beliefs), which we can distinguish from dispositions to acquire dispositions to judge, which are less fully present in one's cognitive economy (e.g., one might need to develop further conceptual resources before one could judge, and it is more difficult to rationalize one's behavior by appeal to these further dispositions).
24. Greco allows for one kind of knowledge where skillful formation of belief is not necessary. This is innate knowledge. He sees this as a "limit case", where "knowledge is true belief that (partly) *constitutes* one's intellectual abilities" (2010, 85), rather than true belief caused by the exercise of one's intellectual abilities. However, I think it would be clearly wrong to think that all tacit knowledge is innate or even constitutive of intellectual abilities.
25. Greco (2010) argues that the etiology of a performance is often (perhaps even always) relevant for evaluations of who is *responsible* for the result. I don't mean to suggest that evaluations of doxastic responsibility are not also central to the topic of epistemic normativity. But I think this is often conceived as a precondition for making evaluations about what one ought to believe (especially negative ones), and praising or blaming those whose beliefs meet or fail to meet these normative evaluations.
26. It is tangentially interesting to note, however, that like Greco, Goldman focuses on the genesis of belief rather than the sustaining of belief in providing more explicit articulation of his view. He writes, "My positive proposal, then, is this. The justificational status of a belief is a function of the reliability of the process or processes that cause it" (1979/2012, 37).
27. See, for instance, Plantinga (1993b, 61, n22), Dummett (1993, 420–421), Burge (1997, 47, n14), Huemer (1999, 349), Goldman (2009, 323), and Jackson (2011, 569–570).
28. In later work, I describe these activities as *autotelic* rather than atelic, since there is a sense in which they involve their own ongoing completion. This still means that they are not performances and so do not fit the structure of performance normativity, but it makes better sense of the fact that they can be done in order to achieve something. For more discussion, see Chrisman and Hubbs (forthcoming).

29. In the previous chapter, I considered the example of live motionless statues. To repeat, maintaining a pose for a certain period of time is a performance; it has a constitutive end. But this is different from the bare idea of maintaining a pose or maintaining a belief.
30. In this regard, there may be an interpretation of something in the vicinity of Sosa's and Greco's virtue epistemology, where the focus is not on telic movements of the mind such as *belief-formation,* but rather on the *whole complex* of having a state of belief plus all of the cognitive activity that goes into sustaining that state through time. We could stipulatively call this complex a "performance", and then of course it would follow that the normative evaluation of this complex is an instance of the normative evaluation of a "performance". However, we should then be careful not to be misled by the stipulative label into thinking that the "performance of believing" can be evaluated by essentially instrumental standards like the telic action of shooting an arrow at a target. The "performance of believing" would rather be atelic, like the activity of maintaining a belief or a system of beliefs; this is a version of the kinds of view I explore in more detail in the next chapter. Thanks here to an anonymous referee for helping me to see this possible interpretation of virtue epistemology's approach to doxastic agency along lines more like those I develop in the following chapter.
31. For example, Soteriou (2013, chs 10–14) develops a detailed account of the activity of thinking and the role this can play in the formation of belief. And Fairweather and Montemayor (2017) explore in detail how attention works in human psychology and develop an attractive theory of the integrative role this plays in the sort of cognitive agency relevant to knowledge. These are the sorts of approaches to cognitive agency I believe will make progress on identifying the various doings that are both closely connected to believing and plausible candidates for prescriptive epistemic norms. In my view, some of these will be telic and so are plausibly called cognitive performances because it makes sense to evaluate success in terms of whether the external aim of the performance has been achieved. However, others will be atelic and so are more plausibly conceived as the sorts of cognitive activities I go on to discuss in the next chapter, where success is internal to the doing itself.

4
The Activity of Maintaining Beliefs

4.1 Introduction

Throughout the first part of this book, I have been assuming that knowledge attributions imply a robust normative evaluation of beliefs, where what it means for these evaluations to be "robust" is that they presuppose, as the normal case, that people generally manifest some agency in or over what they believe excised. I think this assumption reflects a Cartesian heritage in many of the ways epistemologists tend to think about belief and knowledge. However, as soon as we accept the involuntarist idea that belief is *not* like action in being subject to voluntary choice, we face a challenge locating the assumed agency in or over our beliefs. Moreover, this challenge deepens to the degree that we take seriously a broadly naturalistic philosophy of mind that traces most of our beliefs to quick and automatic cognitive processes that have been biologically evolved and socially conditioned.

In the previous chapters, I considered two closely related but subtly different ideas, viz., that doxastic agency is exercised mainly in the performance of believing, and that doxastic agency is exercised mainly in the performance of forming beliefs. As long as such performances are manifestations of epistemic virtues that can be credited to persons rather than merely to subpersonal cognitive mechanisms, we might plausibly regard them as exercises of someone's agency in or over belief, while also appreciating that they remain different enough from paradigmatic action to comport with the intuitions behind involuntarism and naturalistic approaches to the mind. I argued, however, that both of these ideas are problematic in instructive ways.

In this chapter, I proceed to consider two further ways to account for agency in or over our beliefs. The first account turns on the claim that we exercise agency not mainly *on* our beliefs, considered as empirical conditions of our minds, but *in* believing, considered not as a performance but as an ongoing subjective commitment to how things are. According to proponents of this view, paradigmatic belief involves a kind of essentially first-personal, non-alienated, and active ongoing endorsement of a proposition. There is an important kernel of truth in this idea, but I will argue that it is wrong to view belief *itself* as an active exercise of agency, for some of the same reasons (given in Chapter 2) that it is wrong to view belief as a performance, and for additional reasons to do with the holistic nature of our subjective take on how things are.

The second account I consider in this chapter locates much of the activity involved in doxastic agency in *belief-system maintenance*, rather than in belief itself. This is my preferred account. It allows for a picture of belief as a non-active state that is stably present in one's mind over a period of time, but which can nevertheless be seen as a *manifestation* of one's cognitive agency to the extent that its existence depends on an essentially first-personal, non-alienated, and active ongoing activity of belief-system maintenance. One of the goals of the chapter is to say more than is usually said about the nature of belief-system maintenance, and to encourage more focus on this activity in making sense of doxastic agency and epistemic normativity.

Although it may not be immediately apparent, the distinction I draw between doxastic activities and states is meant to be foundational for my contribution to the Craigian constructivist project (see Chapter 1)—more specifically, the project of explaining the concepts of belief and knowledge in terms of their role in interpersonal interactions occurring in mostly cooperative social circumstances characterized by limited individual access to necessary information that is diversely distributed (more on this in Chapter 7). The account of beliefs and doxastic agency advanced in this chapter also fits better with the related interpersonal practices of rationalizing each other's past, present, and future actions, thoughts, and feelings as a part of understanding each other. I see this as a central part of the Sellarsian idea (see Chapter 1) that attributing knowledge to someone is taking up the sort of stance toward them that involves "placing them in the space of reasons" (more on this in Chapter 9).

4.2 Belief as Active Self-Determination

Some philosophers have recently argued that although belief is not voluntarily chosen like action, it is still something wherein we are *active*, in the sense that we exercise our agency in belief itself rather than in actions or other activities that lead up to or affect what we believe. For example, Raz writes, "We are active when our mental life displays sensitivity to reasons, and we are passive when such mental events occur in a way which is not sensitive to reasons.... In these terms beliefs are...on the active side of our mental life" (1997, 218). Hieronymi writes, "I think believing is an activity done for reasons, though not something that can be finished or completed" (2009, 172). Boyle writes "The fact that believing that P is not something one does...does not rule out that believing that P is itself an exercise of agency" (2011, 16). And Moran writes, "The sense in which I see belief and other attitudes as forms of activity is deeply related to the fact that they are not matters of choice for the person, and hence the agency involved here is not that which is exercised when, say, a person chooses to raise her arm and then does so" (2012, 213).

These philosophers recognize of course that we often act so as to cause other people—and sometimes even ourselves—to have certain beliefs. But they draw a sharp contrast between such "managerial" relations to a belief and the normal way subjects are related to their own beliefs. In this vein, Hieronymi argues that beliefs are in a special class of attitudes that embody a subject's answer to a question or set of questions, and she claims that "one can exercise control or agency over such attitudes by coming to or revising one's answer to the relevant question(s)" (2009, 141). And Boyle argues that we normally expect ourselves and others to be able to answer for what we believe in a distinctively direct and first-personal way. His idea is that, when someone believes that p, it usually makes sense to ask them why they believe that p, where this is not a question about what external causes affected what they believe. It's not even a question about what actions they performed that had believing-that-p as the result. Instead, it's a question about the reasons they take to speak in favor of believing that p.[1]

These philosophers use this idea to explain how beliefs are importantly different, in relation to a person's agency, from other mental states, even ones to which we have first-personal privileged access, such as pains or headaches. We control our pains or headaches by managing them in more-or-less the same ways we might manage someone else's pains or headaches by seeking to alleviate their physiological causes, and in this sense these mental states are subject to managerial control; but beliefs seem to be subject to our rational agency in a deeper and more direct way. Accordingly, Boyle writes, "we do not merely suppose that cognitively mature human beings can, in the normal case, give expert testimony on what they believe and why. We treat them as in some sense *in charge* of what they believe and why, not merely specially knowledgeable about these topics" (2009, 123). In this way, our beliefs seem to be manifestations of a power for self-determination rather than an aspect of ourselves that we merely control.

Given the discussion in Chapter 2 of the difference between states and events, one might object to the idea that we actively exercise agency in belief itself, by insisting that "beliefs are states, not occurrences" (Bach 1981, 355). Similarly, Setiya complains that, "This way of framing things ignores a metaphysical contrast that is essential to action theory, between states, like being tall, and things that can be finished or completed and in that sense done" (2008, 38). And since part of what it means to be in a state is to be unchanging or nondynamic in some respect, one might object that someone can't literally be active in believing that p.

Hieronymi and Boyle both respond to this objection. Hieronymi argues that it is wrong to view belief as "a state that we create in ourselves, for reasons," such that one could ever be "finished with the part of believing done for reasons" (2009, 175). That would represent a kind of managerial control, and she claims that believing is better viewed as an ongoing activity rather than the completed result of some past action. Similarly, Boyle suggests that we need to recognize a form of agency "whose exercise [does not] consist in actively changing things to produce a certain result, but in actively being a certain way" (2011, 19).

Initially, this may look like a slightly odd way to use terms such as 'activity', 'active', and 'being a certain way', but Boyle seeks to motivate it via Aristotle's distinction between *kinēsis* and *energeia*.[2] In general terms, *kinēsis* refers to an active change constitutively directed toward some telos (e.g., becoming thin or running a mile); in contrast, *energeia* refers to a kind of activity that is not constitutively directed toward some telos (e.g., reflecting on some topic or running in place).[3] More specifically, as Boyle glosses Aristotle, a *kinēsis* is an "actualization of something's capacity to change in respect of place, quality, or quantity.... Any such change, Aristotle holds, proceeds from something to something: there is a condition from which it starts and a result toward which it proceeds" (2011, 19). Because it requires telic change, a *kinēsis* involves a sort of incompleteness: "while a *kinēsis* is occurring, the relevant change has not yet reached the result toward which it is proceeding, and when the result is reached, the *kinēsis* itself is no longer extant" (2011, 19–20). In contrast, Boyle glosses *energeia* as "an actualization of a capacity 'in which the end is present': one whose existence does not consist in the unfolding of a process toward a certain result, but rather in a moment of the completion of this activity" (2011, 20). The actualization involved in *energeia* is, so to speak, complete at every moment of its occurrence.

Given this distinction, Boyle suggests that believing that p is itself "an 'energetic' *act* of rational self-determination" (2011, 22–23, emphasis added). And although she doesn't employ the Aristotelian apparatus, Hieronymi intones a conception of belief as active and continuing: "My beliefs are...my present, ongoing take on what is so" (2009, 126). These suggestions provide an initially attractive account of the target of normative epistemic evaluations of belief. When assessing whether someone knows something, as I argued in Chapter 3, we seem to be evaluating the epistemic quality of what they believe here-and-now—which may or may not relate to the epistemic quality of the way they got into that state. As we saw in Chapter 2, however, the idea of believing isn't an idea of something that itself progresses toward some external end. This was the basis for my argument that the normative evaluation of belief itself cannot be in terms of the categories of performance normativity. So, if belief is conceived instead as an "active state" or an "ongoing take" of a kind that is enduring but doesn't unfold toward some end like a performance, then perhaps it could count as an exercise of a person's agency that is not performance-like. This would provide a way to retain belief at the center of here-and-now normative epistemic evaluations

Moreover, although defenders of the active state view of belief stress the sort of *rational* self-determination involved in believing *for reasons*, their views do not locate doxastic agency solely in intellectual actions such as inquiry and deliberation. The enduring act of holding p to be true can be done implicitly, habitually, or even unreasonably, but as long as the subject has the capacity to respond to what they take to be reasons for belief (i.e., they can answer the question whether p is the case, for themselves), defenders of this view will think the subject is exercising agency in believing that p. Such agency is conceived not as the agency of explicit choice but as the agency of responding to reasons. This goes some way toward addressing the deontological puzzle of how it makes sense to normatively evaluate beliefs even though they are not objects of voluntary control. Also, it promises to find doxastic agency in most of our beliefs, rather than only in the beliefs that have been or could be subjected to explicit inquiry and deliberation.

4.3 Challenges for Beliefs as Active States

It is an important insight of the active state view that believing, unlike shooting an arrow or running a marathon, is not something that could be underway at one time, only to be completed at some later time. (I discuss in more detail the apparently competing idea that belief aims at the truth in section 2.4 in Chapter 2 and Chapter 5.) Nevertheless, I want to press three related challenges to the idea that beliefs are active states. First, even if we were to concede that beliefs are active states, that wouldn't explain why they comprise direct rather than managerial exercises of agency, since there are other conditions that people can merely manage which are nevertheless enduring actualizations of a capacity. Second, I think there is an implausible hint of epistemic atomism in the suggestions that believing is an enduring act of being persuaded that p is true or a subject's ongoing take on the answer to the question of whether p is true. Our subjective take on the world doesn't typically come belief by belief, but as a holistic package, and this makes it doubtful that one exercises a rational capacity for self-determination in each individual belief, considered as an atomistic act. Third, in our ordinary conception of things, not only is believing not telic, it is also not dynamic. Belief is a state, namely, a way people *are* over a period of time, rather than something that people *do* during a period of time, which means that belief doesn't involve the sort of movement or change implied by describing something as active. In the remainder of this section, I flesh out these three challenges, which serve as the basis for the alternative view I begin to develop in the following section.

As I have indicated, I don't think that beliefs themselves are active, but I'd concede that there is a fine line between conceiving of something as a state (and so not something that happens) and thinking of something as an actualization of some capacity (and so something that happens).[4] We sometimes describe situations in one way that makes it seem like they could just as aptly be described in the other way. For example, a chemical compound might be said to be in a gaseous state, or it might be might be said to consist of a collection of molecules currently actualizing their capacity to move about at such a rate that the compound has the properties of a gas.[5] A person might be said to be in a manic state, or they might be said to be currently actualizing abnormal capacities to frenetic emotive excitement and uncontrollable bursts of energy. An animal might be described as being in a state of fear, or they might be said to be currently actualizing a capacity to increase blood flow to particular brain areas and to characteristic changes in galvanic skin response that in turn dispose them to various sorts of actions.

In light of this concession, perhaps we should grant proponents of the active state view that belief should be understood as the actualization of a capacity rather than as a state that grounds such activity. I don't really want to grant this, but even if we do, I think we should note that this idea would not fully explain how we exercise non-managerial agency in belief itself. For there are other states that could similarly be described as "active", at least in the sense that they can be correctly described as actualizations of a capacity, but which are clearly not examples of non-managerial exercises of agency. For example, being addicted to drugs or being anxious might both be thought of as "active states" that can be correctly described as a subject's actualization of a capacity. However, these states are mainly empirical conditions of a subject rather than parts of their subjective take on what is the case. Because of this, people in these states may exercise agency in seeking to manage or indirectly control them, but we don't suppose they normally are, in Boyle's sense, "in charge" of them.

Thus, something more than the idea that beliefs are active states is needed to explain the distinctive kind of agency we exercise with respect to our beliefs. Boyle suggests that beliefs are active states of "rational self-determination," and Hieronymi suggests that beliefs are active in that they represent the subject's "answer to a question." But I see these ideas as *labels* for the phenomenon we want to *explain*. Later, inspired by but also adapting Boyle and Hieronymi, I'll suggest that, unlike being addicted or being anxious, believing is a state for which the subject can have reasons, where believing on the basis of reasons is a matter of being disposed to do various things. So, were I to develop the active state view, this is where I'd be inclined to take it.

However, there is a related worry, which is my second challenge. Energetic states, if we want to recognize this category, seem to me to be importantly holistic in their structure. The sorts of examples usually given of such states—e.g., being happy with one's career, being in love with one's children, understanding poverty, being alive—are not single enduring atoms, but manifestations of a complex compound of activities, actions, and other constituting mental dispositions. There may be certain acts that manifest one's being in such states, but it's difficult to identify any particular act that is necessary to count as being in these states. And the constitution of these "active" states seems to be much more web-like than any particular belief that p.

For this reason, I think it is misleading to talk about individual beliefs as enduring acts of holding p to be true, or as settling for oneself the answer to a question about whether *p*. To be sure, philosophers sometimes talk about "maintaining" a belief that *p*, and perhaps there is little conceptual difference between believing that *p* and maintaining the belief that *p*. However, for any individual proposition *p* that we might say someone believes, there is usually a whole host of other propositions that the individual must also believe in order for it to be correct to say that they believe that *p*. And not just other *beliefs*. To count as believing that *p*, I think one must be disposed to engage in various cognitive activities, perform various intellectual actions, and automatically acquire and maintain other states in light of changing circumstances.[6] So I suspect it is wrong to think of ourselves as cognitively active mainly with respect to individual beliefs, considered as atoms of the mind.[7] Insofar as we are active with respect to our beliefs, it is with respect to groups or webs of interconnected beliefs, which means that it isn't in believing that *p*, considered alone, that one should be said to be active. So, again, were I to develop the active state view, I would want to find a way of incorporating the essentially holistic and evidentially interconnected nature of rational self-determination with respect to one's subjective take on what is the case.

The reason I'm not inclined to develop that view further, however, is that I think our understanding of beliefs for the purposes of normative epistemology is, primarily, of them as states, and only secondarily of them as actualizations of capacities. I'll say more later about the qualification "for the purposes of normative epistemology," but my driving thought here is that part of the function of belief is to stick around, to lie in wait through time, while other things in our environment and minds change. And, quite generally, the idea of stativity involves persistence, being unchanged in some central respect through time, whereas the idea of activity involves dynamicity and change over time.[8] Beliefs seem to me to fit more cleanly in the former category.[9] As Peirce wrote, "belief does not make us act at once, but puts us into such a condition that we shall behave in a certain way, when the occasion arises" (1877, 6). Peirce's claim is not strictly inconsistent with the idea that belief is active, yet the longer any particular believing is supposed to be "happening", and the more things are supposedly changing in the background, the less plausible it seems to me that we're talking about something dynamic or active.[10]

This is why, in the end, I think belief is not dynamic, neither in the way of telic events that involve progress toward some end, nor in the way of atelic activities that involve movement or change during a period of time but which are not directed at some external end. I recognize that this may sound like a stubborn stipulation rather than an argument against the active state view. So, I'll sketch a more substantive account of belief in the next section which I hope makes sense of why it is useful to treat belief as a state which persists unchanging for a period of time. But first I'd like to recall that the stative nature of belief is both crucial to standard conceptions of belief in philosophy and is presupposed in the way we use the word 'believes' in ordinary language. This is what I take to be manifested in the aspectual distinctions available for the words we use to speak about things that are stative and dynamic. Recall the verb phrase aspect typology canvassed in Chapter 2 (see Figure 4.1, an expansion of Figure 2.1, with extra examples).

English verb phrases[11] describing paradigmatically dynamic things, such as 'eat healthily' or 'build a house', admit of the progressive form '*S is f-ing*', whereas verb phrases describing paradigmatically stative things, such as 'be tall' or 'desire tea', do not typically admit of this progressive form.[12] This is because they are not things that the subject is actively doing during a period of time, but ways that the subject *is* over a period of time.

Intuitively, belief doesn't fit with other activities. We don't say things such as "I am believing that it is sunny today." Furthermore, it is notable that the verb 'believe' is often one of the examples linguists use of a paradigmatic state verb when distinguishing state descriptions from activity and event descriptions. Boyle concedes "that we will not accept 'I believe that P' as an answer to 'What are you doing?'" (2011, 16). But he seems to think this is an unfortunate quirk of English rather than a hint about how we tacitly conceive of beliefs when we use this term. He continues, "but that is merely because the formulation of the question here demands an answer in a continuous tense, and 'to believe' is a stative verb that is

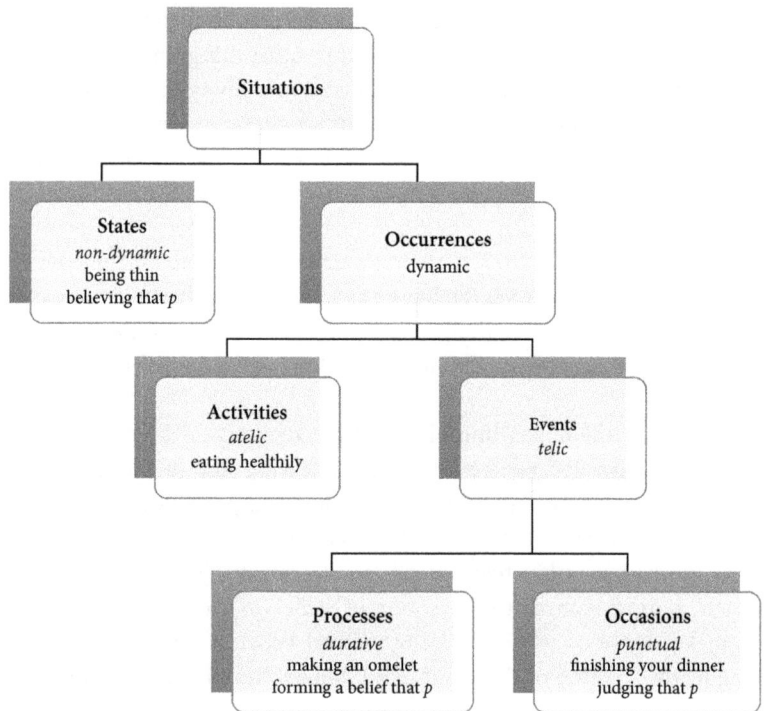

Figure 4.1 Verb phrase aspect typology (expanded)

not ascribed in the continuous tense" (2011, 16). That's right, but I think there's no *merely* about it. I think the best explanation of why we use a stative verb to refer to belief is that belief *is* ordinarily conceived as something stative rather than active. This isn't an accident of English but, as I will try to motivate more in the next section, something we should recognize even if we were to doubt the sort of linguistic evidence given earlier.

That is not to say, of course, that our beliefs don't alter in light of changing external circumstances or developing internal thought processes. But, as B. Williams writes, "if they change too often... they will not be beliefs but rather something like propositional moods" (2002, 191). Williams sees this stability as crucial to the development of cooperative activity in epistemic communities: "The basic mechanism depends on the fact that there are others who need to rely on our dispositions, and we want them to be able to rely on our dispositions because we, up to a point, want to rely on theirs" (2002, 192).

Activities, such as eating healthily, running, or daydreaming are all described with verb phrases that pass tests for being dynamic but atelic, which is why they get classified as occurrences, but not as the kind of occurrences which progress toward some endpoint. Activities involve movement or change during a period of time, but no progress toward some endpoint. By contrast, states are neither telic nor dynamic; they are conceived as a way someone *is* over some period of time, wherein one neither progresses toward some end nor moves or changes with respect to the state.[13] On the assumption that an *exercise* of agency must be active, and whatever is active is dynamic rather than static, this means that belief itself cannot be both a state and an exercise of cognitive agency.[14]

4.4 What Is Belief Anyway?

I suspect part of the motivation for thinking that beliefs are active states is the assumption that if we are not active in belief then we must be passive. And if we're passive with respect to what we currently believe, then epistemic normative evaluations can't really pertain to what we believe here-and-now, but could at best pertain to how we formed our beliefs. Belief-formation is a performance and so dynamic, but I think Boyle is right that any account locating doxastic agency only in such performances would be one in which "beliefs can at most 'store' the results" of our cognitive activity, which would mean that "a person's agency can get no nearer to her beliefs than to touch them at their edges" (2009, 121). So, how do we develop a picture of our minds that retains a kind of activity with respect to our beliefs, but without construing beliefs themselves as active, and *also* without construing them as passive, touched by our cognitive agency only at their edges?

To start, I think we need a fuller account of what belief is than has been provided so far. For reasons mentioned later, I won't attempt to offer a full answer to the question "What is the nature of belief?" But I will try to outline some of the philosophical controversies packed into this question and indicate where I stand on them.

Some philosophers argue that belief is a type of occurrent idea with particular phenomenological characteristics such as vivacity, tenacity, and conviction, whereas others argue that it is a dispositional state that can lie dormant to be only sometimes occurrently cognized.[15] Some philosophers argue that belief is a specific kind of neurological representation encoded in the language of thought and located in a module of the human mind, whereas others argue that belief is anything with a particular psycho-functional role, wherever exactly that is realized in various sorts of minds.[16] Some philosophers argue that there are no beliefs and that belief-talk is a convenient fiction, whereas others argue that beliefs are theoretical posits of mental entities that are presumed to be real, and which we make as part of rationalizing what other people do, think, and feel.[17] Some philosophers argue that belief is essentially the manifestation of conceptually articulate, reasons-responsive, and potentially self-conscious thought of the sort in which mainly only humans engage, whereas others argue that belief is any state in an animal's mind that carries information in a way that allows the animal to act on the information.[18] Some philosophers argue that belief is a fundamentally different sort of mental state from faith, credence, conviction, and delusion, whereas others argue that these states are just some of the many types of belief.[19] Some philosophers insist that belief must have propositional content and that it constitutively aims at truth, whereas other philosophers doubt that we can always identify a precise propositional content for beliefs, and others still wonder whether truth is even a coherent "aim" for belief.[20]

This theoretical space contains a dizzying array of cross-cutting distinctions. I'm not at all confident that we know how to go about investigating the nature of belief to be able to settle the questions represented in this array. Also, I think we should be careful not to tacitly assume that belief is a substance which might be studied by doing something akin to cutting open people's heads and subjecting what we find to biological analysis. And, while I've argued that reflection on the semantic properties of the word 'belief' reveals some common properties of all things called "beliefs", I suspect that traditional kinds of conceptual analysis promise little in the way of answers to the controversial questions alluded to in the previous paragraph.

Instead, I think we should accept that different conceptions of belief are going to be appropriate for different purposes. We should respect the semantic properties of the word 'belief' in order to avoid changing the topic or talking past one another, but we should also try to articulate our specific theoretical purpose before saying anything more specific about what belief is.

So, what is my purpose in this book? At the most simplistic level, I treat belief as the primary object of normative epistemic evaluation because I think of epistemology as centered on the study of knowledge, and I am assuming that knowing that *p* requires truly believing that *p* plus meeting some normative standard. Moreover, I assume that when we're talking about whether someone *epistemically* ought or ought not to believe that *p*, we are primarily concerned with rules or standards, conformity to which is necessary for someone to count as knowing that *p*. Hence, in epistemology's focus on knowledge and a related epistemic conception of 'ought', I think we already assume belief to be the primary target of normative epistemic evaluation.

As we have seen, however, there is controversy amongst epistemologists regarding how to think about what belief is (a performance, the result of a performance, or an active state, etc.). In my view, for understanding both the distinctive value of knowledge and the susceptibility of belief to robust normative evaluations, it is important to treat belief as a state that persists unchanging for some period of time, unlike action which involves change. Hence, knowledge-relevant norms for belief are not properly conceived as norms for action (as I will discuss in Chapter 6); in evaluating whether someone believes as they ought to believe, we are not generally evaluating actions they are engaging or have engaged in, or even the performance of acquiring the relevant belief. We care about knowledgeable belief is, in part, because we rely on it to stick around, unchanged for a period of time.

Despite this, I think beliefs are a special kind of state, the possession of which can be said to *manifest* the active exercise of someone's cognitive agency. Digging into how this could be so is the key to developing a conception of belief suitable for epistemological purposes. The tricky task, as I see it, is to connect an epistemological conception of the state of belief with other nearby and more obviously active processes, such as inquiry, inference, and deliberation, *but also* with all of those more automatic cognitive processes involved in the maintenance of one's overall system of beliefs. To this end, we should organize and extend some insights from accounts discussed earlier.

I think proponents of reliabilist virtue epistemology are right to argue that an important aspect of our epistemic conception of belief is that beliefs are denizens of person-level cognitive systems, rather than merely subpersonal psycho-neurological systems.[21] Moreover, proponents of the active state view are also right to argue that an important aspect of our epistemic conception of belief is of belief as an essentially subjective, first-personal, and usually non-alienated take on what is the case. However, I also want to emphasize the way that attributions of such states figure in irreducibly first-personal plural and second-personal ways in the sort of interpersonal communication and sensemaking involved in social cooperation. We attribute beliefs to one another and avow beliefs in ourselves as part of rationalizing actions, attitudes, and other beliefs. Furthermore, we do this not usually out of idle curiosity but for the purpose of engaging with each other in the attempt to improve and spread knowledge within a group of people.

So, as much as anything, I think these *interpersonal* aspects of belief-system maintenance are what makes beliefs appropriate targets of the robust normative evaluation implicit in knowledge attributions. From the first-personal subjective perspective, it can be difficult to achieve distance between what one takes oneself to believe and what one takes oneself to know, without thinking of oneself in an alienated, third-personal way. But, as soon as we think about what *each other* believe and know, it is quite easy to realize that not all of our beliefs meet the normative standard necessary to count as knowledge. For example, we might appreciate that the reason why someone is reluctant to vaccinate their kids is that they believe what many of their friends on Facebook say about the risks. Then thinking about why these beliefs don't meet epistemic standards for knowledge can lead further to self-evaluation of our own grounds for believing that vaccinating our kids is safe and important. In this way, believing as one epistemically ought to believe, and hence knowing something, can be seen to be more important than the things some of us merely happen to want.

One might worry that this conception of belief presupposes too much conceptual articulateness amongst people to whom we attribute beliefs. For instance, is there really a specific proposition that people who are skeptical of vaccinating their kids believe; do people forming beliefs based on what friends say on Facebook really aim at the truth when considering such matters?[22] I'll have more to say about the idea that belief aims at truth in Chapter 5, where I'll argue that belief should be thought of as subject to a constitutive norm of truth, but that it's wrong to think that *believers* typically aim at standing in the belief relation to a proposition just in case it is true. My idea is that to have truth as a constitutive norm means that it always makes sense to ask of any belief whether it is true and, if it isn't true, to regard it as incorrect. But I take that idea to be consistent with thinking that believers don't typically aim directly at the truth in their thinking, or that they require a fully articulate grasp of the concepts involved in proposition p in order to be properly said to believe that p.

In my view, we attribute belief not mainly in order to predict the future behavior of others, but rather to make sense of each other and to figure out where and how we might cooperate or at least coordinate action.[23] This means that we posit beliefs from first-, second-, and third-personal perspectives, and I think that privileging any of these perspectives over the others is likely to distort the picture of belief needed to make sense of knowledge. Moreover, we often make such attributions with an eye not just on external behavioral dispositions, but also on cognitive, emotional, and phenomenological dispositions.[24] And I think we're not only interested in the downstream causal upshots of belief, but also the upstream causal antecedents of belief. Because of this, I embrace a functionalist conception of belief as a dispositional state constitutively subject to normative evaluation.

In sum, for my epistemological purposes here, I treat beliefs as dispositional states constitutively connected to processes of belief-formation, activities of belief-system maintenance, and occasions of judgment; these states in turn integrate broader functional connections to inputs in perception and attention, as well as to outputs in the phenomenology of conviction and various sorts of emotional and behavioral reactions. And all of this is apt for normative evaluation in virtue of the interpersonal practice of making sense of each other and the world in our ongoing attempts to act together. Unlike many other states of ourselves, belief is a state with propositional content which we can hold for reasons and avow on the basis of those reasons; we can also posit it in others, with varying levels of conceptual resources, as part of collective sensemaking. And we do all of this in the hopes of learning about the world and cooperating over time in pursuing our aims.

4.5 Doxastic Agency in the Maintenance of Systems of Belief

With a fuller conception of belief on the table, we should now ask: where's the agency? The typology in Figure 4.1, laying out the different aspectual categories of situations, provides a clue. If beliefs are classified as *states* because they are atelic and nondynamic, it is easy to think of nearby doxastic *events*, which are telic and dynamic, such as the formation of a belief. But that leaves the following question unanswered: What could be the nearby doxastic *activities* that are dynamic but atelic?

I think normal beliefs should be regarded as particular manifestations of the general activities that sustain them. What are these "doxastic" activities? Surely, they are diverse, but we can refer to them generically under the heading of *belief-system maintenance*.[25] And I want to propose an account according to which a central and important form of doxastic agency is exercised in this activity; on this account, it is only to the degree that individual beliefs are *sustained* by this activity that they count as manifestations of our agency. In my view, individual belief is not the right focus for understanding doxastic agency and epistemic normativity. This echoes something Moran writes: "what we call a person's beliefs are the precipitate of her ongoing rational activity. It is only derivatively that a person is 'active' with respect to a particular attitude itself" (2012, 219). We sometimes posit individual beliefs as part of rationalizing explanations; however, we don't hold our own beliefs individually but as part of broader rationally integrated systems.

So, in the way I am thinking of it, maintaining a system of beliefs involves not just holding a set of many individual beliefs, but basing some of those beliefs on other of those beliefs (and potentially other aspects of our cognition) in an ongoing fashion.[26] And in a more fine-grained way, it involves a kind of ongoing modulation of one's degree of confidence in particular propositions, in light of one's changing degrees of confidence in *other* propositions, and updates to one's implicit understanding of the relations of probabilistic and rational support between them.[27]

There are surely some sub-agential (mainly physiological) processes that have to be functioning well for a person to maintain a system of beliefs, but I am thinking of such maintenance as a dynamic, agent-level phenomenon. Moreover, such belief-system maintenance is not typically something that one does *to* oneself, considered as an empirical condition of the world to be acted upon, but rather part of what it is *to be a self*, to have a first-personal perspective on what is the case. That doesn't mean that the activity of maintaining a system of beliefs has to be conscious, indeed much of it might be relatively automatic in the sense of "habitual" (rather than "passive"). Nevertheless, some of it could be conscious and deliberate, e.g., where one maintains a system of beliefs by endeavoring to learn new things about the world, which then bears on how confident one is about specific beliefs and how well one understands the reasons for holding them.[28] And this possibility explains why we typically think of our beliefs as *up to us* in a more intimate and direct way than mere empirical conditions (e.g., our weight or headaches).

This is a holistic picture. Belief-system maintenance may involve various acts, but there needn't be a specific act which constitutes belief-system maintenance. Indeed, maintaining a belief system may require no conscious or intentional attention for a period of time; there may even be periods when the relevant habits lie dormant or are temporarily inactivated. Moreover, although intentional action resulting in the formation of a state can be an important part of maintaining a system of such states, we needn't assume that a person must voluntarily choose to form a particular belief in order to count as active in the maintenance of this belief as part of a system of beliefs. Sometimes people consciously seek to answer a question about whether p, and answer it in the formation of a belief, which is then maintained; but other times, they simply find themselves believing that p and then maintain this belief as part of their overall system of beliefs. Either way, this manner of exercising agency with respect to one's beliefs seems to me to be importantly different from the sorts of "Pascalian" actions which we might imagine someone performs *on* their belief systems when they endeavor to make it the case that they believe that p. Maintaining a system of beliefs, as I am thinking of it, is not manipulative or managerial in that way; one exercises paradigmatic doxastic agency *in* maintaining a system of beliefs, not in extra-epistemic acts *on* one's system of beliefs.

As the verb phrase suggests, 'maintain a system of beliefs' is dynamic rather than static. Maintaining something (e.g., your fitness or your garden) can be a grammatical (albeit slightly weird) answer to the question "What are you doing?" And, as the verb phrase suggests, the activity of maintaining something is spread out in time like a process, but, *unlike* a process, it is atelic, i.e., lacking an external endpoint. More specifically, maintaining a system of beliefs involves continually re-examining what one believes in light of the evidence that one has and continues to acquire. This activity can be more or less deliberate and conscious. For example, sometimes we reflective adult humans think hard about a question, or explicitly re-evaluate the inferential or evidential relations between our beliefs.[29] Other times, though, we are more similar to animals and young children, merely manifesting a low-level disposition for credence in a proposition to go up or down in light of new beliefs that we acquire automatically.

In sum, I think the notion of maintaining a system of beliefs provides something active (in the sense of being dynamic) but atelic (in the sense of not progressing toward some end) that deserves consideration as a primary locus of doxastic agency.

I suggested in section 4.3 that a challenge for the active state view was to explain what distinguishes doxastic activity from other actualizations of capacities, such as being anxious or being addicted to drugs. My answer to that challenge is twofold. First, I think that part of what makes a cognitive activity *belief*-system maintenance is that the states maintained have to be reactive to epistemic reasons.[30] In other words, the system will change in light of the believer's coming to appreciate new considerations which they (often implicitly) take as bearing on whether individual beliefs are true.[31] This is weaker than the idea that believers must be responsive to the real reasons that there are for believing one thing rather than another. Believers can actively maintain a system of beliefs that is deeply deluded or misguided. Second, belief-system maintenance allows for the good case where believers base their beliefs on the epistemic reasons they take themselves to have. That is, a believer can base their beliefs on considerations which (they assume to) bear on the truth of the belief. This basing of a subject's beliefs on their reasons will usually be implicit and often unconscious, and there may well be beliefs that are baseless. But my idea is that, in the paradigm reflective person case, one counts as maintaining a system of beliefs to the degree that one is regarded as a proper target of the question "Why do you believe that?" (conceived as a request for justification rather than causal explanation).[32]

For most things a person believes, it makes sense to ask about the reasons for which they believe them, and this is a way of presuming believers are in charge of their beliefs via the activity of maintaining their system of beliefs. However, being a proper target of this question doesn't mean that people always know or can easily find out what they believe about a topic. Except in relatively simple or explicitly deliberated cases, I doubt that people can just look "transparently" to the world in order to figure out whether they believe that p, or to discern the reasons they base their belief that p on.[33] As I will discuss more in Part II, we often depend on interaction with our epistemic community in order to develop clearer views about what we believe and why.

So far, I have been stressing the active and holistic nature of the activity of belief-system maintenance because it is key to explaining how my preferred view of doxastic agency locates it not in individual states of belief, but in the wider cognitive activity of integrating that state of belief with other aspects of one's subjective take on what is the case. I think we do normatively evaluate individual beliefs when we make knowledge attributions, but this evaluation presupposes a kind of agency that can be exercised only at the level of systems of beliefs. (More on the nature and content of these norms in Part II.)

In presenting this picture, I may have given the impression that I think of belief-system maintenance as a mainly solitary affair, but I don't. Part of what I think makes a cognitive activity *belief*-system maintenance (as opposed to some other mental activity), is that the states maintained are such that they ought to be true. This is the beginning of my account of deontological evaluations of beliefs. And, as I will argue in Chapter 5, individual subjects do not normally evaluate their own beliefs for whether they are true (for, to do so would be to try to manage one's beliefs as an empirical condition of one's mind, rather than as constituting one's subjective take on what is the case). Rather, I think reference to the truth or falsity of someone's beliefs is how *other people* identify whether what someone is up to is *belief*-system maintenance.

Moreover, as I will discuss more in Chapter 7, a key element of the way human belief states get their characteristic stability is the sort of corrective and supportive interactions people have with their community. This occurs both because we challenge each other when beliefs differ on some topic of mutual concern, and because we depend on each other for various bits of knowledge about the way things are and what we ought to do, think, and feel about the way things are. Here I am echoing something B. Williams writes:

> If what I uninhibitedly declare at a given moment can be taken by myself or anyone else as a declaration of something which I believe, that is because there is a practice that firms up the expression of the immediate state into something that has a future, it is what enables us, most of the time coherently to make such declarations as declarations of belief, and to read them in what other people say.
> (2002, 192)

4.6 Conclusion

In Chapter 1, I suggested that one central puzzle about epistemic normativity is that we normatively evaluate beliefs, and normative evaluations presuppose the ability to exercise some kind of agency connected to the object of normative evaluation, but believers don't normally exercise voluntary control over our beliefs. Given the very natural assumption that exercises of agency are active, this deontological puzzle about epistemic normativity seems to force anyone who wants to recognize the robustly normative evaluations in epistemology into a difficult theoretical choice. Either belief itself is an active exercise of agency, or we exercise agency only in the process of belief-formation. In this chapter, I've argued this is a false dichotomy. I've offered an alternative account of doxastic agency, which I've claimed is consistent with an attractive way of conceiving what belief is for the purposes of normative epistemology.

More precisely, I have argued that doxastic agency is exercised mainly in the activity of maintaining a system of beliefs. This is a cognitive activity involving webs of multiple inferentially and evidentially connected mental states that ought to be true. I've claimed that locating doxastic agency here, rather than in individual states of belief or in the performance of forming them, captures the active, atelic, and holistic aspect of doxastic agency better than competing accounts. And the assumption that this activity normally involves a subject's being regarded as open to the justificatory, rather than (merely) causal, question "Why do you believe that?" for any state maintained, is a way of differentiating the activity of belief-system maintenance from other subpersonal activities. This provides a way to respect the robustness of epistemic normative evaluations of belief, while recognizing both that they presuppose some kind of agency with respect to beliefs and that we do not normally voluntarily choose our beliefs. I think the active state view is right that believers exercise doxastic agency in their ongoing and atelic reactivity to reasons, but where believers do this is *not* in the state of belief itself (conceived somehow as an active atom of the mind) but in the activity of maintaining a system of beliefs.

A natural response to my suggestion that doxastic agency is located mainly in the activity of belief-system maintenance is that this idea is not *so* different from the other views I have considered in this part of the book. Perhaps, for example, defenders of the performance view will think that they can easily incorporate cognitive activities alongside cognitive performances in their overall account of cognitive agency; then maybe we'd just need to update the name of the view to the performance-and-activity view. Or, similarly, a defender of the active state view might think that beliefs count as "active states" precisely because they are partially constituted by their manifesting the activity of belief-system maintenance in something like the way that I have suggested. The devil is in the details, of course, but I'd welcome such company, as long as it didn't require us to conceive of beliefs as something other than cognitive states, or to reject the conception of states as themselves stative rather than dynamic. And I'd want to push proponents of these accounts to reflect more on the social character of belief-system maintenance through interpersonal first-person plural and second-personal normative evaluations of beliefs.

If doxastic agency is exercised (at least mainly) in maintaining systems of belief, as I suggest, we avoid the idea that subjects exercise agency only *on* beliefs, considered as merely empirical conditions of their minds. This approach also makes sense of the possibility of agential involvement in beliefs acquired in some way other than actively engaging in inquiry and deliberation. Such beliefs can still be based on and serve as the basis for other beliefs in one's belief system, and so can be actively maintained as part of maintaining that system. As we acquire new information, we also adjust our understanding of the evidential relation between various beliefs without ever giving up those beliefs, and we change our disposition to inquire further to try to confirm or disconfirm beliefs that don't seem to cohere well together, even if we cannot quite say why. Cognitively, much of this may happen through relatively automatic processes of Bayesian updating; still, I don't think that means we should conceive of ourselves as *passive* with respect to these processes, since we implicitly recognize them as our own (insofar as our endorsement of our beliefs constitutes an enduring subjective take on what is the case).

I was initially drawn to the idea that activities of belief-system maintenance are of central importance to understanding doxastic agency because it seemed to be truer to the phenomenology of epistemic norm-governance, as reflected (albeit incompletely) in the language we use to talk about epistemic matters. When we talk about what someone ought to believe, or we ask ourselves what we ought to believe, we don't usually think of this as targeting a specific act of judgment or action of inquiry, but rather as targeting a web of interconnected cognitive activities. But I also think this more complex picture I have developed, which gives pride of place to the cognitive activity of belief-system maintenance, is ultimately going to be crucial to making sense of ourselves as believers in a distributed information-managing *community*, especially as imperfect information-storing beings with diverse perspectives on the world. This, in turn, is what will fund a more social account of the distinctive value of knowledge. As I will argue further in Chapters 7 and 9, we care about knowledge more than unknowledgeable belief, and we think it is especially worth pursuing, largely because of the special role it plays in the collective regulation of our distributed information-managing communities.

Rather than asking simply about the rules of judgment, or about the norms of individual inquiry and deliberation, I think we should ask about the various normative standards whose application to our beliefs, maintenance of belief systems, belief-formation (including by perception, testimony, and deliberation), and judgment, is what makes all of these things integrated parts of human cognition in our *essentially social* environment. So, in the next part of the book, I turn to the social nature of epistemic normativity, and in particular to explaining the axiological status of knowledge within epistemic communities, given the ways in which it makes sense to deontologically evaluate states such as belief.

Notes

1. Drawing on Anscombe's (1957, 9) much discussed special sense of the question "Why?" For discussion, see Moran (2004), Thompson (2008), Hubbs (2013), and Teichman (2015).
2. Boyle cites Aristotle's *Metaphysics* IX. 6 (1048b 18–35).
3. One can of course engage in an activity such as reflecting on some topic or running in place *for some purpose,* such as satisfying one's curiosity or wining a prize. But the point is that these purposes are not *constitutive* of such activities in the way that being thin or having run a mile are constitutive of the events of becoming thin and running a mile.
4. Koziolek (2018) argues that belief is a state rather than an activity, but he suggests that belief is an actualization of rational capacities involved in having the faculty of reason. In my view, however, he does not show how belief itself can be the actualization of a capacity; rather, he shows how the *acquisition* of a belief can be the actualization of a capacity. As I discussed in Chapter 3, belief acquisition and formation are active and telic, but not plausibly regarded as the main locus of doxastic agency.
5. In connection to the idea that belief is a state, Steward (1997, 69) discussed the idea that a chemical can be in a gaseous state because of the activity of all of the molecules. She argues, convincingly in my view, that we should see the state of the chemical as dependent on the activities of the molecules even though the activities of the molecules are not parts of the state.
6. Compare Currie and Juredini (2001) for discussion of delusions and an argument that some aren't beliefs because of not being properly integrated with other aspects of the believer's cognition. See also Hetherington (2012, 83–85) who argues that states of knowledge are constituted by the ability to be manifested in various forms of activities. Similarly, I suspect the constitutivist route provides a way to make sense of what Rohrbaugh (2015) calls "inner achievements", like sobriety and marriage, which seem to me to involve both states and activities constitutively related. However, as far as the account in this chapter goes, I think one might back off from the metaphysical claims of constitution, and instead insist on conceptual claims about what one who attributes belief (and knowledge) is committed to in virtue of our concepts of these things and of the various actions and activities intimately related to them.
7. For related reasons, I think a reliabilist account of epistemic justification that focuses on the reliability with which beliefs are sustained (rather than on the etiology of belief-formation as we saw with Greco in the previous chapter) is going to need to examine the reliability of belief-*system* maintenance, rather than the reliability of sustained particular beliefs considered as atoms.
8. See Comrie (1976, ch. 1) and Brinton (2009, ch. 1).
9. Compare Meylan (2020) for a related objection based on the idea that states do not have temporal parts. Her paper targets performance-based views, but I think it applies to the active state view as well.
10. Hieronymi objects to a picture of beliefs as stored information or standing dispositions. She writes, "My beliefs do not sit in my mind as last week's lecture sits on my hard drive, recording what I once thought.... My beliefs are not like the 'out of office reply' feature that I set up for my e-mail account: they are not something I create and then

allow to affect things on my behalf " (2009, 176). I think it is right to say that beliefs are not *merely* stored information or *only* standing dispositions, but unless beliefs store information and dispose one to act in various ways, it is unclear how we can explain agents' behavior by appealing to something they believe though aren't currently thinking about. Moreover, if beliefs didn't tend to have the kind of stability to them of a standing disposition, it'd be hard to make sense of the way we can explain why an agent will act the way that they will by appealing to their stable beliefs. For these reasons, I think we should allow that beliefs often store information and function as standing dispositions, while insisting that one's first-personal relation to one's own beliefs is not as a merely empirical condition that one can notice and potentially change, but as something that is part of an overall system that one is, in an ongoing way, always maintaining. I go on to develop this thought further in the next section.

11. I acknowledge that this is an argument based on one particular language during one particular phase of its historical evolution. Different languages operationalize the conceptual distinctions between stative vs. active, telic vs. atelic, and durative vs. punctual, and these won't always be grammaticalized in the semantics of particular verb phrases. Still, I think the English verb phrases provide a window into that aspect of our conceptual scheme, which is widely attested in human languages.

12. Although it doesn't matter for the argument I go on to make, it is important to note that the distinctions in verbal aspect I'm appealing to are semantic not grammatical. The distinction between verbs that do and don't admit of transformation into the grammatical progressive is idiolect-relative and historically contingent, which makes it an imperfect guide to the semantic distinction between verbs that describe something dynamic and verbs that describe something stative. For instance, standard English deploys the grammatical progressive with verbs used to describe states considered somehow temporary, e.g., "The statue is standing in the driveway," but this is still semantically considered a state description. Some people have suggested to me that 'believe' admits of an atypical use in the progressive, as in, "For a second there, I was believing you were dead." In my idiolect, 'believe' never takes the grammatical progressive, but even if it did in a case like this, I think that is just an example of how English uses the grammatical progressive to refer to states that are considered somehow temporary. See Goldsmith and Woisetschlaeger (1982) for useful discussion of the English progressive used to make state descriptions.

13. What about Aristotle's distinction between *kinēsis* and *energeia*? I don't object to placing things into theoretical categories in whatever way suits one's theoretical purposes (and, to be clear, I think Aristotle's terminology marks a philosophically important distinction). However, by also using ordinary language to refer to things that go in those categories, one risks importing alternative and incompatible criteria implicit in the use of terms such as "state" and "activity". In order to be active, something must be dynamic, in the sense of conceived as involving change or movement; my claim is that this is incompatible with being conceived, for the purposes of normative epistemology, as a state. That is ultimately why I demur at the idea that belief is an active state. For what it's worth, I suspect Aristotle's category of *energeia* is better conceived as within the typological category of activity (dynamic so not state-like, but atelic so not event-like). And I could imagine a version of Boyle's view that finds a distinctive kind of

doxastic agency in the activity of maintaining beliefs instead of the state of belief. Changing his view in this way would move rather close to the view I go on to develop later.
14. Perhaps proponents of the active state view will insist that, in spite of philosophical orthodoxy and linguistic custom, the verb 'believes' refers to something that isn't really a state, if states have to be nondynamic. For example, Miracchi (2015, 30) suggests that all mental states are actually activities of some sort. Or maybe Boyle and Hieronymi should be read as proposing to change our way of speaking and thinking so as to treat *believe* as an activity verb rather than a state verb. Either of these ways of defending the view would involve radically revisionary claims about the metaphysics of mind and/or ordinary language—claims which would have to be evaluated by comparing the theoretical and practical usefulness of our current metaphysics and ordinary language to the suggested alternative. I don't think this is actually what Boyle and Hieronymi have in mind, and I'm not going to discuss further here the possibility of giving up on the orthodoxy that belief is a mental state. I argue for the orthodoxy in more detail in Chrisman (2012a).
15. Some philosophers follow Hume, who famously defines 'belief' as "a lively idea related to or associated with a present impression," (1978, 96); see also J. Marušić (2010) for discussion. She cites MacNabb (1951, 69–81), Everson (1988, 401–413), Armstrong (1973, 70–72), Stroud, (1977, 74), and Loeb (2002) for dispositionalist readings of Hume and arguments for dispositionalism more broadly. See also Braithwaite (1933), Price (1969), Lycan (1986), and Crane (2013) for useful discussion of occurrentism vs. dispositionalism about belief.
16. For defenses of the something like the former idea, see Fodor (1975, 1981), Dretske (1988), and Mandelbaum (2016), and for the latter idea, see Putnam (1975), Loar (1981), and Leitgeb (2017). These aren't obviously incompatible positions. See especially Fodor (1981, 1990) for discussion.
17. See Churchland (1981) and Jenson (2016) for defenses of eliminativism. See Dennett (1987, 1991) for discussion of instrumentalism and development of his idea that beliefs are posited as part of certain kinds of folk-psychological explanations.
18. Compare Gendler's (2008a, 2008b) distinction between belief and alief, and the critique of the idea that the latter aren't beliefs discussed in Hubbs (2013), Mandelbaum (2013), and Wilkinson (2013). See also Frankish (2004, 2007, 2009, 2012) for someone who distinguishes the consciously formed and deliberative beliefs of system-1 cognition from the unconsciously formed beliefs of system-2.
19. See Bayne and Pacherie (2005) and Bortolotti (2009), who argue that delusions are beliefs; see Berrios (1991), Currie and Jureidini (2001), Egan (2009), and Schwitzgebel (2012) for counterarguments.
20. See Baracan Marcus (1990).
21. See Steward (1997) and Hunter (2001) for important defenses of the idea that beliefs are states a person is *in* rather than states *inside* of a person.
22. See Zimmerman (2018, ch. 3) for discussion of some of the reasons philosophers and cognitive ethologists have been skeptical of over-intellectualizing the attribution of belief by insisting that it is always an attitude toward a specific proposition.
23. Compare Dennett (1969) and the discussion in Hornsby (2000).

24. See Schwitzgebel (2002).
25. As we learned in Chapter 2.4 when discussing the motionless statues, the idea of maintaining something for a specific period of time is telic, but the ongoing and unbounded maintenance of something is an atelic activity.
26. Initial formation of belief can involve basing it on something, and so the epistemic quality of belief-formation can indicate the quality of basing. In the way I am thinking of it, however, basing is an ongoing and sometimes evolving relation between a belief and its basis. So, one's current belief that p may be based on evidence which one did not possess when one originally formed the belief. See the cases of improved bases discussed in Chapter 3.3, which I think generate problems for views of justification focused exclusively on the quality of belief-formation. See Nottelmann (2007, ch. 5) for a similar appeal to the relevance of basing in exercising agency to meet epistemic demands.
27. Compare Nolfi (2018) for a congenial view that doxastic agency is located most centrally in the cognitive processes manifesting our belief-regulating dispositions.
28. I'm not completely sure what to say about the beliefs of animals and young children, but I am inclined to think it is a matter of degree how self-conscious and rationally deliberate a belief is maintained, and any discontinuities are not about *whether* animals and young children maintain beliefs, but about which of their beliefs can be brought to self-consciousness and maintained in a rationally deliberate way. Even for adult humans, I suspect not all of our beliefs can be easily brought to self-consciousness and maintained in a rationally deliberate way.
29. Compare Nolfi (2014) for an account of how normative judgment about what one ought to believe might plausibly be involved in belief-system regulation.
30. B. Marušić (2015, 136–143) distinguishes a category of beliefs he calls "practical beliefs" which pertain to one's own future behavior, e.g., the gambler's belief about whether he will gamble again in the future. He argues that these can and should be reactive to the person's practical reasons for resolving to behave in certain ways in the future. As he points out, it is important for how we think about practical reasoning that we regard these as beliefs, but equally they often seem, even to the believer, to be theoretically irrational. These represent an interesting special case, and I'm not sure what to say about them. But even if such practical beliefs can and should be maintained for partly practical reasons, they are not maintained *only* for practical reasons. For example, the believer has to believe that the relevant future action is possible.
31. McHugh argues that we are responsible for a belief only if we have what Fischer and Rivizza (1998) term "guidance control" with respect to that belief. On McHugh's way of developing the idea, guidance control requires that the believer be receptive and reactive to reasons. Being "receptive" requires that the believer recognizes reasons for and against the belief across an appropriate range of scenarios (even if she fails to do so in some particular scenario). Being "reactive" requires that, in an appropriate range of scenarios, the believer "reacts to the reasons she takes herself to have by forming the doxastic attitude they seem to her to dictate" (2013, 143). This may be right, though I worry that it is too atomistic, because I doubt we can understand receptivity and reactivity with regard to single beliefs absent integration with wider webs of belief. Nevertheless, what's important here is that I haven't made any claims in the discussion

about when believers are *responsible* for their beliefs. This is because I think believers can exercise agency with respect to beliefs, even if conceiving of them as responsible isn't yet appropriate (e.g., because they are children), or if responsibility has been undermined or mitigated in some way (e.g., because they have been brainwashed). Moreover, even if responsibility requires receptivity to (actual) reasons, I suspect doxastic agency requires only reactivity to what the agent takes to be reasons. Also, as discussed in the previous chapter, I think there are many cases where it is unclear whether a belief was *formed* as a reaction to what the believer took to be reasons, but where they go on to maintain the relevant belief as part of their overall system of beliefs in a way that is reactive to reasons.

32. This is where I think Anscombe's much discussed "certain sense of the question 'Why?'" (1957, 9) is relevant. (See references in note 1 of this chapter.) For congenial use of this distinction in an account of the relation of an attitude or action being based on something, see Neta (2019) and Keeling (2021, 2023). For related dispositionalist accounts of when a belief is based on reasons, see Sosa (2015, 201–205). I think the beliefs of young children and some animals should be regarded as based on reasons, because, even if those subjects are not capable of understanding the question "Why do you believe that?", they can still be treated as holding beliefs that are rationalizable by others. In other words, the "why" question can be answered on their behalf by others, as is the case when we seek to articulate someone else's justifying reasons for believing something rather than the factors that merely caused them to believe it. For discussion of Anscombe's justificatory why-question and its difference from various kinds of psychiatric explanation in the case of mental illness, see Wilkinson (2014).

33. Here I reference the so-called transparency of belief to the world. I think there is definitely something right about the idea that, when subjects are asked what they believe about some topic, it would be abnormal and alienated to consider one's mind as an empirical object and introspect its contents. However, I suspect there is a false dichotomy in the idea that we would answer the question "Do I believe *p*?" *either* by introspection *or* by looking to the world. When it comes to more complicated beliefs (e.g., do I believe structural racism is responsible for the race wealth gap in the United States, do I believe climate change is likely to create terrible disasters for our children and grandchildren, do I believe I'll finish this book and it will be well received?), I think looking to the world often doesn't settle the question, and neither does introspecting our own minds. I suspect we have to do a bit of both, as well as a lot of talking to other people, to ascertain how convincing our reasons for various beliefs are and to gather feedback about the coherence between the beliefs we profess to have and the ways we tend to behave. For further development of this idea, which postdates the writing of this chapter, see Chrisman and Marušić (forthcoming).

PART II
EPISTEMIC NORMS

5
The Aim of Belief and the Goal of Truth

5.1 Introduction

In Part I, I suggested that beliefs are best conceived as not merely empirical conditions of our minds but also as manifestations of our subjective take on what is the case. Because of this, I focused on locating and explaining the distinctive sort of agency we exercise with respect to our beliefs. This is interesting in its own right, but I think understanding doxastic agency is also important for the theory of knowledge, because counting someone as knowing that *p* involves evaluating them by epistemic norms of a sort that presuppose the existence of agency. So far, however, I haven't said much about the nature of those norms or the source of their applicability to believers. So, in Part II of the book, I proceed to consider the nature and source of epistemic normativity.

I argued that beliefs are states rather than performances in Chapter 2. Toward the end of that chapter, I considered a natural rejoinder to this argument, which is to say that even if beliefs are not strictly performances, they still "aim at the truth." I argued that it is wrong to think that this popular metaphor licenses applying the categories of performance normativity directly to belief itself. However, I didn't explain why I nevertheless think there is an important truth in this metaphor.[1] In this chapter, I address that question in a way that begins to flesh out an account of the nature of epistemic norms and why we value compliance with them. This continues my investigation of the deontological and axiological dimensions of epistemic normativity.

Even granting that truth is not a target we shoot at with our beliefs, there are still many epistemologists who would insist that true belief is the fundamental goal relative to which various epistemic conducts can be evaluated normatively. The influence of this idea traces to Quine's characterization of naturalized epistemology as "the technology of truth-seeking" (1986, 664); BonJour provides another prominent early articulation, writing, "What makes us cognitive beings at all is our capacity for belief, and the goal of our distinctively cognitive endeavors is truth.... the basic role of justification is that of a means to truth, a more directly attainable mediating link between our subjective starting point and our objective goal" (1985, 7–8). Many other philosophers have endorsed the basic idea that being orientated toward the end of true belief distinguishes *epistemic* justification, reasons, rationality, warrant, and/or virtue from other varieties of these normative notions.[2]

So, the first task for this chapter is to assess and refine this idea, which I will do by considering an argument for the claim that truth *cannot* be an end at all, whether epistemic or otherwise. By carefully examining an argument for this radical conclusion, I think we can learn why truth doesn't have to be a *goal* that individuals set their sights on in forming beliefs in order for truth to be an *end* that helps to define what it is for a normative notion to be epistemic. More to the point, I think the role of truth in this theoretical context is better conceived as a *constitutive aim* rather than as an external goal; indeed, the end of truth partly determines what it is for something to count as part of the activity of *belief*-system maintenance, and correlatively what it is for a mental state to be a belief.[3] The radical argument against truth's being an end ignores this possibility.

The second task for this chapter is to consider the truth norm of belief in more detail. There is a tendency in many discussions of this norm to assimilate it with what are sometimes called "evaluative" norms in order to distinguish them from the "prescriptive" norms that are more familiar in ethics and other practical domains. I think there's something right about the idea that epistemic norms of belief, including the truth norm, do not tell individual believers what to believe. This is what the radical argument gets right, and it is a reflection of the fact that epistemic reasons for belief are different from practical reasons for action (including actions that might be involved in forming a belief). However, a fuller understanding of the role of epistemic *communities* in normatively evaluating belief will reveal that the goal of getting *each other* to believe more truths is a key source of epistemic normativity. In my view, we care about whether people know things, and correlatively whether they comply with epistemic norms, in large part because we are collectively engaged in epistemic practices that are partly constituted by a tacit mutual commitment to valuing compliance with epistemic norms. The radical argument that I consider also ignores the possibility of using the truth goal to evaluate *other people's* belief-forming practices—as do many others that treat truth as a merely "evaluative norm" of belief.

5.2 The Radical Argument Outlined

There are two prominent critical reactions to the idea that truth is the fundamental epistemic end. The first is to argue that truth is not the *only* or *main* end that plays the role of distinguishing epistemic normativity from other sorts of normativity, as there are other distinctive epistemic ends such as knowledge, understanding, and wisdom.[4] I want to focus here, instead, on a second, more radical argument made by those who think there is something altogether wrongheaded about conceiving of truth as the end of our cognitive endeavors. Their idea is roughly that, in order for truth to be a genuine end, we'd have to be able to tell when we achieve it, but, since we are always fallible in our beliefs and only ever have other beliefs to go on, this is impossible. So, truth cannot be a goal or aim and *ipso facto* cannot be the fundamental "epistemic" end.

Rorty suggests something like this argument, writing that truth "is not what common sense would call a goal. For it is neither something we might realize we had reached, nor something to which we might get closer" (1995, 39). And Davidson echoes the sentiment when writing that "we know many things, and will learn more; what we will never know for certain is which of the things we believe is true. Since it is neither a visible target, nor recognizable when achieved, there is no point in calling truth a goal" (2000, 67). In my view, however, the most comprehensive case for thinking that truth cannot be a definitive epistemic end is made by Jay Rosenberg (2002) in an underappreciated book, *Thinking about Knowing*. He claims that "no notion of truth, neither a transcendent notion of objective truth nor a minimalist notion of immanent truth, can play any determinative role at all in our epistemic activities" (2002, 229). And because of this, when it comes to understanding epistemic normativity, he concludes that "we would do well to stop talking about truth altogether" (2002, 229).

Rosenberg's argument proceeds through two lemmas, depending on how one is conceiving of truth, whether in an "enquiry-transcendent" way or a "minimalist" way. In the first case, truth is treated as something that could always in principle go beyond what we might discover. Truth is a property that a statement or belief has when it matches, or correctly pictures, the way things really are, which is thought to be sometimes beyond our ability to discover. On this conception, we might say that the putative truth goal is to believe that p iff p is *objectively* true.

In the second case, truth is not treated as a substantial property that our beliefs may or may not have, but rather as something we understand through tacitly accepting the minimal schema that p is true iff p (for any proposition we can believe or assert). Minimalists about truth argue that it is useful to have a predicate conforming to this schema to generalize over truths (e.g., "Every claim in this book is true") and to move between object-level and meta-level discussions of particular truths; however, they deny that truth has a substantial nature in relating beliefs and statements to objective reality. On this conception, we might say that the putative truth goal is simply to believe that p iff p. Of course, proponents of more substantial accounts of truth can endorse this claim too, but minimalists would insist that there is no *more* substantial and general goal to make our beliefs match objective reality. This allows for various levels of subjectivity and intersubjectivity to enter into the determination of whether p, and it fits naturally with views that are skeptical of objective or enquiry-transcendent truth.

In light of this distinction, Rosenberg's argument is as follows. If one is thinking of truth along enquiry-transcendent lines, then truth transcends our beliefs in that there is "no epistemically accessible *truth-determinative* feature of beliefs" (2002, 214).

This is because we can never "get outside" of our belief system to check, in a non-question-begging way, whether believing for the reasons that we do brings us closer to or farther away from believing what is objectively true. On the other hand, if one is thinking of truth along minimalist lines, then truth is immanent to any given belief system in that "*whatever* we currently believe, we hold true" (2002, 228). So, there is nothing more to the pursuit of the putative goal of truth about a particular proposition *p* than the pursuit of belief as to whether *p*, which means that "the ostensible goal of immanent truth is…a goal in name only, [since] it does not exert any constraints on the actual concrete conduct of our enquiries" (2002, 228–229).

What follows is a somewhat detailed exposition of Rosenberg's argument (so some readers might want to skip ahead to the beginning of section 5.4).

(1) There is no epistemically accessible feature of beliefs about the world that determines whether they are objectively true.
(2) If there is no epistemically accessible feature of beliefs about the world that determines whether they are objectively true, then there is no way to ascertain whether our belief-forming methods result reliably in our having objectively true beliefs about the world.
(3) If there is no way to ascertain whether our belief-forming methods result reliably in our having objectively true beliefs, then there is no reasonable way to evaluate the efficacy of these methods for achieving the end of our having objectively true beliefs about the world.

First lemma: There is no reasonable way to evaluate the efficacy of our belief-forming methods for achieving the end of our having objectively true beliefs about the world.

(4) We accept each of our beliefs to be true.
(5) If we accept each of our beliefs to be true, then we take each of our belief-forming methods to generate beliefs we accept to be true.
(6) If we take each of our belief-forming methods to generate beliefs we accept to be true, then there is no reasonable way to evaluate the efficacy of these methods for achieving the end of our having beliefs which we accept to be true.

Second lemma: There is no reasonable way to evaluate the efficacy of our belief-forming methods for achieving the end of our having beliefs which we accept to be true.

(7) Some end can be a genuine goal or be capable of constraining our policies or procedures only if there is a reasonable way to evaluate the efficacy of our methods for achieving that end.

Thus,

(8) Neither our having objectively true beliefs about the world nor our having beliefs that we accept to be true can be a genuine goal or be capable of constraining our epistemic policies or procedures.

5.3 The Radical Argument Explained and Defended

In this section, I attempt to defend several of the premises from criticism. This is not because I think the argument is ultimately successful, but rather because identifying more precisely where it fails is helpful for understanding the complex role of the end of truth in epistemic normativity.

Premise (1) says that there is no epistemically accessible feature of beliefs about the world that determines whether they are objectively true. I think this should be understood as denying two things. First, it denies that there are self-evident beliefs about the world. Perhaps there are self-evident beliefs in tautologies or about the contents of one's own mind. That's debatable, but we should set these aside. When we form a nontautologous belief about the outside world, according to premise (1), this belief never comes with an infallible marker of its truth. Second, it might be thought that one of the epistemically accessible features of our beliefs is our reasons for holding them. If so, I think (1) should be understood as denying that these reasons can ever *guarantee* the truth of the beliefs they support.[5]

As Rosenberg is thinking of the premise, these two denials embody a commitment to a sort of epistemic fallibilism. He characterizes a *"fallibilist* understanding of the notion of justification or warrant" as "one which allows that a person may be justified or warranted in believing a proposition which is nevertheless false" (2002, 136). Many philosophers take fallibilism to reflect a "realist" commitment to the mind-independence of the world, or similarly the idea that how we take things to be in the world, and our reasons for doing so, must always be distinguished from how the world really is. For his part, Rosenberg suggests that fallibility is "the epistemic reflection of objectivity", i.e., "that the fact that someone believes that *p*, or even the fact that everyone believes that *p*, does not imply that it is true that *p*" (2002, 217). To fail to recognize this distinction, many think, is to commit to a crude form of idealism.

However, even while disavowing a crude idealism which would reject the mind-independence of the external world, other philosophers will object to fallibilism (and premise (1) of the argument reconstructed in section 5.2) based on a certain view of what our reasons for belief can be. They will say that sometimes you believe that *p* because you see that *p* or you hear that *p* or you figure out that *p*, etc., and you cannot see, hear, or figure out that *p* unless *p* is true. This means that beliefs formed for these reasons are not fallible. If one's reason for believing that *p* is that one sees that *p*, that reason *does* guarantee the truth of the belief.[6]

If one is sympathetic to this idea, then one may want to reject premise (1) of Rosenberg's argument. However, before doing so, notice that philosophers more sympathetic to Rosenberg will worry that, even if there is a sense in which seeing, hearing, or figuring out that *p* are genuine reasons for believing that *p*, they are not reasons that are epistemically accessible features of the beliefs that they support, since we often think that we have seen, heard, or figured out that *p* only later to discover that we were mistaken. In the cases where we were mistaken, it's natural to think that *our* reason for believing that *p* was that we *thought that* we saw, heard, or figured out that *p*, but this thought turned out to be false. But why then shouldn't that be the story about reasons in the good cases as well?

I think it should, but not all philosophers would agree.[7] In any case, the key point is that the difference between the good case and the bad case is not discriminable from within a single believer's perspective, which means that it doesn't constitute an "epistemically accessible" feature of the beliefs that determines whether they are objectively true. And, if that's right, then parties to this debate cannot reject (1) on the basis of rejecting the fallibilism about reasons it embodies.

Premise (2) says that, if there is no epistemically accessible feature of beliefs about the world that determines whether they are objectively true, then there is no way to ascertain whether our belief-forming methods result reliably in our having objectively true beliefs about the world. Rosenberg's idea is not, I think, to deny that we can use one belief-forming method to check the results of another. For, surely, it is commonplace to discover that, relative to an assumed background method, some candidate belief-forming methods are more reliable than others. If, for instance, we come to doubt the veracity of the reporting on the propaganda channel, and so check it against the independent news channel, we may find out that forming beliefs based on what is reported on the propaganda channel is not a very reliable way to form true beliefs, at least not as judged by the reporting on the independent news channel.

Instead, the idea behind (2) must be that, in relying on one method to check another, we have to simply assume that the former is reliable. This means that when we check the reliability of a particular belief-forming method, we are not checking whether it is *absolutely* reliable, but merely whether it is reliable *relative* to the outputs of some other method. After all, if we had instead started by doubting the veracity of the reporting on the independent news channel and then checked it against the propaganda channel, perhaps we would have reached exactly the opposite verdict. And if we checked both against our actually witnessing the events reported on, we may discover that the independent news channel is more reliable than the propaganda channel, but only relative to the outputs of our actually witnessing the events.

What we seem to need in order to tell whether a belief-forming method is absolutely reliable is a way to compare its results directly to the objective facts. But, given (1), we are only ever able to compare the results of one belief-forming method to the results of some other belief-forming method, which means that we can never tell if we have objectively true beliefs about the facts. I think this is why Davidson writes:

> Truths do not come with a 'mark', like the date in the corner of some photographs, which distinguishes them from falsehoods. The best we can do is test, experiment, keep an open mind... Since it is neither a visible target, nor recognizable when achieved, there is no point in calling truth a goal. (2000, 67)

In response to Davidson, Lynch suggests that claims like (2) trade on the false assumption that "we can't recognize whether a belief is true or false unless we can compare it to the naked facts" (2004, 25). He thinks that the idea of comparing a belief to the naked facts is a strange sort of requirement, and that there is a more natural sense of recognizing when a belief is true, by which it should be a truism that we can and often do recognize when a belief is true. He writes:

> The most natural interpretation of what it means to 'recognize when a belief is true' is that to recognize a belief as true or false is either to confirm that it is based on adequate grounds or note that it is not.... In this sense of 'recognize' I clearly *can* recognize when my beliefs are true or false—it amounts to noticing whether or not they are justified. (2004, 26)

However, unless Lynch means to reject premise (1) by following those philosophers who claim that there are some ways of noticing a belief to be justified which *guarantee* to us that the belief is true, I can't see how confirming that a belief is based on adequate grounds, or noting that it is not, can count as ways of "recognizing that it is true or false." After all, even beliefs based on adequate grounds can turn out to be false, and a belief not based on adequate grounds can turn out to be true.[8]

Indeed, I think the fallibilism embodied in (1) is animated by the idea that an adequately grounded belief may nevertheless be false and a poorly grounded belief may nevertheless be true. If we accept that idea, then, although Lynch is of course right that we can check a doubted belief's grounds or justification, this won't provide a way to check the absolute reliability of any belief-forming method. It will provide only a way to check one method against another, like checking the propaganda channel against the independent news channel. This will produce beliefs that we take to be true—in the minimalist sense of truth—because we take all of our beliefs to be true; but it won't ever put us in a position to recognize the objective truth of our beliefs. I believe this is precisely Rorty's point in writing:

If I have concrete, specific doubts about whether one of my beliefs is true, I can resolve those doubts only by asking whether it is adequately justified—by finding and assessing additional reasons pro and con. I cannot bypass justification and confine my attention to truth: assessment of truth and assessment of justification are, when the question is about what I should believe now, the same activity.

(1995, 281)

Premise (3) says that, if there is no way to ascertain whether our belief-forming methods result reliably in our having objectively true beliefs, then there is no reasonable way to evaluate the efficacy of these methods for achieving the end of our having objectively true beliefs. I take this to be the least controvertible premise of the argument. If there is no way to tell when we have achieved a particular end, then surely there is no way to tell which means are best for achieving it. And, likewise, if there is no way to tell whether a candidate means for achieving an end like having objectively true beliefs about the world results reliably in this end, then surely there is no way to evaluate the efficacy of that candidate means. That's the simple idea behind premise (3).

Premises (1)–(3) entail the first lemma. So, if we accept them, we're committed to acknowledging that there is no reasonable way to evaluate the efficacy of candidate belief-forming methods for achieving the end of *objective* truth.

It's worth pausing to notice how radical this conclusion will at first appear from the point of view of commonsense realism. Can we really accept that it's impossible to reasonably evaluate our attempts to hone and improve the ways we form beliefs? If that's what the first lemma of Rosenberg's argument comes to, agreeing to it may seem to involve avoiding crude idealism at the steep cost of pointless skepticism.

Yet I don't think this is what the first lemma comes to. Recall the idea that Lynch and Rorty apparently agree on, viz., that trying to determine whether one of our beliefs is true or false amounts to nothing more than trying to determine whether or not it is based on adequate grounds. If we accept this, then we may think Rosenberg's talk of "objective truth" imputes a much stronger position to proponents of truth as the definitive epistemic end than they really need. Perhaps, believing truly doesn't have to be identified with infallible contact with the naked facts in order for the goal of believing truly to structure our epistemic policies and procedures. Maybe all we need is a less lofty idea of truth to make sense of Lynch's idea that "recogniz[ing] when my beliefs are true or false... amounts to noticing whether or not they are justified" (2004, 26).

It is in these terms that I think we should understand Rosenberg's claim at (4), viz., that we accept each of our beliefs to be true. This follows from the fact that believing that *p* entails accepting that *p* is true. So, to interpret truth in this way is, in effect, to transition to the second horn of Rosenberg's original dilemma, according to which truth is conceived on minimalist grounds, or what Rosenberg sometimes refers to as the "enquiry-immanent" understanding of truth.

In light of this, premise (5) may seem uncontroversial (but see later and in section 5.5 for an objection). It says that, if we accept each of our beliefs to be true, then we take each of our belief-forming methods to generate beliefs we accept to be true. This links a platitude about beliefs to a correlative conceptual fact about our belief-forming methods. If it's part of believing that we take each of our beliefs to be true, then it's part of something's being one of our belief-forming methods that we take it to generate something, i.e., beliefs, which we take to be true.

Premise (6) says that, if we take each of our belief-forming methods to generate beliefs we accept to be true, then there is no reasonable way to evaluate the efficacy of these methods for achieving the end of truth. I think the idea is that, since it's part of their being instances of *belief*-forming that these methods lead to our accepting some proposition as true, there is no meaningful sense in which we can evaluate them as more or less reliable for achieving this end. Insofar as they are methods that form *beliefs*, they will *always* achieve the end of accepting some proposition as true, so there is no way that they can serve as constraints on actual epistemic policies and procedures. As Rosenberg puts the point, "the ostensible goal of immanent truth is a goal in name only.... [For] nothing can count as a reason to believe that we have *failed* to reach or realize the putative goal" (2002, 228).

However, premises (4)–(6) entail the second lemma. So, if we accept them, we're committed to acknowledging that there is no reasonable way to evaluate the efficacy of our belief-forming methods for achieving the end of our having beliefs which we accept to be true.

That leaves premise (7), which says that some end can be a genuine goal or be capable of constraining our policies or procedures only if there is a reasonable way to evaluate the efficacy of our methods for achieving that end. I suspect this premise wrongly equates the general idea of ends with a more specific idea of goals capable of constraining our policies and procedures, but I'll postpone criticism till the following section so that I can finish explaining the argument. For, even if we agree that epistemic ends must be goals capable of constraining our policies and procedures, some people have objected to this premise's conception of *goals*.

In his review of Rosenberg's book, Fantl objects to the idea that for something to be a genuine goal, it must be possible to check whether we've achieved it. He writes, "Why buy into the premise that the only thing that can count as [an epistemic] goal is something that can constrain our epistemic practices or that we can confirm we've reached?" (2007, 231). As a counterexample, Fantl asks us to consider his goal that his children thrive after his death. He writes, "Regardless of whether my life goes worse if that goal is not achieved, there is a clear sense in which I have it as a goal and a clear sense in which I have failed to achieve that goal if they do not thrive after I am dead" (2007, 231). In my view, however, this criticism misses the point of premise (7) in the argument.

The point is not to deny that some of our goals are for ends that we will not, as a matter of fact, be able to confirm have been achieved. The point is rather that, in the case of the alleged definitively epistemic goal of truth, it would be either impossible to tell that we have achieved it or impossible to tell that we have not achieved it. It's quite clear how Fantl could tell whether he had achieved his goal that his children thrive after he is dead. He'd just have to wait a sufficient amount of time after his death and then check on how his children are doing. To be sure, that isn't humanly possible, but it's pretty clear what "checking whether the goal had been achieved" looks like. By contrast, opponents of the putative goal of truth think it's very *unclear* what it would take for us to check that we had achieved the goal of having objectively true beliefs, and that it is utterly pointless to check that we had achieved the goal of having beliefs that we take to be true.

Nevertheless, we might still worry about premise (7) for related reasons. For it may seem that it is enough, in order for something to be one of my goals, that I *take* it that some means are better than others. Consider, for example, the ostensible goal of getting into heaven. Suppose, for the sake of argument, that this is something we cannot even in principle ascertain whether we have achieved (maybe heaven is pure ego-less bliss and devoid of any unified consciousnesses). In this case, (7) implies that getting into heaven cannot be a genuine goal; however, it seems clearly possible to have this as one of our goals and to let it prescribe particular conducts (e.g., praying, going to church), insofar as we *take* these practices to be encouraged by having that goal.

This is a better version of the sort of objection Fantl is suggesting. I think Rosenberg's initial answer to this objection comes in the distinction he draws between a motive and a goal:

> a *motive* is whatever *in fact* moves someone, and there's no in-principle limit to the sorts of mental goings-on that might *in fact* give rise to activities that we'd recognize as enquiry—a desire for money or fame or respect... In *this* sense, a desire for objective truth might indeed motivate enquiry. But it doesn't follow that objective truth can function as the *goal* of enquiry, and that becomes clear when we observe that, unlike such other potential motivating desires as those for money or fame or respect, a desire for objective truth is one that we can't ever determine has been *satisfied*. (2002, 219fn.)

If a motive is whatever *in fact* moves one to act, then what is a goal? The causal-psychological description of a motive suggests that the contrasting notion of a goal could be understood in terms of the distinction between motivating and justifying reasons. A motivating reason is part of the best psychological explanation of why an agent acts as she does, and a justifying reason is what the agent might appeal to in order to justify a particular action.

In order to evaluate this interpretation and to see whether it supports (7), we need an account of "justifying reasons" in the context of the question of whether truth is the distinctive *epistemic* goal. What are the relevant actions that may or may not be justified in this case? To begin to answer this question, Rosenberg proposes the following:

> The specification or formulation of a goal... is characteristically the first step in a process of *means-ends reasoning*. In traditional terms, it yields the major premise of a practical syllogism:
> (P1) I/We shall achieve E
> (P2) The only/best means for achieving E are M
> (P3) So, I/we shall adopt M. (2002, 206)

The idea here is to define the sense of "goal" that is relevant to the argument in terms of the functional role of goals in practical syllogisms. With respect to the activity of inquiry, Rosenberg is specific about what he thinks it would take for truth to be the relevant goal. He writes:

> What we need, to make sense of the idea that true belief is the goal of enquiry... is an instantiation of this general practical syllogistic form which establishes a connection between a commitment to that goal and the actual *conduct* of enquiry; that is, which shows *how* our having the goal of truth can structure our actual concrete cognitive-epistemic practices. (2002, 207)

The general idea seems to be that some end E can provide a validating reason for doing M only if we can produce an instantiation of the practical syllogistic form which establishes a connection between doing M and achieving E.

Whether this idea supports (7), however, will depend on what it means to "produce" an instantiation of the practical syllogistic form which establishes a connection between doing M and achieving E. For, in one sense, it has to be trivial that, if some of our belief-forming methods are indeed objectively reliable, then it is logically, physically, and epistemically possible that we can formulate an instantiation of the practical syllogistic form where the minor premise is objectively true. This instantiation would then, in a sense, "establish" a connection between these methods and attaining the goal of objective truth. It would not, however, show *us* the objectively correct way to pursue the end of believing p iff p.

More generally, with (7), I think Rosenberg means that, in order for an end E to be capable of rationally constraining policies or procedures, it must be possible for one who has that end to produce an instantiation of the practical syllogistic form which they *can tell* successfully establishes a connection between engaging in particular conducts M and achieving E. I'll challenge this idea in the next section, but if it's right, then (7), along with the first and second lemmas, entails Rosenberg's conclusion, viz. (8): Neither our having objectively true beliefs about the world nor our having beliefs that we accept to be true can be a genuine goal or be capable of constraining our epistemic policies or procedures.

This completes my explanation of the argument suggested by Davidson's and Rorty's famous claims, developed most thoroughly by Rosenberg, against the idea that truth is an epistemic end. I've attempted to motivate each of its premises, though I've already said that I think there are problems with premises (5) and (7). I want to turn now to spelling out these problems.

5.4 Constitutive Aims and Evaluative Norms

Consider again premise (7):

(7) Some end can be a genuine goal or be capable of constraining our policies or procedures only if there is a reasonable way to evaluate the efficacy of our methods for achieving that end.

As we have seen, Rosenberg assumes that ends are goals that can serve as the first premise in a practical syllogism establishing the reasonableness of some conduct to pursue this end. I think this is misguided in the present dialectical context, because it assumes that one who thinks that some end (such as truth) may help to distinguish epistemic norms, reasons, and justifications from other sorts of norms, reasons, and justifications, must be conceiving of those norms, reasons, and justifications as fundamentally related to some *performance*, or more specifically to some epistemic-cognitive *conduct directed at some goal.*

As I argued in Chapters 2 and 3, however, it is doubtful that the primary objects of epistemic evaluations are performances. Beliefs themselves are states, not performances, and although we are sometimes interested in the normative quality of the etiology of a belief, I argued that the normative epistemic evaluations relevant to whether someone knows something are about the mental *states* that persist through time, rather than the cognitive performances of forming them. And as I explained in Chapter 4, this is why I think the primary locus of doxastic agency is not in the performance of forming beliefs but in the activity of maintaining states of belief as part of one's system of beliefs. Because activities are atelic, in the sense of not rightly being conceived as pursuits of some external goal, it is wrong to think they are normatively evaluable in terms of a connection between engaging in the activity at one time and achieving the relevant goal at some later time. But this is precisely what Rosenberg's means-end practical syllogism seeks to do.

To see more precisely why it is wrong to think an end has to be conceived as a goal along the lines of the means-end practical syllogism, notice that the logical form of premise (7) is a conditional embedding a disjunction in its antecedent. The two disjuncts are (a) some end E can be a genuine goal, and (b) some end E can be capable of constraining our policies or procedures. In effect, I think Rosenberg has incorrectly assumed that (a) and (b) come to the same thing. On his conception, a goal is an end capable of constraining our policies and procedures; he is assuming that an end capable of constraining our policies and procedures just *is* a goal. However, I want to argue that not all ends are "goals" in his sense. This is because there are ways that ends can constrain our policies and procedures *other* than by structuring a practical syllogism that validates performing particular actions.

Beside *regulative goals*, I think we should recognize *constitutive aims* of what one is doing.[9] Appeals to constitutive aims can be used to determine whether or not one is engaged in some specific type of performance or activity, and doing so has an indirect impact on what sorts of further normative evaluations are appropriate.

How can the idea of constitutive aims be connected to beliefs? Unlike most who link truth *directly* to belief as a constitutive aim, I think we should make the connection through doxastic *activities*. I argued in Chapter 4 that belief itself is not an activity, but that there is a conceptually nearby activity of maintaining a system of beliefs. This involves basing some beliefs on other beliefs, modulating confidence in various beliefs in light of changing evidence, and confirming or disconfirming various hypotheses. In my view, all of this hangs together in an activity which is not itself directed toward some external goal. This is borne out by the-ing/-ed test: if we think S is maintaining a system of beliefs, we can immediately infer that S has maintained a system of beliefs. That doesn't determine what it is to maintain a system of beliefs as opposed to (say) a system of assumptions or desires, but, we're now in a position to distinguish belief-system maintenance from these other activities, with the idea that truth is the constitutive aim of belief-system maintenance.

That's consistent with, and indeed supports, the more general idea that truth is not just any old standard; it's a standard whose applicability distinguishes beliefs from other mental states such as hunches, suppositions, and preferences.[10] Accordingly, for what one is doing to count as the activity of maintaining a system of *beliefs*, the states of mind which one maintains must be correctly evaluable by reference to the norm "x ought to be true".[11] Some philosophers may think that objective truth is the constitutive aim of belief-system maintenance, but all that is required for this way of identifying the activity of belief-system maintenance is the minimalist idea that one ought to believe that p iff p.

So, one of the key lessons I think we can learn from Rosenberg's argument is that truth doesn't have to be a *goal* pursued by individuals in order for it to be an "end" that is partly definitive of what it is for a normative notion to be epistemic. The maintenance of a system of connected mental states counts as the activity of *belief*-system maintenance only insofar as it is conceived as the maintenance of states that ought to be true. (Later I will explain how I think we can determine when the norm is met.)[12]

In some respects, my idea here is similar to the suggestion that belief is subject to a norm of truth which is *evaluative* rather than prescriptive. The distinction between evaluative and prescriptive norms traces back, firstly, to Sidgwick's (1874/1907) distinction between the "political" 'ought' of what state of affairs would be best for some purpose and the "agentive" 'ought' of ethics that he presumed to prescribe individual actions, and also to Moore's (1903, §90) distinction between statements of what ought to be the case and what people ought to do.[13] Drawing on this distinction, one might think that it is somehow a good state of affairs when a belief is true, even if one denies that there is anyone who is prescribed the action of bringing this state of affairs about.[14]

However, my thought in arguing that truth needn't be a goal in order to be normatively relevant to evaluating belief is not that true belief is merely good in some sense. Rather, my point is that evaluability relative to the standard of truth is part of what makes a mental state a *belief* and, more fundamentally, what makes things we do count as elements of the activity of *belief-system maintenance*. So, if truth is an evaluative norm of belief, it's a *constitutively* evaluative norm.

This is similar to the idea that some things are constitutively evaluable by norms deriving from their function. For example, it's a commonplace that the stomach is for digesting food, which we might express with the ought-to-be claim: "The stomach ought to be disposed to digest food." Maybe we could then appeal to this constitutive norm of stomachs to distinguish digestive norms from other species of norms. For instance, one might think it follows that the stomach's pH range ought to be between 1 and 3. This is not meant to be a prescriptive claim about what some agent ought to do, but is rather an evaluative claim deriving from the constitutive evaluative norms of stomachs.

Would a similar picture work for the truth norm and any epistemic norms of belief it implies? The idea would be that our belief system is for having true beliefs like our stomach is for digesting food. McHugh suggests something like this, writing, "Acting in the world requires you to have a representation of how the world is, so that you can select and guide the behaviour that will bring the world in line with how you want it to be. A representation that does not aim to be correct does not count as playing this role" (2012, 23). McHugh is not suggesting here that epistemic standards for belief get their normative force from a person's *individual* and *particular* desires. Rather, he casts the normative evaluation of belief within an account of our essential "nature as intentional, moral, and rational agents," according to which "the function of...the activity of regulating [our] doxastic attitudes...is to form and maintain true beliefs, and not false ones, about the propositions under consideration" (2012, 23). By construing the truth norm as constitutively evaluative and deriving from the function of belief systems, this account nicely avoids the assumption in Rosenberg's premise (7) that truth has to be a goal one pursues in order for it to be a normatively relevant end.[15] However, I don't think the resulting picture is right.

Our belief systems are importantly different from our stomachs. Evaluative norms applying to our stomachs are purely physiological and can be identified by considering the biological function of stomachs. I don't doubt that we can consider the biological function of our belief systems and can identify some norms of belief that derive from this function. Maybe we'll even conclude from such considerations that the function of beliefs is to store information that may be useful in navigating the world in pursuit of our desires. However, I doubt that what our belief system is *essentially* for is selecting and guiding behavior that will bring the world in line with how the believer wants it to be (moral beliefs, religious beliefs, philosophical beliefs, and pure mathematical beliefs are salient challengers to this picture).

Moreover, I think this picture leaves out an important social basis for the normative evaluation of beliefs in epistemic terms. We rely on each other in epistemic communities in ways that suggest that the function of some beliefs is to store information for guiding behavior that promotes *other* people's interests, rather than the satisfaction of the believer's own desires. Indeed, prior to promoting interests or satisfying desires, it is often important for finding common aims, and for planning the mutual pursuit of those aims, that people believe what they epistemically ought to believe—and not just about the way the world is but also about how we ought to treat one another. (More on this later and in the next chapters.)

So, in advancing the idea that truth is a constitutive aim of belief-system maintenance, I don't mean to suggest that "S ought to believe that p iff p" is merely an evaluative norm deriving from the biological function of belief systems. One of the key claims I want to advance in this part of the book is that the constitutive norms of belief derive from social epistemic conditions, and indeed in some cases from the preconditions of our social-political community. Furthermore, I think the kind of agency presupposed in evaluating beliefs with respect to those social epistemic conditions distinguishes epistemic norms from biofunctional norms. Neuro-physiological functions of belief systems are of course relevant to our ability to conform to the norms, but I think the picture needs to be much more richly social to help us move forward in making sense of the role of truth in epistemic normativity.

5.5 Social Epistemic Goals

I'll discuss the social basis of epistemic norms in more detail in Chapters 6 and 7, but to begin to get a sense of how this might interact with the idea that truth is a norm of belief, let's turn back to Rosenberg's argument, specifically premise (5). Here it is again:

(5) If we accept each of our beliefs to be true, then we take each of our belief-forming methods to generate beliefs we accept to be true.

The problem I see with this premise stems from an ambiguity in the term "our belief-forming methods". Premise (5) is trivially true if this means "each of our own actually and currently deployed belief-forming methods"; for, part of what it is to be one's actually and currently deployed belief-forming method is to be a method which generates a mental state in the person who deploys it which this person currently accepts as true. However, if we separate belief-forming methods across members of a population, or across time-slices of an individual person, we can generate a different reading of the term "each of our belief-forming methods" that makes premise (5) much less plausible. For instance, if that term means "each of the belief-forming methods that are deployed by some of us at some time" then, surely, we don't take each of our belief-forming methods to generate beliefs that we (all) accept as true.[16] After all, some of us form beliefs by watching the propaganda channel, and, as we have already seen, this generates beliefs that those of us who watch the independent news channel will not accept as true, and vice versa. Likewise, someone may have formed beliefs in the past by watching the propaganda channel, which they *then* accepted as true, but, after becoming a devotee of the independent news channel, they will not take it that forming beliefs by watching the propaganda channel is a reliable way to generate beliefs that they *now* accept to be true.

So far, all this suggests is that Rosenberg's argument needs the reading of "our belief-forming methods" to mean "each of our own actually and currently deployed belief-forming methods" in order for premise (5) to be plausible. However, recall that (5) is a premise in the second lemma of Rosenberg's argument. This had to do with whether truth, conceived minimalistically, could be a genuine goal of our cognitive-epistemic practices. Someone who thinks that minimalist truth is a goal of our cognitive-epistemic practices might reasonably insist that they don't mean for us to use this goal to evaluate the efficacy of one's actually and currently deployed belief-forming methods, but rather for us to use it to evaluate *candidate* belief-forming methods (such as those used by others, those we used in the past, and those we might use in the future). Generally, it is not true that the belief-forming methods used by others, our past selves, or our future possible selves are ones that generate beliefs that we now accept as true. So, if the goal is to believe p iff p, then candidate belief-forming methods could be meaningfully evaluated with respect to this goal.

What this means is that, although Rosenberg is of course right that each of us accepts our own individual beliefs as true, he is wrong that this implies that there is no reasonable way for us to use the ostensible goal of minimalist truth to evaluate candidate belief-forming methods. To be sure, as long as we have accepted premises (1) and (2), such evaluations will always transpire relative to an assumed background of belief-forming methods, and so will never get at the "absolute" reliability of candidate belief-forming methods for achieving the end of objective truth. Because of this, as long as objective truth is understood as inquiry-transcendent, I'm inclined to accept the first lemma of Rosenberg's argument. The only way to ascertain the efficacy of our belief-forming practices is to engage in inquiry that results in forming or revising beliefs. However, the second lemma is not concerned with such inquiry-transcendent truth. Moreover, it does seem that, relative to a background method, a candidate method (such as trusting the propaganda channel) can be judged to be less reliable than some other method (such as trusting the independent news channel) for forming true beliefs.

The reason I think this is relevant to understanding the relation of truth to epistemic normativity is that I think it shows how, although doxastic activity as a whole has truth as a constitutive *aim*, some of the individual actions involved in doxastic activity can have minimalist truth as a *goal*. These won't be the actions of individual believers with respect to their own current beliefs (for reasons Rosenberg explains), but they could be the actions in which members of an epistemic community engage with respect to the beliefs of other members of the community. We teach our children and friends not just what we think is true, but also what strategies we think are most effective for forming true beliefs about various topics. This sort of means-ends reasoning—constraining cognitive-epistemic conducts toward the end of people in one's epistemic community believing *p* iff *p*—is consistent with thinking that individual believers do not directly pursue the goal of believing the truth when forming beliefs. Accordingly, as part of a broader social understanding of the activity of interpersonal belief-system maintenance, I think the idea that beliefs ought to be true implies some more specific goal-directed rules of action related to what we do when we teach each other about things. Again, we need a much more richly social conception of deontological evaluations of people's beliefs in order to make sense of the role truth plays in understanding epistemic normativity.

5.6 Conclusion

I began this chapter with the idea that the end of truth can be used to distinguish epistemic norms, reasons, and justifications from other sorts of norms, reasons, and justifications. I have considered in depth one of the most detailed arguments against this idea, which I hope has helped to clarify several issues. Most importantly, it has helped to distinguish the idea that truth is an external goal pursued by engaging in various cognitive performances, from the ideas firstly that truth is a constitutive aim determining what it is to engage in the activity of belief-system maintenance, and secondly that evaluability by the truth norm is partly constitutive of something's *being* a belief.

The account of the relation of truth to epistemic normativity that I've sought to advance in this chapter does accept the contention that truth isn't a goal individual believers pursue through their cognitive conducts, such that normative epistemic notions such as justification and reasons can be understood in terms of means to this end. However, crucially, I've argued that conceiving of truth as a *goal* is not the only way this putatively definitive epistemic end might be thought to relate to normative notions relevant in epistemology. By treating truth as a constitutive *norm* of belief, we can identify certain activities as elements of *belief*-system maintenance. Moreover, once this way of thinking of the end of truth is in view, I think we can also recognize how some cognitive conducts might have truth not only as their constitutive end but also as their goal. Generically, these are the cognitive conducts by which we influence and regulate the beliefs of others in our epistemic community, when we do so with the goal of them coming to believe p iff p.

However, even if this account of the complex normative role truth plays in epistemic evaluations is correct, it is not yet clear why we tend to think that knowledgeable belief is distinctively valuable, or why we ultimately care whether others and ourselves comply with epistemic norms. So, the axiological puzzle about epistemic normativity remains with us. In Part I, I suggested somewhat vaguely that we value knowledge in the way that we do in part because it is a particular kind of state—a belief one ought to have—and as such persists through time, remaining available for repeated use by believers and their epistemic community. In order to make that idea more precise, we need to think more about the types of normative evaluations we make of states.

So, in Chapter 6, I return to the puzzle about why we normatively evaluate beliefs which are assumed to be outside the scope of voluntary control, and build on the idea that belief constitutively ought to be true, in order to develop a broader account of epistemic normative evaluations as adverting to "state" norms rather than action norms. Then, in Chapter 7, I'll use this to develop an alternative account of the value of epistemic norm-compliance, which is based in our intersubjective sociality. This is meant to incorporate the idea that there are evaluative norms of belief deriving from the fact that beliefs are such that they ought to be true. However, it situates this idea in a broader social understanding of the value of knowledge.

Notes

1. For discussion of this claim as a metaphor, see Wedgwood (2002) and Shah and Velleman (2005).

2. Similarly, Moser characterizes epistemic justification as "essentially related to the so-called cognitive goal of truth, insofar as an individual belief is epistemically justified only if it is appropriately directed toward the goal of truth" (1985, 4). Other writers defending something like this idea include Goldman (1986), Foley (1987), Alston (1989), Lehrer (1990), Sartwell (1992), Haack (1998, 203), Beckermann (2001), Hofmann (2005), Lynch (2009, 2013), and Phillips (2020).
3. This is a version of "normativism" about belief, which I was previously inclined to reject but which I now embrace. See Chrisman (2016b). See McHugh and Whiting (2014) and Fassio (2015) for a useful survey of the recent literature and some of the key issues.
4. See DePaul (2001), Kvanvig (2003a, 2005), Riggs (2002a, 2003), Pritchard (2010), and Perrine (2017).
5. In a related vein, Glüer and Wikforss (2009, 2013) suggest that norms are supposed to be prescriptive or at least capable of guiding us, and, on this basis, they argue against the idea that belief is constitutively normative in its being subject to a norm of truth. Like Rosenberg, they think that a truth-norm could never guide us directly; in their view, this is because we'd have to already believe p in order to follow a rule such as "You ought to believe p, only if p!"
6. Compare McDowell (1982, 1986), Martin (2002, 2004), Williamson (2000), Littlejohn (2012, chs 3–4), and Pritchard (2012).
7. See, for example, defenses of disjunctivism, McDowell (1982, 1986), Millar (2007, 2008), Neta (2008b), and Pritchard (2008, 2012).
8. This is what many think, anyway, though it is controversial. See Littlejohn (2012) for a book-length argument for the claim that a belief cannot be fully justified and yet false.
9. For discussion, see Velleman (2000, 247–252), Wedgwood (2002), Steglich-Petersen (2006), Lynch (2009, 81), McHugh and Whiting (2014), and Fassio (2015).
10. For defense of this more general position, see Wedgwood (2002), Engel (2013), McHugh and Whiting (2014), and Fassio (2015). For criticism of this idea, see Glüer and Wikforss (2013) and Vahid (2009).
11. This is related to, but importantly weaker than, a suggestion Velleman makes for distinguishing beliefs from other propositional attitudes. He argues that an important difference between belief and desire is that, for a propositional attitude to be a belief, it must (at least) involve regarding its propositional object as true, whereas for a propositional attitude to be a desire, it must (at least) involve regarding its propositional object as to be made true. But, although this so-called "difference in direction of fit" distinguishes belief from desire, Velleman thinks that more is needed to distinguish belief from other cognitive attitudes such as assumptions or imaginings. This is because these, too, involve regarding a proposition as true, just not seriously or in earnest. So, according to him, "What distinguishes a proposition's being believed from its being assumed or imagined is the spirit in which it is regarded as true, whether tentatively or hypothetically, as in the case of assumption; fancifully, as in the case of imagination; or seriously, as in the case of belief" (2000, 183). The reason my proposal is weaker is that I do not require that the subject of a belief that p have any particular view on the spirit in which they regard p as true. Of course, I think Velleman is right that, when a subject has a view about whether they are regarding p as true tentatively or fancifully rather

than seriously, that will make a difference to whether this attitude should be counted as a belief. But since one of the defining features of state norms is that their logical subjects needn't be the same as the logical subjects of the implied action norms, we could allow for subjects who lack any second-order take on the spirit in which their first-order attitudes are held. As long as these attitudes are still regarded by the relevant community as ones that ought to be true, they will count as beliefs on my view, and what the subject does with respect to them will count as maintaining beliefs, rather than maintaining assumptions or preferences.

12. It is interesting to note that, when Rosenberg comes to developing a positive account of the epistemic-cognitive conducts, he does not appeal to backward-looking issues about the etiology of beliefs, but rather to forward-looking issues about putting oneself in a position to justify one's beliefs if challenged. He writes, "the relevant executable epistemic conducts can be specified only generically, as whatever is necessary to put one into a position to justify one's beliefs if they are legitimately challenged" (2002, 213). So, on a conciliatory note, I'd like to say that this positive idea seems to me to be partly right. What I think is right about it is that the action norms implied by "S ought to believe that p" will often include doing things structured around the aim of being in a position to justify the belief that p. However, I regard these actions not as performances whose normative quality can be evaluated by reference to some external goal they pursue, but rather as activities whose end (believing p iff p for whatever one believes) is always already present. As long as we accept the sort of fallibilism implied by premise (1) of Rosenberg's argument, I think we have to accept that we're never finished with putting ourselves into a position to justify beliefs. This is an activity partly constituted by the aim of believing truly.

13. See also Humberstone's (1971) discussion of two sorts of 'ought', Harman's (1973, 1986, 131–132) distinction between 'ought-to-do' and 'ought-to-be' sentences, and B. Williams's (1981) discussion of "deliberative" and "non-deliberative" 'ought's. The precise semantics for this distinction is controversial. See Wedgwood (2007, 117–126), Schroeder (2011), and Chrisman (2012c, 2016a, ch. 5) for discussion. Many epistemologists have suggested that beliefs are subject to an evaluative norm of truth, though not all of them highlight the distinction between evaluative and prescriptive norms. See McHugh (2012) and Fassio (2011) for explicit discussion; see also Goldman (1999) and Lynch (2004, 2009).

14. Compare Engel (2013).

15. McHugh (2014b) changes his position, arguing that constitutive norms of belief are species of "fittingness" norms for attitudes rather than evaluative norms. For others discussing something like the evaluative norm picture, see Bird (2007), Nolfi (2015), Sullivan-Bisset (2017), Graham (2011, 2012), Simion, Kelp, and Ghijsen (2016), and Simion (2019, 2025).

16. B. Williams (2002, 147–48) makes a similar point in response to Rorty.

6
Doxastic Involuntarism and 'Ought to Believe'

6.1 Introduction

We do not have the same sort of control over our beliefs as we do over our ordinary actions. Sometimes, this is highlighted (e.g., in Alston 1988, 263) by noting that, when offered a reward for performing an action such as turning on the light, you can at least in normal circumstance just turn on the light in order to collect the reward. By contrast, when offered a reward for believing a proposition, such as that the number of stars in the Milky Way is even, you cannot at least in normal circumstances just believe that the number of stars in the Milky Way is even in order to collect the reward. Let's isolate this intuitive contrast in the following *no rewards principle*:

(NRP) No matter how large the reward, a person S cannot usually decide to believe some proposition p in order to collect that reward.

Because of this intuitive contrast with simple action, many philosophers endorse *doxastic involuntarism*, i.e., the view that what one believes is not within one's direct voluntary control.[1]

This has led some epistemologists to conceive of belief as more like pain than action in its interaction with the will.[2] One may have *indirect* control over what one believes in that there may be actions within one's direct voluntary control that have foreseeable effects on what one believes, just as there are actions within one's direct voluntary control with foreseeable effects on whether one feels particular pains. However, we seem to lack the sort of direct control over these mental states that we have over ordinary actions.

Nevertheless, many claims about what we ought to believe seem to state robustly normative truths, which is not the case for claims about what pains we ought to feel. For example, you ought to believe that you are reading this text right now, and most people ought not to believe that the NASA moon landing was a hoax. We can of course make claims about whether someone ought to feel pain. For example, a dentist who has numbed your nerve might say that you ought not to feel pain in your tooth. This kind of claim appears to be about what a person with a normal or well-functioning nervous system would feel, whereas our normal practices of attributing knowledge—considering whether other people are justified in their beliefs, wondering what we ourselves should believe—seem to presume that subjects are in charge of their beliefs in a way that they are not in charge of their pains. Let's isolate the intuitive contrast with the following *epistemic normativity principle*:

(ENP) Some robustly normative claims about belief are true.

This principle leads some philosophers[3] to endorse a *deontological conception of epistemic normativity*, i.e., the view that people's beliefs are proper objects of robustly normative epistemic ought claims.[4]

To many who are impressed by the idea that 'ought' implies 'can', however, the deontological conception of epistemic normativity seems to be in tension with doxastic involuntarism. This leads to a situation in which, on the one hand, proponents of doxastic involuntarism[5] argue that the deontological conception of epistemic normativity must be false, and are thus forced to explain away the intuitions behind the epistemic normativity principle, while on the other, proponents of the deontological conception of epistemic normativity argue that doxastic involuntarism must be false,[6] and are thus forced to explain away the intuitions behind the no rewards principle.

My primary purpose in the rest of this chapter is to sketch a theory of doxastic 'ought's that achieves an attractive middle ground between these extremes. The key will be appreciating the fact that not all normative ought claims presuppose that we have direct voluntary control in or over the object of the evaluation. I will construct my account as an attempt to improve on other accounts in this vein (especially those due to Richard Feldman and Hilary Kornblith). The new idea (in a telegraphic slogan) is that normative epistemic claims about what someone ought to believe articulate state norms, which are logically distinct from, but also interestingly connected to, action norms. The distinction between state norms and action norms provides a way to understand the phrase 'ought to believe' that is consistent with both doxastic involuntarism and the deontological conception of epistemic normativity. Moreover, my account of the connection between these two sorts of norms provides a novel way to incorporate a believer's epistemic community into our understanding of the scope of epistemic norms. This is foundational for my more social conception of the force of these norms and the value of knowledge.

6.2 Rejecting "Ought Implies Can"

In the literature about doxastic involuntarism and the deontological conception of epistemic normativity, there are a variety of ostensible counterexamples to the idea that 'ought' implies 'can'.[7] For example, it seems true that you ought to pick up your friend on time, even if, because you left too late, you can no longer do so. Also, it seems true that your friend ought not to steal, even if, because she is a kleptomaniac, she cannot help herself.

In my view, however, these sorts of counterexamples are a red herring in the debate between doxastic involuntarists and deontologists about epistemic normativity. They are illustrations of kinds of actions that all participants to that debate would agree can, in principle, be under our direct voluntary control, even if there are cases when they are not. The vexing thing about beliefs is not that there are *some* situations where we ought to have a particular belief, even though we do not happen to exercise voluntary control over our doxastic attitudes in that situation. What's vexing, rather, is that doxastic attitudes are *never* under our direct voluntary control, yet some robustly normative evaluations of what someone ought to believe still seem true.

This point is relevant for evaluating two prominent ideas about doxastic control and epistemic normativity. The first comes from Feldman, who argues that doxastic 'ought's are akin to role 'ought's (2000, 675), which are normative claims applying to someone in virtue of their occupying a particular role. And, crucially, role 'ought's seem like they can be true even if the person to whom they apply lacks voluntary control over compliance. For example, Feldman writes, "Teachers ought to explain things clearly. Parents ought to take care of their kids. Cyclists ought to move in various ways" (2000, 275). But of course, we all know of teachers who lack the capacity to explain things clearly, of parents who cannot take care of their kids, and of cyclists who don't have sufficient control over their movements. According to Feldman, this doesn't mean that these role 'ought's are false when applied to those teachers, parents, and cyclists. Instead, he argues that the normative claims are articulations of a way in which someone fails to live up to the standards of the relevant role.

If doxastic ought claims were similar, the fact that we do not have direct voluntary control over particular beliefs would not undermine the idea that there are some true normative epistemic claims about what we ought to believe. Feldman writes, "we form beliefs in response to our experiences in the world. Anyone engaged in this activity ought to do it right. In my view, what they ought to do is to follow their evidence (rather than wishes or fears). I suggest that epistemic oughts are of this sort" (2000, 675).[8]

One should worry, however, that the relevant epistemic ought claims seem to be categorical, whereas Feldman's examples of role 'ought's are not categorical. Even if you do not want to believe the truth about what you are doing right now, you ought to believe that you are reading this text right now.[9] In contrast to optional roles such as teacher, parent, or cyclist, in

> the epistemic case, we not only want to say that if someone wants to be a good believer, he or she should believe in certain ways; we also wish to endorse the

claim that individuals ought, without qualification, to believe in those ways which, as a matter of fact, flow from good performance of the role of being a believer. (Kornblith 2001, 237)[10]

Feldman's only means for explaining this contrast is the fact that, unlike the roles of teacher, parent, and cyclist, we have no choice about whether to take on the role of being a believer. But I think this is an insufficient explanation. The kleptomaniac may also have no choice about whether to take on the role of a thief, but we would not want to say that she categorically ought to steal. Exactly the opposite: she categorically ought not to steal. So, the mere fact that "it is our plight" (Feldman 2000, 676) to play certain roles cannot explain the apparent categoricity of doxastic 'ought's.

Kornblith argues that what Feldman is right about is that some 'ought's come from evaluations of what counts as a good performance. Thus, the cogency of such 'ought's clearly does not require voluntary control to do what they prescribe or proscribe, as illustrated by role 'ought's deriving from roles such as teacher, parent, and cyclist. But, according to Kornblith, this is also true of *ideals*. He writes:

> An appropriate human ideal must in some ways be responsive to human capacities. Ideals are meant to play some role in guiding action, and an ideal that took no account of human limitations would thereby lose its capacity to play a constructive action-guiding role. At the same time, our ideals cannot be so closely tied to what particular individuals are capable of that we fail to recognize that some individuals at some times are incapable of performing in ideal ways. There is a large middle ground here, and it is here that reasonable ideals are to be found. (2001, 238)

So, for example, if respecting the legitimate property of others is plausibly thought to be a moral ideal, from this ideal we might conclude that the kleptomaniac ought not to steal, even if she can't help herself.

Kornblith argues that this helps to preserve the deontological conception of epistemic normativity in the face of the no rewards principle. He writes, "once we recognize that our ideals must lie somewhere within this large middle ground, we see that the defensibility of the oughts that flow from our epistemic ideals does not require the level of voluntary control over our beliefs that Alston and Plantinga insist upon" (2001, 238). But because these 'ought's flow from ideals rather than roles, their normative force can be categorical, unlike the role 'ought's discussed by Feldman. Kornblith writes:

> Although the role of being a slave might be performed well, it is perfectly reasonable to suppose that being a slave, whether the role be performed well or

badly, is no part of any acceptable human ideal. It is for this reason that oughts which flow from human ideals have a degree of normative force that is not shared by role oughts. (2001, 238–239)

I think Kornblith is right that doxastic 'ought's derive from our epistemic ideals. And it is certainly correct that human ideals can transcend particular humans' capacities without undermining the 'ought's that derive from them. Nevertheless, I doubt that Kornblith's comparison of doxastic 'ought's to moral ideals can resolve the apparent tension between the epistemic normativity principle and the no rewards principle. This is because the no rewards principle turns on the idea that believing is not the sort of thing *anyone* has direct voluntary control over—not just something that *particular* humans lack a capacity to control because they fall short of some ideal. Again, the upshot here is that particular action tokens that provide ostensible counterexamples to the idea that 'ought' implies 'can' are not suitable as models for epistemic normative evaluations of what someone ought to believe in the face of the no rewards principle, which seems to indicate that we never exercise direct voluntary control over our beliefs.

6.3 Sellars on State Norms

I think Sellars (1969) offers a clue for resolving the tension between the no rewards principle and the epistemic normativity principle. He distinguishes between claims about what some agent ought to *do* and claims about how some thing (inanimate objects, cultural artifacts, institutions, people, etc.) ought to *be*. He sometimes uses the labels "rules of action" and "rules of criticism" for this distinction, but I prefer the labels "action norms" and "state norms".[11] Whatever exactly we call it, the key point is that only the former category seems to presuppose voluntary control on the part of the logical subject of the normative claim. To adapt one of Sellars's examples, a clock repair-man might point out that "The clock chimes ought to (be disposed to) strike on the quarter hour," or the camp counselor might tell her campers that, "The beds ought to be made by 8am every morning." These ought claims can surely be true despite the fact that the disposition of the clock chimes to strike, or the state of the campers' beds, are not, properly speaking, things that are in someone's *direct* voluntary control.[12] This is not because we (or some of us) happen to lack control over a particular sort of action; rather, it is because the disposition of the clocks and the state of the beds are not ways of acting—they are ways of *being*.

We might worry that if claims about how something ought to be do not presuppose direct voluntary control on the part of the subject, then they aren't robustly normative. But I think we observe this distinction between action norms and state norms even in the most paradigmatically "robust" normative domain:

ethics. Action norms such as, "One should not steal," "One should pay back debts," and so on are familiar from everyday ethical life. However, it takes only a moment's reflection to think of ethical norms pertaining to states: for example, "Playgrounds should be free of drugs," "Hospitals should be accessible to the infirm," and so on. These are norms pertaining to states outside of the agents who are assumed to be (at least partially) responsible for the states. But there are also ethical norms pertaining to states of the agents who are assumed to exercise some kind of agency (at least partially or potentially) in or over those states: for example, "One should feel guilt for wronging another," "One should want one's children to be happy," and so on.

Unlike action norms, the validity of both of these kinds of state norms does not rest on the assumption that their logical subject can choose or directly control whether to conform to the norm. To take the most extreme example, playgrounds and hospitals do not choose or control anything—they are inanimate objects. Likewise, it seems to me that individual people do not choose, in particular cases, whether to feel guilt for wronging others or to want their children to be happy. The idea that these claims are robustly normative would, I think, come into question were there no discernable connection between things that people can choose to do and conformity to state norms; however, that's consistent with thinking that the connection is often indirect, complicated, and perhaps even uncodifiable.

Sellars boldly claims that, "though ought-to-be's are carefully to be distinguished from ought-to-do's they have an essential connection with them. The connection is, roughly, that ought-to-be's imply ought-to-do's" (1969, 508). According to him, the general form of the implication is material (rather than formal)[13] and involves a heavy *ceteris paribus* clause. I take the core idea to be that statements of the form "X's ought to be in state F," where these are not predictive or "merely evaluative" uses of 'ought', materially imply statements of the form, "(Other things being equal and where possible) S ought to bring it about that X's are in state F."

Sellars operationalizes this distinction in a general account of language-use as thoroughly rule-governed, even though he accepts that most language-use isn't action done following a rule. His key move to make this idea work is claiming that most language-use is the manifestation of linguistic dispositions (states in which language-users ought to be yet over which they do not exercise direct voluntary control), while recognizing that there are various special cases of linguistic actions done following a rule (such as happens when one explicitly learns a second language or corrects a child's grammar).

On this basis, Sellars suggests that a possible rule governing basic perceptual reports is that, "When exposed to red objects in sunlight, one ought to *be disposed to utter* 'this is red' under appropriate prompting."[14] Although this alleged rule of criticism applies to speakers of a language and to those who are in the process of learning a language, it is important not to confuse it with the (merely putative) rule of action, "When exposed to red objects in sunlight, one ought to *assert* 'this is red' under appropriate prompting." In Sellars's view, this rule of action can be understood only by those who already have the concepts of red, object, sunlight, and what it is to assert something. So, importantly, Sellars thinks this rule could not constitute a rule that language-learners genuinely follow in *acquiring* the concept of red (or, for that matter, the concepts object, sunlight, and assertion).[15] But that does not mean that the rules of criticism governing linguistic activity are akin to the dentist's ought-claim about feeling pain in the example in section 6.1, because Sellars treats them as robustly normative in their connection to rules of action. Indeed, as we saw, he thinks rules of criticism *imply* rules of action. In particular, he suggests that the earlier claim about how English speakers ought to be implies the following claim about what people ought to do: "One ought to bring it about (*ceteris paribus*) that when people are exposed to red objects in sunlight, they are disposed to utter 'this is red' under appropriate prompting."

The 'one' here is vague, and making it more precise will help to distinguish between three possible views about the connection between state norms and action norms. One relatively deflationary idea is that state norms materially imply certain conditional rules of action. Generically,

(1) X ought to be F

materially implies

(2) If someone is responsible for X's being F, then they ought to do what they can (*ceteris paribus*) to bring it about that X is F.

Call this the *conditional view* of the logical relationship between state norms and action norms.[16] A much stronger view sees state norms as materially implying universal action norms—generically, that is, (1) implies

(3) Everyone ought to do what they can (*ceteris paribus*) to bring it about that X is F.

Call this the *universal view* of the logical relationship between state norms and action norms. A third, middle view treats state norms as materially implying nonconditional but also nonuniversal action norms—generically, that is, (1) implies

(4) Someone ought to do what they can (*ceteris paribus*) to bring it about that X is F.

Call this the *existential view* of the logical relationship between state norms and action norms. On this view, a true normative claim about how someone ought to be implies that someone is responsible for making the subject of the state norm be the way it ought to be.

Sometimes Sellars seems to be adopting the universal view of linguistic rules of criticism. This seems to me to be the correct view of moral state norms, such as "People ought to feel outrage about genocide," which then might be said to imply that everyone ought to do what they can (*ceteris paribus*) to bring it about that people feel outrage about genocide.[17] However, Sellars's leading example about clocks suggests the conditional view instead. That is to say, the claim "Clock chimes ought to be disposed to strike on the quarter hour" seems to imply at most that, if someone is responsible for the (relevant) clock chimes, then that person ought to do whatever they can (*ceteris paribus*) to bring it about that the chimes are disposed to strike on the quarter hour. This is made clearer by noticing the parallel to "Bombs ought to be disposed to spread shrapnel widely," which hopefully does not imply anything more than the conditional that, *if* someone is responsible for the bomb's spreading shrapnel widely, then that person ought to do whatever they can (*ceteris paribus*) to make the bomb disposed to spread shrapnel widely—a conditional whose antecedent is, at least morally speaking, usually false.

However, the intuitive idea of teaching our children things by doing what we can to get them to conform to particular rules of criticism suggests to me neither a universal action norm nor a merely conditional action norm. If it is true, for instance, that my son ought to be able to tie his shoes by age seven, then it would seem also to be true that someone (me and his mother, but not everyone) has an obligation to teach him to be this way. This suggests the existential view.

Which is the correct view of linguistic rules of criticism—the unconditional view suggested by the moral outrage example, the conditional view suggested by the chiming clock example, or the existential view suggested by the shoe-tying example? I don't really want to take a stand on that question here, and it doesn't matter for what follows whether language is rule-governed in the way Sellars imagines. My point in discussing Sellars's idea was only to explain the conceptual possibility of each of these three sorts of logical relations between state norms and action norms. What is important for what follows is that, in one way or another, Sellars's idea of rules of criticism, or what I've been calling "state norms", might provide a good model for understanding normative epistemic claims about what someone ought to believe, given our assumption of doxastic involuntarism.

6.4 Ought to Believe as a State Norm

In developing an account of robustly normative claims about what someone ought to believe, my strategy is to treat these as adverting to a species of state norms. For instance, the claim, "You ought to believe you are reading this text right now" could be understood to be an instance of the general form, "*S* ought to be in doxastic attitude *A* toward proposition *p* under conditions *C*." Then, the crucial observation is that some such normative claims seem to be true, just like:

> Clock chimes ought to be disposed to strike on the quarter hour,
> The beds ought to be made by 8am every morning,
> A child ought to be able to tie their shoes by age seven,
> People ought to feel outrage about genocide,

and

> When exposed to red objects in sunlight, one ought to be disposed to utter 'this is red' under appropriate prompting.

Yet these true normative claims don't presuppose that *their subjects* be capable of voluntarily following the rule. So, modeling doxastic 'ought's on these kinds of claims provides a way to respect both the epistemic normativity principle and the no rewards principle (introduced in section 6.1 at the beginning of the chapter).

As Sellars's account of linguistic rules of criticism reveals, however, none of this implies that believers cannot be agents. We just have to appreciate that they do not exercise direct voluntary agency in believing what they believe. Given the result of Chapter 4, this should not be surprising. If we assume that exercising agency is dynamic, whereas belief is a state and so nondynamic, we should already know not to look for exercises of agency in belief itself. But my approach is consistent with the idea that our beliefs *manifest* our agency and that we have the capacity to exercise agency *with respect to* our beliefs, e.g., in the activities of belief-system maintenance. By respecting both the epistemic normativity principle and the no rewards principle, this approach avoids the drastic choice between doxastic involuntarism and the deontological conception of epistemic normativity with which I began. Moreover, I think it surpasses the accounts of doxastic 'ought's suggested by both Feldman and Kornblith. Let me explain.

Regarding Feldman: Even though he does not make this point, presumably some role 'ought's derive from state norms rather than action norms. For example, the claim, "Teachers ought to be interested in their subject" seems to articulate a way that teachers ought to *be* rather than any particular action they ought to perform. Nevertheless, such role-driven state norms are not plausibly thought to be categorical. As we've seen, good performance of the role of a kleptomaniac may require that one *be* cunning, but it is not a categorical state norm that one ought to be cunning if one is a kleptomaniac. Rather, we want to say that, if one is a kleptomaniac, one ought to be treated by a psychiatrist. But, while this later claim is perhaps categorical, it is not a role-ought. And, likewise, doxastic 'ought's conceived of as state norms seem to be categorical in a way that Feldman's role 'ought's are not. So, by treating doxastic 'ought's as deriving from state norms that are not role 'ought's, my account gains important resources for explaining the apparent categoricity of doxastic 'ought's which Feldman's account lacks.

Regarding Kornblith: Doxastic 'ought's do seem to me to derive from epistemic ideals, but not on the model of the derivation of typical *moral* 'ought-to-do's from *moral* ideals. This is because the lack of voluntary control we have over our beliefs is not the same as the lack of voluntary control of someone who, because she falls short of a moral ideal, is incapable of acting in the morally required ways. Even when we are epistemically ideal, we appear to lack direct voluntary control over our beliefs. So, the possibility of being nonideal does not explain why the no rewards principle is true. By contrast, seeing doxastic 'ought's as epistemic state norms does explain why the no rewards principle is true: Doxastic 'ought's are 'ought-to-be's and we cannot directly decide *to be* this way or that—being is not a form of doing.

On this approach, then, the epistemic ideals which underwrite doxastic 'ought's would be analogous to moral ideals about what we should feel. Perhaps, for example, the moral ideal of generosity implies that one ought to feel pleasure when giving to charity. If so, this can be true even though one does not have direct voluntary control over whether one does indeed feel pleasure when giving to charity. Because one lacks direct voluntary control, it does not make sense to offer to reward someone for having this feeling, just like it does not make sense to offer to reward someone for having a particular belief. However, we can of course sometimes decide to do something that has as an indirect consequence that we are this way or that. So, it can sometimes make sense to reward someone to perform an action with indirect influence over their states of feeling or belief. None of this is inconsistent with Kornblith's account of doxastic 'ought's as deriving from epistemic ideals, but it moves beyond that account, by providing a way to understand the difference between ideal-based 'ought's that apply to actions and 'ought's that apply to beliefs.[18] The former are action norms, while the latter are state norms.

So far, modelled on Sellars's view of linguistic rules, I have argued that doxastic state norms imply *ceteris paribus* action norms. But his account was unclear about the content of the action norms implied. So, it is fair to wonder: What action norms are implied in the epistemic case? This is a complex and difficult question that I do not hope to settle with any serious precision here, but some speculative thoughts might help to flesh out how I am thinking about epistemic norms of belief.

When we say that a hospital ought to be accessible to the infirm, we imply (defeasibly) that the hospital's architect should design it that way, and/or the builders should use techniques ensuring accessibility, and/or the manager should correct any problems with accessibility, and so on. These are things that agents can choose to do in order to put the hospital in the state it should be in. Because of this, we can say that the connection between this state norm and action norms is *exclusively other-regarding*. When the relevant state is the state of an agent, however, it seems that we can also have a self-regarding connection. When we say, for example, that a person ought to feel guilt for wronging another, we often imply (defeasibly) that she should perform certain actions, such as reflecting on the pain she has caused, considering the plight of the victim, discussing her wrongdoing with others, seeking psychological help if she does not feel guilty, and so on. In this way, state norms pertaining to the states of an agent can be different from the state norms with exclusively other-regarding connections to action norms, since they can imply things about what the logical subject of the state should do. In this way, my account of epistemic normative claims about what people ought to believe is meant to comport with the account of doxastic agency defended in Chapter 4, where I argued that believers can normally exercise agency with respect to their own beliefs by engaging in the activity of belief-system maintenance.

Based on this idea, it can be tempting to think that the normative force of "ought to believe" derives entirely from the normative prescriptions that such claims imply for the subject of the belief. The idea would be that when we make normative claims of the form "S ought to believe that p," this has robust normative force insofar as it implies that S ought to do or have done things that would make it the case that they believe that p.[19]

However, this can't be right. For, claiming that someone epistemically ought to believe that p doesn't seem capable of guiding their action in the same way as claiming that someone ought to be in one of those other states over which subjects plausibly exercise indirect voluntary control. If I come to think, for example, that I ought to be clear-headed on the morning of an exam, I can take steps to pursue this (abstain from alcohol); or if I think I ought to be asleep in the middle of the night, I can take steps to ensure that is the case (take pills). By contrast, if I come to think that I epistemically ought to believe that p, normally I either already believe that p or I thereby begin to believe that p.[20]

Moreover, I suspect we miss an important part of the picture of normativity if we ignore the fact that state norms pertaining to an agent often imply things about what others in the agent's community should do. For example, when we say that a person ought to feel guilt for wronging another, we can also imply that the person's friends should help them to see the plight of the victim, and/or that their parents should have inculcated this emotional capacity, and so on. In this way, state norms with a self-regarding connection to action norms can also have other-regarding connections. So, the value of the distinction between action norms and state norms is not just that the latter don't presuppose direct voluntary control, but also that they make sense of a kind of sociality among the agents who are responsible for making it the case that someone is in the state that they ought to be in.[21]

Accordingly, although epistemic norms pertaining to beliefs are state norms that often imply normative claims pertaining to the action norms governing the activities involved in individual belief-system maintenance, I also think we miss an important and developmentally more primary part of the picture if we ignore the fact that epistemic norms pertaining to beliefs can also imply things about what others in the subject's community should do. This becomes clear when we think about children. There are things that young children ought to believe, but because they are too young to be responsible for these states, it would be wrong to think that these norms imply actions of inquiry that the child ought to perform. But even when someone is old enough to be a mature epistemic subject, and we say that they should believe some proposition, I think we often imply (defeasibly) that their parents should have taught them the truth of this proposition, and/or their friends should correct belief in the opposite proposition, and/or their colleagues should provide evidence of the truth of this proposition, and so on.

Broadly speaking, these are the actions that constitute the practice of instruction (testimony, criticism, reporting, and the like). And my suggestion is that epistemic norms pertaining to beliefs bear an important connection not only to the self-regarding norms of belief-system maintenance, but also to the other-regarding norms of *instruction*. (This is a further reason why I think it is wrong to hold that the biological function of an individual belief system is the sole or even main source of the epistemic norms governing belief.)

So, as I am thinking of them, beliefs are states of mind subject to epistemic state norms, which have both self- and other-regarding connections to action norms. I think this idea explains why we use a form of words aspectually classified as stative (see Chapter 2) to talk about the object of central epistemic norms, namely, the norms of belief. Moreover, it makes it at least intelligible why we would make robust normative evaluations of beliefs. And this is how my account of doxastic 'ought's offers a framework for addressing the deontological puzzle about epistemic normativity with which I started this book.

What about the axiological puzzle about why we value knowledge more than true belief and think it is something people should pursue? When we attribute knowledge to someone, we evaluate this person's belief state as conforming to norms about what they ought to believe. These norms are inferentially related to the epistemologically relevant action norms pertaining to inquiry and/or instruction, but it would be a mistake to conflate epistemic state norms with those action norms. This is because there may not often be an identifiable connection between an epistemic state norm and a set of specific actions that exhaust the state norm's normative force. That is to say, there may be no general or straightforward way to link state norms pertaining to beliefs to specific action norms pertaining to belief-system maintenance and instruction. Still, the validity of each specific application of a state norm may still depend on the validity of a corresponding set of action norms pertaining to the believer themselves, but also to others in their epistemic community.

I think this is key for explaining the distinctive way we value knowledge. So, in the next section and in the following chapter, I will further investigate the connection between what someone epistemically ought to believe and the various self- and other-regarding doxastic activities that are required for someone to have knowledge. Insofar as these activities function to keep beliefs responsive to reasons, this approach offers a way to make sense of Sellars's oft-cited claim that "in characterizing an episode or state as that of knowing, we are not giving an empirical description of that episode or state; we are placing it in the logical space of reasons" (1956, sec. 36). Crucially, on my interpretation, the person who knows that p doesn't have to be able to justify their belief that p. Because instruction is a way that members of one's epistemic community can help a believer to maintain a belief grounded in reasons, it is possible for a belief to be "placed in the space of reasons" even when the believer isn't capable of robust forms of reasoning (e.g., because they are a young child).

6.5 Conclusion

In this chapter, I have sought to explain how understanding the distinction between action norms and state norms can generate an account of robust epistemic norms that doesn't presuppose that we exercise direct voluntary control over our beliefs. This is a way to embrace both the no rewards principle and the epistemic normativity principle. In the larger narrative of this book, that means that there are promising routes between the pitfalls of Cartesianism and the impoverishment of reliabilism when it comes to thinking about epistemic normativity and doxastic agency. And these routes do not require succumbing to the temptation to treat belief itself as a kind of performance or as an active state, which I warned against in previous chapters.

Moreover, an account of doxastic 'ought's that treats them as state norms, on the model of Sellars's rules of criticism, fits well with the observation that belief and knowledge are two of the most important cognitive states for us to keep track of in order to understand and cooperate with others in a common environment. Each of us has only an incomplete set of information about the features of our physical and social environment, but luckily each of us also has a different set of information. This means that we can often share information with one another and broaden the information on the basis of which we make particular decisions about how to behave. But to do that, as Craig (1990) suggested, we need some way of keeping track of who has which pieces of information, and whose informational states contain systematic or idiosyncratic errors.

In virtue of being state descriptions, our ordinary belief and knowledge attributions are well suited for this task. When I do not know, for example, where the food is, it will surely be a step in the right direction if I understand that you *do* know where the food is; then, I only need to convince you to share that information with me. And even when I do know, for example, that the water is over the hill, if I am looking for you to tell me where the food is and I think you may be fetching water, then I can form a strategy for finding you: look over the hill. If my discussion earlier is moving in the right direction, then belief and knowledge are both cognitive states, but in the environment in which it is useful to keep track of these things, it is plausible to think that they play different roles. If I am looking for the food, then, if you have knowledge about where the food is, you will prove more useful than someone who merely has a belief about where the food is.

As Socrates already pointed out in the *Meno*, assuming that both you and the other person have correct beliefs about such matters, the instrumental value of finding out your beliefs may prove identical in that specific case. However, we are often interested in keeping track of each other's cognitive states not only for a *present* purpose, but also for purposes of unspecified *future* exchanges of information. Hence, even if you and someone else agree about where the food is, it will prove useful to me to be able to keep track of the fact that you merely believe this and the other person knows this. For in the future, it will probably be a better strategy to seek information about where the food is from the other person than from you. Alternatively, even if I think that both of your opinions are false, if I think one person's opinion amounts to justified belief, whereas the other's does not, then I will have some idea of who to go to first in the future, and also some idea of whose practices of inquiry to emulate when it comes to such matters.

In light of these simplistic ecological observations, the answer to the axiological puzzle about epistemic normativity does not seem to me to lie in any special idea of "performance normativity" or distinctively "active states". Rather, the value of knowledge will depend precisely on the fact that it is *not* a performance. As a cognitive state, it is the sort of thing we can count on being available to depend upon, even as other things change. Of course, belief falling short of knowledge is also a state, and we depend on such states when we have to. But because the long-term functioning of our information economy depends on the difference between knowledge and other sorts of belief, we depend on these states in different ways. This difference should be reflected in the connections between epistemological norms of belief, and the action norms governing actions that constitute the practices of belief-system maintenance and instruction. Hence, it will be something about this difference which explains why we value knowledge more than beliefs falling short of knowledge. And this is how my framework conceptualizes the axiological puzzles about epistemic normativity. In the following chapter, I turn more directly to the question of why we value epistemic norm-compliance so highly in our information-sharing communities.

Notes

1. B. Williams (1973) endorsed the stronger principle that the formation of one's beliefs cannot be within one's voluntary control. He thought that this is an implication of the idea that belief aims at truth. There has been much discussion of what to make of this idea and the conclusion Williams drew from it. See especially Bennett (1990), Scott-Kakures (1993), Radcliffe (1997), Velleman (2000), Shah (2003), and Shah and Velleman (2005). For my purposes here, however, the weaker form of doxastic involuntarism stated in the text is strong enough; in Chapters 2 and 5, I discuss further my reservations about the idea that belief aims at truth.
2. Raising one's hand is an action over which we have what Alston (1988) refers to as "basic voluntary control", because it is something we can just do. Turning on the light is an action over which we have "nonbasic immediate voluntary control", because it is something we can do right away by doing something else (such as, flipping the switch). By and large, these details will not matter here, but it is worth mentioning that Alston claims that we have neither sort of voluntary control over our beliefs, although he allows that we have what he calls "nonbasic indirect voluntary control" of a very weak sort over our beliefs, comparable to the sort of control we have over our blood pressure. Feldman (2000) argues that there are some beliefs over which we exercise nonbasic immediate voluntary control. His example is the belief that the lights are on in his office. If offered a high reward to believe this, he could collect the reward by turning on the lights in his office and thereby coming to have the belief right away. Alston might respond that this is indirect rather than direct nonbasic voluntary control, but what is important here is that (as Feldman recognizes) the sort of voluntary control over beliefs that his example illustrates is something we have over only a small class of potential beliefs: just the beliefs for which we have the power to make their propositional contents true. For the purposes of my discussion here, this class of beliefs may be bracketed, since the sorts of ordinary normative claims about what someone ought to believe that generate the tension between doxastic involuntarism and the deontological conception of epistemic normativity far outstrip this class of beliefs.
3. See especially Ginet (2001), Steup (2000, 2008), and Ryan (2003).
4. I adopt the label "deontological" from Alston (1988) and subsequent discussion, although I think it can be misleading in two important ways. First, the term "deontology" is sometimes taken to imply a commitment to the idea that the relevant object of evaluation is strongly rule governed and not merely rule conforming. However, Alston and his critics are not concerned with whether believers explicitly follow rules in forming beliefs, they are concerned with the prior issue of whether it even makes sense to make robust normative claims about what people ought to believe. Second, deontology is often contrasted in ethics with consequentialism and virtue theory in terms of their respective views on the source of ethical normativity or the structure and justification of normative ethical evaluations of action. However, all of these views hold that action is a proper object of normative ethical evaluation. It is the parallel claim about belief that is being investigated here. A more genuinely epistemic deontology might rightly be thought to involve something more to distinguish it from epistemic consequentialism, and epistemic virtue theory. See Turner (2004); see Berker (2013) for

a critique of teleological conceptions of epistemic normativity and a (partial) defense of a purer form of epistemic deontology.
5. See especially Plantinga (1993b) and Alston (1988, 2005).
6. In earlier versions of this material, I discuss some rather detailed arguments from Steup (2000) and Ryan (2003) against doxastic involuntarism. I believe their arguments usefully highlight distinctions that were often run together in previous debates about involuntarism, especially between voluntary choice/decision, something's being within our voluntary control, and something's being free. See Chrisman (2008) and Weatherson (2008) for further discussion.
7. For discussion of several epicycles, see Ryan (2003), drawing on Stocker (1971) and Sinnott-Armstrong (1984). See also Chuard and Southwood (2009).
8. Later in Feldman (2008), he makes a compatible proposal, suggesting that "S ought to believe that p" should be analyzed as "Believing that p is the epistemically appropriate response to S's evidence." He takes this to be a way of spelling out the evidentialist idea that in one's role as a believer, one ought to follow one's evidence. Whatever way we spell out the details, I still think Feldman's proposal falls prey to the criticisms I go on to articulate earlier.
9. For a similar point, compare Kelly (2003).
10. Kornblith might not want to call these "categorical" 'ought's, but rather a sort of hypothetical ought, where the hypotheticality is cancelled for any agent with any desires—for the full view, see Kornblith (2002, ch. 5).
11. For a similar distinction, compare Humberstone (1971). My idea of applying this distinction to belief and knowledge here is similar to Owens's idea in writing, "Some norms are not there to guide action, to govern the exercise of control: their function is to assess what we are" (2000, 126).
12. This distinction may seem to be unavailable if we follow the standard view in deontic logic and treat 'ought' as a unary modal operator applying to propositions. On a very schematic version of this view, all ought-statements with a particular subject can be transformed into impersonal constructions beginning with "It ought to be the case that..." in a way that elides the distinction between 'ought-to-do's and 'ought-to-be's (McNamara 2006). Treating 'ought' as this kind of unary modal operator is helpfully simplifying for developing the semantics and proof theory for deontic logic; in the present context, however, this way of proceeding seems to wash away the distinction between ought claims which might reasonably be thought to presuppose voluntary control and those which do not. This is why I want to resist the idea that 'ought' is just a unary modal operator applying to propositions. However, that does not commit me to saying that 'ought' is never a unary modal operator on propositions. 'Ought' clearly has a non-normative use in sentences such as, "Given how the sky looks tonight, it ought to rain tomorrow". Moreover, some uses of 'ought' may be merely "political" as Sidgwick (1874/1907) calls them (to distinguish them from "agential"). The idea is that some things ought to be the case because they are generally desirable, although no particular agent ought to do anything to make things this way. See Chrisman (2012c; 2016a, ch. 5) for further discussion of how to incorporate a distinctive 'ought-to-do' into a semantics for 'ought' considered as a modal operator.

13. That is to say, it is not merely in virtue of the logical form of the statements that an inference from one rule to the other is correct; rather, it is in part because of the nature of the concepts deployed in the statements that such an inference is correct. For example, the inference from "X is a triangle" to "X has three sides" is materially correct. (Compare Sellars (1953) on the materially correct inference from "Pittsburgh is to the west of Princeton" to "Princeton is to the east of Pittsburgh".)
14. I have changed Sellars's example slightly to make it more intuitive and to make it more clearly fit the general formula stated earlier. He wrote, "(Ceteris paribus) one ought to respond to red objects in sunlight by uttering or being disposed to utter 'this is red'" (1969, 511).
15. What about the linguistic rule "One ought not to use unattached participles", which seems true even if the person to whom it applies does not have the concept of an unattached participle? Sellars would insist that if this really is a true linguistic rule applying to all English speakers, we should view it as a rule of criticism (perhaps more precisely stated as: "One ought not to be disposed to use unattached participles"). And if it is rather meant as a rule of action, then it cannot apply to subjects who lack the relevant conceptual resources to follow it. The technical distinction between rules of action and rules of criticism is (in part) defined by whether the rule presupposes that the subject has the conceptual resources to follow it. (Thanks to John Broome for pressing me to make this point clearer.)
16. While "conditional", it would be wrong to think of the resulting 'ought-to-do's as therefore "hypothetical". The sense in which they are conditional is not that they are conditional on the agent's antecedent ends/desires, which is what hypotheticality requires. The conditional–unconditional distinction cuts across the hypothetical–categorical distinction.
17. Sellars uses a similar example where I think intuitions are less clear: "One ought to feel sympathy for the bereaved." He suggests that this materially implies that one ought (*ceteris paribus*) to bring it about that people feel sympathy for the bereaved. See Sellars (1969, 509). It is important to remember that the *ceteris paribus* clause might be relied on quite heavily in cases in which there are other obligations to mind one's own business, or to do something else more important than influencing people's feelings about genocide.
18. It also makes sense of Owens's claim that, "Some norms are not there to guide action, to govern the exercise of control: their function is to assess what we are" (2000, 126). Because he thinks this, Owens argues that not all responsibility presupposes freedom to choose—in particular, epistemic responsibility does not presuppose voluntary choice of our doxastic attitudes. I agree with this. However, I would say that epistemic responsibility is intimately related to responsibility to do things over which we do have voluntary control. The conceptual connection between rules of criticism and rules of action that I have been urging allows one to make this connection.
19. For discussion and defense of versions of this idea, see Heil (1983), Leon (2002), Levy (2007), Altshul (2014), Meylan (2015, 2017), and Peels (2016). Vierkant (forthcoming) argues for a conception of control over one's beliefs as one of "tinkering" on the mind with various cognitive and symbolic tools (including some that lie outside the head) in perfectly ordinary ways.

20. Compare Nolfi (2014) for a more realistic account of how normative evaluation of belief might sometimes affect one's stance toward this belief and the formation of other beliefs. I regard this as a special case and by no means the usual way that belief is formed.
21. This is related to the difference between attributable and accountable senses of "responsibility" (see Watson 1996), since one can be responsible for something (e.g., a belief) that it is incorrect to attribute to someone. But the way in which state 'ought's advert to the responsibilities of other people needn't be connected to reactive attitudes of blame. Compare Young's (1990, 124, 151; 2006) forward-looking "social connectionist" conception of responsibility. In this book, I am not really concerned with what it is to hold people responsible for or to blame them for their beliefs. But see the end of Chapter 7 for brief discussion of responsibility.

7
Social Foundations for Epistemic Normativity

7.1 Introduction

On an influential traditional picture in epistemology, belief can be and often is chosen through deliberation, i.e., consciously weighing up and responding to reasons. This fits well with the observation that we normatively evaluate people's beliefs and, when we do, we are assuming that they have the capacity to exercise agency with respect to what we evaluate. However, as I explained in Chapter 1, the sort of doxastic involuntarism that is now dominant in epistemology rests on powerful arguments *against* thinking that belief is normally (if ever) produced by deliberation resulting in choice. And recent work in cognitive and social psychology and behavioral economics suggests that most of our beliefs are *not* the product of anything like a conscious weighing up of and responding to reasons.[1]

As a result, I argued in Part I that the primary locus of doxastic agency is not in belief itself, nor in the formation of belief, but in the activity of belief-system maintenance. This idea helped me to make sense of the fact that individual beliefs are not generally chosen and do not by themselves constitute an exercise of agency, while preserving the idea that there is a potentially rational and norm-governed (even if not always voluntary) activity that believers engage in with respect to what they believe. Believers maintain a system of beliefs by engaging in voluntary actions, such as gathering and reflecting on evidence or seeking out new information, but also by engaging in the mostly automatic activity of basing some of their beliefs on other beliefs, updating their tacit appreciation of the inferential and probabilistic support relations between their beliefs, and spontaneously learning new things about the world.

The activity of maintaining a system of beliefs is something I think believers are, in some sense, always already tacitly doing; or, at least, part of what it means to call states of their mind "beliefs" is to assume that they are capable of engaging in this activity to some extent, and that they tend to do so in an ongoing fashion. On this picture, individual beliefs can be seen as the manifestation of a believer's doxastic agency in engaging in the rational activity of belief-system maintenance, even if we deny that believers normally exercise agency in forming a particular belief that p or in simply believing that p.

In Chapter 4, I characterized this activity in primarily individualistic terms, and it is tempting to think that the epistemic norms that we use to evaluate beliefs derive their normative force from something about the way the activity of belief-system maintenance functions to connect individual believers to reality. Indeed, I have claimed that it is by engaging in this activity that one has and develops an ongoing subjective take on what is the case, and a subjective take on what is the case is crucial for individuals to act in the world. So, we might think that complying with epistemic norms is primarily something done by the individual to whom norms of belief apply, which should in principle be something one can do by oneself, relaxing in the proverbial armchair by the fire and thinking about whether one's beliefs are knowledgeable.

However, I think this individualistic picture of doxastic agency and epistemic normativity is missing something important: other people. Even just identifying *what* one believes about many topics seems to me to require intercourse with other people. And, even then, I suspect it is often very difficult, and sometimes humanly impossible, to do this accurately.[2] After all, if most belief-formation is automatic, intuitive, biased, and/or ideologically framed, there is no guarantee that one can just, so to speak, *ask oneself* what one believes and get a straightforward answer. Moreover, if many of the concepts we deploy in believing have an "externalist" character—in that their application conditions depend on connections to things in the world, including the thoughts and actions of other people—then it may not always be possible to tell, solely from the first-personal perspective, which of two (or more) similar beliefs one holds. This is why, when it comes to normatively evaluating one's own beliefs, I think one usually needs to leave the armchair and link minds with other believers as part of investigating the grounds for what we believe.

Because I accept this more social picture of norm-governed belief-system maintenance, in Part II of this book I have started to develop a more social characterization of the nature and source of epistemic normativity. I argued in Chapter 5 that true belief is not just a constitutive aim of individual belief-system maintenance, but also a potential regulative goal for members of a community of believers to pursue for each other. And I argued in Chapter 6 that the state norms, adverted to in claims about what a person ought to believe, should normally be seen as also implying action norms that pertain to members of the person's epistemic community; specifically, those people who bear responsibility for instructing, testifying, reporting, criticizing, etc., in ways that help a believer to base their beliefs on reasons.

In this chapter, I'll rely on the assumption that epistemic norms of belief are definable in terms of truth and are strongly connected to other-regarding norms of action, but what are these norms and how do they get a grip on us? I don't have much to add to the extensive literature on the content of epistemic norms. Evidentialists argue that one epistemically ought to hold those beliefs that are reasonable, given one's evidence; and reasonableness is defined in terms of that which one's evidence renders likely to be true. Reliabilists argue that one epistemically ought to hold those beliefs that are produced and sustained by a reliable process for the environment in which the beliefs are formed; and reliability is defined in terms of what, given one's environment, is likely to maximize true belief while minimizing false belief. Maybe there are other families of views, but the differences between these won't matter here. I will assume ecumenically that epistemic norms of belief pertain to the levels of *reasonableness and reliability* required for knowledge, in order to focus on questions about the *source* of such truth-orientated epistemic norms. My question is why we care, in the way we evidently do, about whether our own and other people's beliefs meet these normative standards; and, relatedly, why do we value a state (knowledge) that requires the reasonableness and reliability of our beliefs in the apparently distinctive way that we do?

As I will discuss more in section 7.5, I don't think of this as quite the same question as: "Why should we follow epistemic norms?" or "How do we justify epistemic norms?" These questions, at least as they are usually posed, seem to assume the stance of a skeptic or agnostic who imagines we face a choice of whether to care about epistemic norms or whether to follow them in forming our beliefs, whereas I doubt we could ever face that choice. So, I approach the issue of the nature and source of epistemic normativity from within the practice of maintaining beliefs and basing them on reasons, and evaluating whether individual beliefs meet the standards of knowledge. Accordingly, when I ask about the "grip" epistemic norms have on us, I am assuming ordinary believers are already tacitly committed to the validity of epistemic norms, in order to investigate what's involved in this commitment.

To answer this question, I will argue here that epistemic norms of reasonableness and reliability get a grip on us not mainly from individuals' subjective relation to reality, but from peoples' intersubjective relations to each other, based in an unavoidable form of epistemic interdependence. The basic idea is that part of what it is to be a fully human person is to be engaged in a joint endeavor with other people of making sense of reality and how to behave within it; this joint endeavor requires tacit mutual concern for the epistemic standards that one must meet in order to count as knowing something.

To flesh out and defend this idea, I first briefly consider five individualistic ways to explain the grip that epistemic norms have on us. None of these are fully satisfactory, in my view, but they provide important lessons for developing two further, more social, accounts of the source of epistemic normativity; i.e., accounts based on the idea that individuals are subject to norms of reasonableness and reliability because of their membership in, and joint endeavors with, a community of interdependent sharers of knowledge. The first "Hobbesian" account may be social enough for some epistemologists, but I'll suggest that a more richly social "Rousseauian" account offers a better overall explanation of the full source of epistemic normativity and the distinctive way we value knowledge.

7.2 Epistemic Norms and Individual Interests

It is a familiar fact that people desire to know the truth about particular topics. And, assuming that believing unreasonably or unreliably tends to take one away from the truth, one might argue that this desire is what explains epistemic norms' grip on us, that it explains why we value beliefs being reasonable and reliable enough to be knowledge. According to this account (the first of five I will consider in this section), one cares about whether one's beliefs are reasonable and reliable because and insofar as complying with these norms is a means for acquiring the knowledge that one wants.[3]

The first problem I have with this account is that it seems to portray the grip of epistemic norms as being at the mercy of whether individuals happen to want knowledge about particular topics. It also implausibly renders the force of these norms subject to the normative force of other cares and concerns that might outweigh or trump someone's desire for the knowledge. In addition to all of the topics about which each of us would profess a desire to know the truth, there are many other topics that we form beliefs about but don't care much about, yet *all* of these beliefs seem to be subject to epistemic normative evaluation.

Moreover, explaining the force of epistemic norms by appeal to the believer's own individual desires makes it mysterious why we value others' compliance with epistemic norms. Yet we do think it is better when other people have beliefs that meet the epistemic standards for knowledge. To be sure, sometimes I care about whether other people get what they want, and sometimes the people I care about want knowledge, but the way we value the reasonableness and reliability of other people's beliefs doesn't seem to be based in an other-regarding concern for the satisfaction of their desires to know particular truths. Often, we don't even know whether someone wants to know something, and sometimes people actively pursue ignorance about specific issues (e.g., the end of a film or the plan for a surprise party). Yet, in all of these cases, it seems that we are still right to evaluate other people in terms of whether they epistemically believe as they ought to believe. And we're right to think that when such beliefs count as knowledge, they are, in some sense, better than mere true belief.

A second answer to our question seeks to explain the grip of epistemic norms in an individual believer's interests *considered generally*, rather than any specific desire to acquire knowledge about some particular topic. The idea is that, whatever exactly one's particular practical interests are, one is going to tend to pursue these more effectively if one's beliefs are reasonable and reliable, and indeed if one is acting on knowledge rather than mere belief. This is because, over the long run, acting on knowledge is more likely to lead to practical success than not, and believing reasonably and reliably is more likely to result in knowledge than not.[4]

However, this can't be the full story. For, although knowledge about topics with an immediate effect on one's practical success is often useful for pursuing the satisfaction of one's interests, it is more difficult to see how to extend the idea to other topics, such as religion, abstruse scientific hypotheses, long-range probabilities, and the like.[5] For most people, it doesn't affect success in pursuing their practical interests to believe, e.g., in Newtonian physics rather than Einsteinian physics, or that the human race will survive for 1,000 more years rather than 2,000 more years.

Of course, sometimes one wants to know the truth about such issues, in which case complying with norms of reasonableness and reliability helps in the pursuit of this practical interest; but that's just a version of the first answer discussed above (namely, that the grip of epistemic norms comes from individuals' desire to know particular things). If one doesn't have an interest in acquiring knowledge about these specific propositions, however, it is difficult to see how complying with epistemic norms applied to beliefs about less practical topics could promote the successful pursuit of one's practical interests, whatever they happen to be. What we need is an account of the grip of epistemic norms and the value of knowledge that applies just as much to those topics as to other topics.[6]

Moreover, it is not clear that practical success is always better promoted by epistemically reasonable and reliable beliefs, in contrast to the sorts of overgeneralized and unhedged beliefs that limited cognitive agents such as ourselves find easier to process, retain, and act on. It is much easier to remember and so act on the belief that snake bites are dangerous than to remember which snakes have deadly poison, which will harm but not kill a person, and which are harmless. If this is right, it again becomes unclear why we would value reasonable and reliable belief.[7] When we evaluate beliefs as part of assessing whether someone knows something, we don't take "close enough for limited beings like us!" as sufficient for knowledge. Instead, we seem to think that, at least sometimes, people should pursue genuine knowledge, even when this isn't necessary for the pursuit of other practical interests. This evaluative practice could of course be based on some kind of normative error, but if it is, this error runs deep in our practice of thinking about what people ought to believe, attributing knowledge, and imputing doxastic agency. My aim throughout this book has been to make sense of this practice, assuming that it is more or less in order.

Both of the first two attempts to explain the grip of epistemic norms, by appeal to an individual agent's practical interests, fail to make sense of the way in which the force of ordinary epistemic normative evaluations goes *beyond* the desires and interests of individual believers. Because of this, we might say that epistemic norms are *categorical*: they don't lose their force just because an individual's desires or interests change.

Accordingly, one might claim that epistemic normativity comes from some objective value. This is the third kind of approach I will consider. For example, some philosophers might say that believing truly simply *is* what it is for one's belief to be objectively good qua belief.[8] On the basis of this idea, one could argue that the objective goodness of true belief is what gives norms of reasonableness and reliability their grip on us. We care about compliance with these norms because and insofar as such compliance manifests, or is connected to, something of objective value. Or, similarly, "knowledge-first" epistemologists might say that knowing that *p* is what it is for one's belief to be objectively good qua belief, and one cares about compliance with epistemic norms because and insofar as this puts one in a position to achieve this objective value.

To my mind, this third account of the source of epistemic normativity doesn't really explain much. The implicit assumption is that we value things insofar as we regard them as objectively valuable. But, even granting this assumption, the answer leaves me wanting to know *why* we regard true belief and/or knowledge as objectively valuable.

A constitutivist account of the grip of epistemic norms might help to overcome this worry. The idea would be to argue that believing that *p* is partly constituted by an implicit recognition of the force of epistemic norms. Accordingly, on this fourth account of the source of epistemic normativity, one doesn't even count as a believer unless one tacitly values compliance with epistemic norms. Sometimes this is explained further in terms of the idea that truth is a constitutive aim of belief, and compliance with those norms is connected to truth.[9]

As I explained in Chapter 5, I think it's right to view truth as a constitutive "aim" of belief, if this means that it is partly by reference to the fact that a mental state ought to be true that we identify that state as a belief. However, in Chapters 2 and 3, I rejected the idea that either belief itself, or the activity of maintaining a system of beliefs, are *performances* (telic) that are successful when they reach the truth. So, I don't think we can say that, simply in believing something, one is *ipso facto* engaged in a performance that commits one to the force of epistemic norms in virtue of the connection between compliance with these norms and the truth. Because of this, I am skeptical that the constitutivist account just mooted really explains why epistemic norms have a grip on us.[10] Maybe it's right that believing that *p* is partly constituted by a commitment to the force of epistemic norms or a tacit concern with reasonableness and reliability, but how does that explain the fact that we go in for forming and maintaining states of mind that give epistemic norms this kind of grip on us in the first place? To answer this question, I think we need to embed the constitutivist idea in some broader explanation of the practice of maintaining systems of belief, which I am ultimately going to argue is an importantly social practice.

I am also sympathetic to the objection to constitutivism that young children and nonhuman animals might be rightly described as believing things, even though it is considerably strained to view them as tacitly valuing belief that is reasonable or reliable enough to count as knowledge. So, below, I will argue that young children and even nonhuman animals can be *included* in an epistemic community, and that this inclusion might require implicitly viewing their doxastic states as subject to categorical norms of reasonableness and reliability, even if they themselves can't (yet or ever) recognize the force of these norms.

Before turning to more social accounts of the grip of epistemic norms and the value of knowledge, however, I want to consider a fifth and final individualistic account, which might seem to improve on the constitutivist idea considered above. Some philosophers argue that an essential function of human cognition is to form and maintain true beliefs. Maybe this is what belief-forming systems are evolved for, or maybe there is some other explanation of the development and perpetuation of belief-forming systems in beings like us that appeals to their capacity to perform this function. Either way, on this basis, one might try to appeal to this essential function of human cognition to explain why beliefs ought to be true.[11] Then, the idea would be to argue that recognizing the grip of norms of reasonableness and reliability just is (or is a consequence of) being someone with a cognitive system with this essential function; and reacting to this recognition is ultimately how we come to know things and why we care about knowledge.[12]

This account is more illuminating than the objective values account, but I still think there's a problem. The problem is that it is not always good for things to perform their essential function well.[13] For example, human reproductive organs are arguably for procreation, but that putatively essential function doesn't explain why the procreative facility of reproductive organs is something valuable. Of course, some people value this because they have certain interests, but other people don't, and there's nothing incoherent about that. Hence, the mere fact that our reproductive organs have an essential function doesn't show how norms pertaining to their good functioning get a grip on us. Similarly, one might hypothesize that race concepts originate and replicate for bolstering evolutionary fitness via in-group cohesion, but that putatively essential function of these concepts doesn't explain why deploying them aptly relative to that function is something we do or should think is good. Indeed, if this is the essential function of race concepts, it seems morally pernicious to value the good performance of this essential function.

In this section, I have briefly considered five possible individualistic accounts of the grip of epistemic norms and the value of knowledge—desire for the truth, an individual's interests considered generally, the objective value of true belief and knowledge, the constitutive aim of belief, and the evolved essential function of cognitive systems. Perhaps some of my reservations about these five attempts to explain the source of epistemic normativity could be avoided by a more careful defense of these views, or resolved through further discussion of the kinds of objections I have offered. However, I won't attempt to consider possible patches and responses, since my goal hasn't been to show that these views are completely wrongheaded about the source of epistemic normativity, but rather to explain why I think they don't get the full picture. In many cases, I think they point to something important. It just needs to be developed in a more social direction.

So, next, I want to explain why I think infusing a social element into our understanding of the source of epistemic normativity will help to fill out the picture. Some philosophers might take it as read that the grip of any norms must ultimately be explained in terms of our essential sociality. Those philosophers can read what follows as an attempt to elucidate that idea in the epistemic case. However, I suspect that many epistemologists still understand epistemic normativity in essentially individualistic terms, as having something to do with an individual's relation to reality. So, another way to read what follows is as an attempt to offer an alternative vision of epistemic normativity, one grounded in our socialized intersubjective understanding of things, rather than in our individual subjective relation to reality.

7.3 Hobbesian Epistemic Normativity

Thomas Hobbes (1651/2016) famously argues that, in the absence of a community where the legitimacy of certain norms of behavior is widely and reciprocally recognized, human life would be poor, nasty, brutish, and short. His basic idea is that such reciprocal recognition is, when well-signaled, why each of us can count on others to uphold agreements of mutual aid, and why we are compelled not to steal basic material resources and threaten the safety of others whenever it seems to suit us. As part of this explanation of the force of moral norms, Hobbes suggests that pre-moral humans in the state of nature would have been radically "free", in the sense that they would not have been limited by any behavioral norms, only impacted by various natural causes. He then conceives of the project of explaining the grip of morality as a project of rationalizing how such pre-moral humans could have transitioned from the state of nature into a society with the legitimate enforcement of things recognizable as moral norms.

In light of this, his approach to characterizing moral normativity is to identify the freedoms that a pre-moral human would be rational to give up, in exchange for the security and cooperation that depend on a set of norms being in force within a community. The reciprocal and well-signaled recognition of the legitimacy of such norms is, he thinks, necessary for there to be enough stability in social behavior for each of us to pursue our own individual interests. Because of this, he suggests that we should think of ourselves (adult humans belonging to a society) as having already implicitly accepted the force of a set of moral norms, and that this is a rational precondition for having and pursuing almost any normal human interest.

That's not to say, of course, that Hobbes thinks there was actually a process in which early humans exchanged natural freedoms for security and cooperation. Indeed, the sorts of lives normal socialized humans are able to lead, and the sorts of things that fit into a normal range of individual human interests, are so vastly different from what would have been available to pre-moral humans that we shouldn't regard Hobbes as offering a historical account of how norm-governed civil society first emerged. Instead, we should interpret him as offering a rational reconstruction, or "just-so" story, that is supposed to show why it is reasonable for us now to recognize the relevant norms as reasons to behave in certain ways, despite the fact that sometimes violating them would be the most expedient way to advance an individual interest. The core idea, as I understand it, is that widespread and reciprocal recognition of the force of those norms is a precondition for the socially cooperative ways of life that make the pursuit of most recognizably human interests possible in the first place. We care about being moral because doing so is necessary for leading the sorts of lives that we normal humans already have an interest in leading.

Whether or not Hobbes is right about what life would be like in a state of nature, I think he offers a template for explaining the grip of some set of norms that appeals crucially to our membership in a society. So, in the remainder of this section, I want to sketch an account of *epistemic* normativity, which is an application of this broadly Hobbesian story about why people care about complying with norms. The important claim will be that maintaining one's *reputation* as a reasonable and reliable believer is crucial for retaining the status of a "member in good standing" in particular sorts of communities—those sustained by widespread and well-signaled (even if only tacit) acknowledgement of the force of epistemic norms.[14] If correct, I think this claim will go some way toward filling in many of the gaps I highlighted in more individualistic accounts of the source of epistemic normativity.

Notably, the claim still traces the source of normativity to people's practical interests, like the very first individualistic account considered in section 7.2 above. However, it does so in a way that doesn't make the grip of epistemic norms *depend* on the relevant believer's specific practical interests. Because of this, it offers some prospect of explaining the way in which epistemic normativity seems to extend *beyond* any specific individual's particular desires or interests.

The central context in which it is important to maintain one's reputation as a reasonable and reliable believer is testimony, where one person tells others something they regard as true. Discussions of the epistemology of testimony often focus on the receiving side of this interaction, the question of what is involved in individuals handling testimonial input reasonably and reliably—whether this is a derivative or *sui generis* source of reasons to believe.[15] However, a more Hobbesian account of the grip of epistemic norms comes into view when we note that individual believers don't just *take* testimony from other people, they also *give* testimony to other people. Moreover, we each modulate our belief systems not only in light of the testimony of others, but also in light of how others react to *our* testimony—do they accept or challenge it, do they seek it out or ignore it in the future?

I think this is a manifestation of the fact that exchanging knowledge is a cooperative, iterative, and internally self-correcting practice. As a result, it is often crucial for an individual believer to maintain a reputation as someone who forms and maintains beliefs reasonably and reliably, and to develop and foster relationships of epistemic interdependence with others who maintain a similar reputation.[16] That's not to say that we should share everything we know, only that when one does share, one has a reason to care whether what one shares contributes to one's reputation as a knower. In this vein, W. K. Clifford famously notes the testimonial risk in not following one's evidence: "Habitual want of care about what I believe leads to habitual want of care in others about the truth of what is told to me" (1877, 294). Arguably, without a good testimonial reputation, most of us would quickly lose the sort of epistemic support we get from others—both as inputs and challenges to our belief systems—that is necessary for pursuing almost any normal human interest or concern.[17]

One might object to this idea, arguing that the availability of epistemic support is consistent with being a notorious bullshitter who grossly flouts norms of reasonableness and reliability but uses other means, such as wiliness or beauty, to benefit from the epistemic cooperation of others. I discuss the free-rider problem later, but if we include everything that an individual testifies to, I suspect that notorious bullshitters still tell the truth most of the time, and we have a very infirm conception of how impossible it would be to live a normal human life without the reputation of someone who testifies knowledgeably and believes reasonably and reliably most of the time.

Accordingly, a Hobbesian might explain why we value knowledge and are in the grip of norms of reasonableness and reliability, by pointing out how this is crucial for maintaining one's reputation as a good-faith sharer of knowledge in an epistemic community, which is itself crucial for securing epistemic support via testimony from other people. The idea, then, is this: since success in satisfying one's own desires and interests so often depends on having such support from other people, individuals have a strong and ongoing reason to maintain their reputation as reasonable and reliable believers. This is why they have a strong default reason to care about whether their beliefs comply with epistemic norms. Not everyone in the community must recognize this for the community to persist; so, young children, nonhuman animals, and some severely deranged people might be *included* in the community, without their recognizing the force of epistemic norms. The Hobbesian would just insist that tacit reciprocal recognition of the legitimacy of these norms must be widespread in a community in order for it to function as an epistemic community.[18]

This Hobbesian view might look like a version of the second individualistic account considered above. But we are now considering a more social version of the idea. The claim is not that one values reasonableness and reliability in one's beliefs (mainly) because believing reasonably and reliably tends to produce true belief which *directly* facilitates satisfying one's own individual desires or interests. Rather, the claim is that widespread, reciprocal, and well-signaled recognition of the legitimacy of epistemic norms is the basis of a community of interdependent knowledge-exchanging agents, membership in which is required for the satisfaction of almost any of a believer's own individual desires and interests.

This answers one of the major challenges to the individualistic accounts. The idea that these communities are sustained by widespread and well-signaled acknowledgement of epistemic norms makes better sense of the way each of us cares not only about our own compliance with epistemic norms, but also about how well other people are complying. It explains why we value not only our own knowledge, but also the knowledge of other people. Moreover, the inclusion of a *social* element in the account of why it is beneficial to individuals to comply with norms of reasonableness and reliability helps to address the other two reservations I raised earlier for the more individualistic versions of this idea.

First, with a better view of the importance of maintaining a reputation as a reasonable and reliable believer within an epistemic community, we can see how the value of reasonableness and reliability extends across *all* of one's belief system. If a belief is potentially something one might tell another person, it will make sense, given our reputation-infused epistemic interdependence, to care about its reasonableness and reliability. Even if one is sure that the question whether p will never matter to pursuing one of one's own desires or interests, for anything one believes, it is possible that someone *else* will evaluate that belief for reasonableness and reliability, which means that it is relevant for maintaining a good epistemic reputation.

Second, the idea that one's epistemic reputation matters for one's position within a community can help to explain why compliance with norms that tend to produce knowledge might be more important than compliance with norms that tend to produce beliefs that are "close enough to true". The latter sorts of beliefs may work in many particular cases, but in assessing one's reputation as a reasonable and reliable provider of information within an epistemic community over time, it is going to be important that one tends not only to have approximately correct information, but that one tends to have knowledge. This is a state that sticks around and can be depended on in a variety of contexts, not just for immediate practical challenges for which "close enough" might suffice.

One might object that the Hobbesian account doesn't make the grip of epistemic normativity universal enough. For one thing, Hobbes's account of *moral* normativity was famously vulnerable to the free-rider objection: In cases where cheating could remain covert and advance an individual's desire or need, the account fails to explain why people shouldn't cheat. So, we might expect that our Hobbes-inspired account of *epistemic* normativity is going to be similarly vulnerable. For another thing, there's nothing in the Hobbesian picture to rule out a relativistic result, according to which different sets of norms emerge as stable points of coordination for different communities. This looks especially objectionable in the epistemic case.

These are good challenges, and they're part of what motivates me to expand on the social grounding of epistemic normativity in section 7.4 below. But let me conclude this section by saying a few things in defense of the Hobbesian view.

First, I think the free-rider challenge is more of a problem for Hobbes's view of moral normativity than for the application to epistemic normativity. This is because—as I've stressed throughout this book—we don't choose our beliefs like we choose our actions. So, it's not like we commonly face a situation where we could choose to believe, e.g., what makes us feel good, instead of what we have strong evidence for. Sometimes of course people believe what makes them feel good rather than what they have strong evidence for, but on the involuntarist picture of doxastic agency I have offered, this is not a choice. We explicitly appeal to epistemic norms much more in evaluating other people than choosing what to do. And in these kinds of cases, the free-rider challenge doesn't really arise.

Second, regarding the possibility of a relativistic result: if it were true that *any* possible rules for belief could be the "epistemic" norms on which a particular community coordinates, then we might imagine fascist or racist conceptions of "reasonableness" and "reliability" to go alongside the more familiar conceptions from epistemology. However, I've been assuming that part of what makes the relevant norms "epistemic" is their connection to truth, which is why satisfying them is a necessary condition on knowledge. So, unless one wants to recognize fascist or racist conceptions of "truth" and "knowledge", I don't think the Hobbesian view supports a radically relativistic account of epistemic normativity. That being said, there is room for debate about whether our conception of truth is equally objective for all domains of human thought and whether we expect our epistemic norms to be the same for all contexts and communities. Reasonableness and reliability come in degrees, and even when these are defined in terms of truth, it seems perfectly in order for one degree of norm-compliance to be demanded in one context or community, and for another degree of norm-compliance to be demanded in another. (I'll discuss the apparent contextuality of knowledge further in Chapter 8.)

7.4 Rousseauian Epistemic Normativity

Many of the things we do are done not merely with other people's assistance or cooperation, but rather *together*, in some richer sense. This observation, which is key to the second, even more social account of the grip of epistemic norms, applies to particular joint actions, such as dancing a tango or playing a game of basketball, but it also applies to broader social practices, such as participating in democratic self-governance and maintaining friendly relations with the neighbors.

On a prominent view of joint action, it is partially constitutive of doing such things that each participant already recognizes, even if only tacitly, a kind of mutual accountability to others.[19] The idea is that successfully doing certain things such as playing a game of basketball or maintaining friendly relations with neighbors, requires that one recognizes various rules or norms as a legitimate reason to do other things, irrespective of one's other desires or interests; just as the other people with whom one acts similarly recognize the legitimacy of those rules or norms.[20]

Something like this idea was the basis of Rousseau's (1762/2002) controversial argument that political morality is grounded in the recognition of ourselves in a General Will. This is sometimes interpreted as the dubious and perhaps dangerous metaphysical thesis that there is a collective rational entity to which we should submit—a being with its own interests, intentions, and even consciousness. But I think there is a more modest interpretation of the argument in terms of what it takes for a collection of individuals to act with each other in a moral community. According to this interpretation, implicit mutual recognition of the legitimacy of some shared set of moral norms is partly constitutive of participation in certain characteristically social ways of life. So, recognizing our *already ongoing* participation in these ways of life can be a way to appreciate the grip these norms have on us.

To see how this works, it is helpful to contrast Rousseau with Hobbes on justifying acceptance of moral norms. Rousseau is skeptical that we are able or need to rationalize the transition from the state of nature to civil society. For one thing, he thinks that life in the state of nature wouldn't be as poor, nasty, brutish, and short as Hobbes imagined; indeed, he points out that people in the state of nature might, in the right material circumstances, have had a greater proportion of their desires and preferences satisfied than people do in a civil society. But he suggests this is because civil society inculcates in people entirely different kinds of interests that are more difficult to satisfy; these include desires to do things together, and needs for the respect and appreciation of others. Moreover, unlike Hobbes, Rousseau doesn't conceive of moral normativity as grounded on whatever might rationally persuade someone to choose civil society over the state of nature. Instead, he argues that many of the activities in which we (fully socialized humans) are already engaged can only be conceptualized in ways that presuppose (tacit) mutual recognition of the force of certain norms. Pre-moral humans may have had no limits on their behavior besides the laws of nature; however, they would not have been in a position to do many of the sorts of things that fully socialized humans do *together* on the basis of mutual recognition of shared reasons for acting in certain ways.

We can extend this idea into an account of epistemic normativity by asking whether there are similar social practices, participation in which plausibly requires mutual recognition of the force of certain *epistemic* norms. In section

7.3, I argued that we are not only deeply interdependent with each other for testimonial input into our individual systems of beliefs, but also that this interdependence makes establishing and maintaining a reputation for being a knower instrumental for the pursuit of our interests, no matter what these happen to be. But now I want to add: we (fully socialized adult humans) commonly also *do things together* in many of our broadly epistemic practices, and because we do so, we already tacitly recognize reasons to comply with epistemic norms, and *this* is manifested in the way we value knowledge over true belief.[21] There are two main reasons I think this is true.

First, each of us depends on other people for many of the sophisticated concepts we humans deploy in forming and integrating various beliefs about the world into a comprehensive belief system. For example, to have and deploy concepts such as that of electoral college vote, p-hacking, or tenure one must cotton onto their extension and significance by interacting with other people who are engaged in certain kinds of collective practices. This makes our use of these concepts subject to ongoing correction and negotiation. Moreover, the epistemic value of these concepts for making sense of some phenomenon, predicting what will happen in the future, and knowing what to do, think, and feel in various circumstances, is influenced in an ongoing way by how other people use these concepts. This might not be a way that young children and nonhuman animals depend on others in their thinking, but it is a way that more mature humans do; I think this kind of dependence radically expands the range of phenomena we are able to think about and integrate into our overall understanding of what is the case.

Second, maintaining one's own belief system often requires integrating different bodies of knowledge along various explanatory and justificatory dimensions, where these bodies of knowledge are socially distributed. For example, no one person knows all of the information relevant to belief about climate change or the optimal treatment of esophageal cancer or the history of money. So, sustaining reasonable and reliable belief about such topics requires participating in the ongoing epistemic practices of discovering new information about them and integrating this with previous understandings. These things are typically done via stratified intellectual negotiation among those with expertise within different subtopics, and ongoing attempts to put forward synoptic ideas about the relevant topics which are continually subjected to epistemic challenge within the community. This process depends at each level on there being certain stable states of belief which are well enough grounded in reasons that their subjects know them to be true. So, arguably, to engage in these practices requires a tacit concern for knowledge.

Hence, the Rousseau-inspired idea is that mutual recognition of the legitimacy of epistemic norms is partly constitutive of participation in practices such as using the concept of electoral college vote or maintaining beliefs about climate change.[22] Although it's most plausible in cases like those, I'm inclined to think this idea applies not only to technical concepts and academic topics, but also to the vast majority of the concepts and beliefs held by an ordinary person. As Clifford puts the point,

> no one man's belief is...a private matter which concerns himself alone...Our words, our phrases, our forms and processes and modes of thought, are common property, fashioned and perfected from age to age; an heirloom which every succeeding generation inherits as a precious deposit and a sacred trust to be handled on to the next one, not unchanged but enlarged and purified, with some clear marks of its proper handiwork. (1877, 292)

Moreover, as I mentioned above, the role of testimony in an epistemic community is not only to trade knowledge, but also to expose one's own beliefs to potential challenge, correction, or modification by one's epistemic peers. Because of this, I think the activity of basing one belief on other beliefs, and adjusting one's understanding of the inferential and probabilistic support relations between beliefs, is not something that happens wholly within an individual's head. Rather, it is something that happens in an epistemic community of people with diverse perspectives and cognitive skills.

According to this picture, the way each of our subjective viewpoints becomes a take on what is objectively the case is through the collective practice of applying shared concepts, correcting each other's application of concepts, and deferring to experts in a community about the implications of these applications. Each of us participates in many overlapping spheres of this kind of cognitive practice, and the knowledge that is central to one sphere is often only peripherally relevant to several other spheres. Because of this, any one person's particular perspective on some topic would be radically impoverished were they not a participant, along with a wide and diverse set of other members of their epistemic community, in complexly overlapping epistemic practices covering most of what that community knows.

On this basis, we might countenance a very abstract epistemic activity of *making sense of what is the case* as a collective epistemic practice, comprising all of the more specific domain-constrained practices involved in maintaining a set of beliefs about particular topics. If that's cogent, and the general Rousseauian picture of the grip of norms is illuminating, then it is plausible to think that tacit commitment to the value of epistemic norm-compliance and knowledge is required for participation in the practice of making sense of what is the case, which is an activity in which we're *all always already* engaged.

To be clear, my idea is not that each person is engaged in making sense of what is the case about everything, or that we're all concerned with exactly the *same* topics. Instead, if we assume that each person's knowledge and conceptual repertoire has a holistic character, whereby the reasonableness and reliability of applying particular concepts in particular circumstances depends on how reasonable and reliable it is to apply other concepts in other circumstances, and we assume that these concepts achieve relative levels of correctness only by virtue of overlaps with other people deploying similar concepts and maintaining overlapping sets of beliefs, then, at an abstract level, I think all of this concept-use should be viewed as participation in the collective practice of making sense of what is the case. To be a concept-user is to engage in this practice and so to tacitly recognize the values which are constitutive of such activity.

If something like that is right, then we get a wide-reaching Rousseauian account of the social source of norms of reasonableness and reliability and the value of knowledge. The idea would be that these norms get their grip on us because and insofar as we are already participating in the joint social practice of making sense of what is the case. The key Rousseauian claim is that this practice is like the practices of democratic self-governance and maintaining friendly relations with neighbors, in that participation in it is constituted by mutual recognition of the force of certain norms (whatever norms must be implicitly accepted amongst participants as legitimate standards for interpersonal evaluation). But it is unlike these examples in that it is a collective practice that we can't help but participate in as soon as we form beliefs, which we do so involuntarily.

Like the Hobbesian account, this Rousseauian account overcomes the worries I raised for the first two individualistic accounts of epistemic normativity. One doesn't need to care about knowing any particular truth, or stand to benefit in some non-epistemic way from reasonable and reliable beliefs, in order to have a Rousseauian, practice-based reason to care about compliance with epistemic norms. Moreover, reasonable and reliable beliefs about things of no immediate practical concern can still be required by norms the implicit acceptance of which is necessary for ongoing participation in the practice of making sense of what is the case.

Note that this account is also consistent with but not dependent on the ideas that knowing the truth is an objective value, or that tacit concern with reasonableness and reliability is constitutive of simply being a believer. It might be interpreted as a socially constitutivist version of the idea that epistemic normativity is grounded in an essential function of human cognition. Above, I objected that individualistic versions of the functionalist idea don't really explain why we would value compliance with norms deriving from the essential functions of one of our psychological or physiological systems. But I think this social version can avoid the objection. Insofar as one is engaged in the practice of making sense of what is the case, and this practice is an unavoidable social practice for us humans that is partly constituted by mutual commitment to the legitimacy of epistemic norms, then one already tacitly values compliance with those norms. This is different from the procreative function of reproductive organs or the in-group cohesive function of race concepts. One can do things with those aspects of one's psychological and physiological systems without implicitly recognizing the legitimacy of norms constituting good functioning of those systems. The same is not true of the function of our essentially social cognition. To even engage in the practice is to tacitly recognize the value of compliance with the norms, and we are obviously already engaged in this practice.

7.5 Responses to Two Objections to the Rousseauian Account

A critic might worry that although we've explained why epistemic norms have a grip on us, we haven't explained why they *should* have a grip on us. Sure, we care about the reasonableness and reliability of people's beliefs, and we value knowledge over true belief, but are we right to do so?

As already mentioned, I think this question unfairly shifts the argumentative burden. The Rousseauian account has highlighted a way in which we already do care, and it rationalized this concern by situating it within a story about cognitive functions and social practices that are partly constitutive of what it is to be human believers in epistemic communities. So, if anything, the question should be: Why *shouldn't* we care? Even if we could imagine a mythical state of nature where "people" weren't bound to each other by mutual recognition of various norms, we shouldn't have to justify the norms whose grip is constitutive of who *we* are in a way that could bring these "people" to care about them. It's not like we face a choice to either revert to the state of nature or continue in civil (epistemic) society, so we don't have to justify one side of this choice.

Of course, a skeptic or agnostic can always ask questions of the form: "I know we do various things, and doing these things requires that we value X, but why should we do *anything* in the first place?" But I doubt it's productive to try to answer such skepticism. It seems to me to be enough to explain from within a norm-governed practice why we are concerned about compliance with various norms, where such concern is constitutive of doing things that we have to do in order to do anything else. Normal human belief-system maintenance already amounts to participation in the collective practice of making sense of what is the case, and insofar as one is non-optionally engaged in this practice, one already manifests implicit recognition of the legitimacy of epistemic norms.

Another kind of critic will worry that some believers and knowers are not full participants in the practice, and so I haven't really explained why epistemic norms pertain to them. But I think the Rousseauian account can handle this idea. Consider two different cases.

First, as indicated above, it's implausible to think of young children and nonhuman animals as recognizing the grip of norms of reasonableness and reliability. On the Rousseauian view, this could mean we shouldn't count them as participants in the practice of making sense of what is the case. However, as

I am conceiving of the view, these subjects could still be thought of as knowers, properly subject to epistemic normative evaluation. This is because they could still be *included* in an epistemic community partly constituted by widespread reciprocal recognition of the norms. That is to say, they could be treated by other members of the community as subjects to be taught things, and as agents whose actions can be rationalized by attributing beliefs to them. A young child can come to believe (and even know) that the bottle contains milk by being taught this by her parents. And a dog's running after a ball can be rationalized by its desire to please its human and its belief that catching the ball will please its human. Moreover, their teachers, parents, trainers, etc., recognize that the relevant beliefs ought to comply with epistemic norms, and so engage with these subjects in ways that encourage compliance. So, in a derivative way, we would still be thinking of their beliefs as subject to epistemic norms grounded in our sociality.

Second, even granting that lots of people participate in joint epistemic practices partly constituted by mutual recognition of the force of certain norms, one might worry about people who want to opt out of such practices. What about someone who refuses to take norms of reasonableness and reliability seriously, and who only pretends to care about knowledge in an attempt to free-ride on the benefits of membership in an epistemic community; or what about someone who openly lies incessantly and professes distrust of everyone? I'm inclined to think neither of these cases is really humanly possible. Maybe we can imagine someone who has a deep disregard for knowledge in certain domains, or someone whose compliance with epistemic norms appears openly weaker than most. Even then, however, I suspect we are imagining someone who still often depends on others for mundane knowledge and who doesn't lie about the little things. Moreover, I suspect we're also imagining someone who uses normal human concepts, including the complex ones whose application conditions depend on richly social-epistemic relationships between members of epistemic communities. A genuine free-rider on epistemic practices, or a nihilist about knowledge—both strike me as fictions borne of exaggerating the scope of epistemic failings, which we all have in restricted ways.

That is not to say, of course, that one couldn't choose to do something that totally undermines one's capacity to participate in the social practice of making sense of what is the case. Maybe enough drugs or headbanging would ruin one's ability to form views on what is the case; but, in doing so, one would cease to live a fully human life. And even if that claim needs further defense, which I will not attempt here, I think we should still recognize that most normal people are engaged in the practice of making sense of what is the case, and this is a practice which the Rousseauian will suggest is essentially social because it is partly constituted by mutual recognition of the legitimacy of epistemic norms and the value of knowledge. So, whether or not the practice is universal, we still get an explanation of the grip of epistemic norms for anyone engaged in this practice.

7.6 Two Clarifications about the Scope of Social Foundations for Epistemic Normativity

So far in this chapter, I have been arguing that we need a more social account of the grip epistemic norms and of the value of knowledge than one typically finds in epistemology. As an example of a relatively minimalistic appeal to our sociality, I sketched an account that adapts Hobbes's attempt to ground moral normativity in our membership in a community, membership that is partially constituted by reciprocal tacit recognition of the legitimacy of certain norms. That may be as social as some epistemologists want to go, but I'm inclined to think a more robustly social account is available and attractive. So, I developed an application of Rousseau's account of the foundations of political normativity as stemming from joint practices for the case of epistemic norms. Both accounts make an appeal to epistemic community in explaining the source of epistemic normativity, an appeal that I find attractive. However, I also find it attractive that neither account construes epistemic norms as simply imposed on individuals by their communities.

Some philosophers will worry that I go too far in seeking the foundations of epistemic normativity in our sociality, because doing so obscures the way that epistemic norms also apply to non-social beings. Other philosophers will worry that I don't go far enough, because I don't show how epistemic normativity is grounded in our *moral* nature as beings that have robust other-regarding obligations to one another. Of course, I think my view is attractively in the middle of these two extremes, so in this section, I offer clarifications that I think reinforce its merits over them.

I've already mentioned how I think the Hobbesian and Rousseauian accounts can handle the inclusion of small children and nonhuman animals in an epistemic community even while recognizing that they can't (yet) appreciate the force of epistemic norms. But we also apply epistemic norms to people who have dropped out of society, and maybe even to people who have never had contact with other people. Robinson Crusoe is imagined to have washed up on a deserted island where he lives quite successfully without interacting with other people. But doesn't he still care about whether his beliefs are reasonable and reliable? Don't we say that he knows some things and doesn't know other things, and isn't this in part because of how well his beliefs comply with epistemic norms? Relatedly, in one version of the famous thought experiment, a brain-in-a-vat is imagined to form beliefs based on sensory input provided by a computer, rather than on normal interaction with the rest of the world (including other people). Maybe norms of reliability cannot be applied to a brain-in-a-vat, but isn't it still epistemically better for this "person" to form and maintain beliefs reasonably? Can't the brain-in-a-vat acquire some a priori knowledge, at least?

In response, I'm happy to grant that individualistic explanations of epistemic normativity capture some of the phenomenon. So, maybe Robinson Crusoe and the brain-in-a-vat should believe reasonably and reliably to the extent that this would advance their ends or they want knowledge.[23] However, my main critical claim in this chapter is that individualistic accounts won't explain the seemingly categorical normative force of our normal epistemic evaluations of each other in epistemic communities. We don't think of Robinson Crusoe, or of the brain-in-a-vat, as someone who can be trusted to be reliable on particular topics, or as someone whose unreasonable beliefs should be countered in discussion, or as someone warranting blame when they reason poorly. But we *do* think of fellow members of our epistemic community in these ways, and those evaluations wouldn't lose their force if we stopped wanting to find out specific truths, or if we realized that unhedged and overgeneralized beliefs are usually just as good for satisfying practical interests. Hence, my suggestion is that we need a more social account of the grounds of epistemic normativity to explain the sort of categoricity of ordinary epistemic normative evaluations. If that's right, then I can grant that we have all of the same sorts of individualistic reasons that Robinson Crusoe or the brain-in-a-vat have to care about reasonableness and reliability of beliefs, but we *also* have *further* reasons to care—reasons that don't depend on one's desires or interests considered in the absence of one's social relations. And it is this basis for epistemic normativity that the Hobbesian and Rousseauian accounts aim to capture.

Going in the other direction, one might worry that the accounts I've sketched are not social enough. I've suggested that the categorical force of epistemic norms derives from our participation in the joint *epistemic* practice of making sense of what is the case. But one might demand further explanation. Why is it that we depend on each other for knowledge, and what is it about making sense of what is the case that is so important that it binds us together in tacit acknowledgement of epistemic norms? I'm familiar with two kinds of answers to these questions. One would pursue a more strongly communal understanding of the basic unit of normative epistemic evaluation. That is, rather than focus on norms for individuals' beliefs, ask about what ought to be believed by the community, considered as an irreducible collective. The other would pursue a more strongly moral understanding of the basis of our epistemic sociality. For example, Clifford famously argues that epistemic norms get their force from what we owe to each other morally.

I don't really see these ideas as objections to what I have argued for in this chapter, but as calls for more thought about how my conclusions integrate with wider theories of agency and normativity. One might think that the epistemic domain is simply distinct from the moral domain, but I hold out hope for a more integrated account in which epistemic and moral norms can both be brought to bear in thinking about what individuals and groups ought to do, think, and feel. Nevertheless, I don't think one need embrace any particular account of this integration in order to accept that epistemic norms derive their categorical grip on us from our participation in social endeavors.

7.7 Conclusion: Speculation on Doxastic Freedom and Responsibility

In addition to providing alternative and richer groundings for epistemic normativity in our sociality, the Hobbesian and Rousseauian accounts of how epistemic normativity is grounded in our sociality can serve as the basis for discussing topics that have so far been largely absent from this book: freedom and responsibility. I have been assuming that someone counts as knowing that p only if they have a true belief that p which they epistemically ought to have. However, I have also granted doxastic involuntarists that we do not normally exercise direct voluntary control over our beliefs. So, I have sought to explain the kind of agency I think is presupposed by the normative evaluation of believers as knowers, as well as the kind of force the implied epistemic normative evaluations has for believers. I have not, however, sought to explain in what sense, if any, we are *free* with respect to our beliefs, and I have not articulated a conception of responsibility on which it could make sense to hold believers *responsible* for what they believe.

Some readers will find this odd, as questions about agency and normativity are so often wrapped up with questions about freedom and responsibility. I agree, but we should recognize cases where someone exercises agency with respect to their beliefs, even if we're reluctant to count them as free in what they believe, or as responsible for whether they comply with epistemic norms. We've seen this already in the way children acquire knowledge by forming and maintaining beliefs in ways controlled by their parents and teachers, and how responsibility for the children's epistemic failures can lie with the adults in their lives, rather than with the children themselves. But I suspect there are many other instances where we might want to say that someone exercises the kind of rational agency with respect to their beliefs that I've characterized in terms of the always ongoing activity of belief-system maintenance, but where we would also contend that their freedom and responsibility have been somehow curtailed or undermined by oppressive forces. This is why I think of doxastic agency and epistemic norm-compliance as more basic than freedom and responsibility.

Nevertheless, the Hobbesian and Rousseauian accounts put us in a position to distinguish interestingly different senses of doxastic freedom and epistemic responsibility. More specifically, these explicitly social accounts of the categoricity of epistemic normativity can be used to inquire about the sorts of freedom that are facilitated by various socio-political arrangements. And, on this basis, questions about epistemic responsibility might be cast not as metaphysical questions about whether people exercise free will or voluntary control with respect to their beliefs, but as socio-political questions about what it takes to be included in an epistemic community of individually responsible believers.[24] In the remainder of this chapter, I want to explore how such a socio-political treatment of doxastic freedom and epistemic responsibility might look. This is a big topic which I plan to address in more detail in the future;[25] my main aim in broaching it here is to highlight the interesting new issues about freedom and responsibility, which more social accounts of epistemic normativity bring into view.

Recall that Hobbes treats moral norms as constraints on our natural freedoms. He thinks it is rational to mutually agree to give up these freedoms in order to sustain a community, membership in which is necessary for having and pursuing many normal individual interests. If the parallel idea is correct about epistemic norms, then we might think that conceiving of one's beliefs as constrained by epistemic norms is a limitation to one's "natural" doxastic freedom—of course, a limitation that it makes sense to embrace for the instrumental value of maintaining a reputation as a good sharer of information. However, I doubt this is a very useful way to think about doxastic freedom. One of the lessons we should learn from doxastic involuntarism is that we cannot generally just believe whatever we want, constrained only by the causal forces on our minds. To think of someone as "doxastically free" because they are unconstrained by norms of reasonableness and reliability is, arguably, to conceive of their mental activity as something other than *belief*-system maintenance.

This is the kernel of truth in the idea that belief constitutively aims at the truth, and it is why I think the Rousseauian account of the grip of epistemic normativity, provides a more fruitful way to think about doxastic freedom. Rousseau argues that it is through tacit mutual recognition of the legitimacy of moral norms that humans achieve the kind of mutual self-rule or "autonomy" needed to pursue the robust joint projects characteristic of a good human life.[27] These projects depend on our ability to act together in pursuit of common goods, which in turn depends on our ability to recognize normative constraints as reasons to act in certain ways irrespective of our individual desires. So, in a sense, by submitting to mutual normative evaluation by one another, we free ourselves from certain individual desires and thereby become autonomous.

By extending this conception of autonomy and norm-governance from morality to epistemology, we can make sense of a more interesting kind of doxastic freedom than is available to the Hobbesian account. Perhaps tacit mutual acknowledgement of the legitimacy of norms of reasonableness and reliability frees us from forming beliefs only in reaction to our immediate environment and to narrowly instrumental needs. In my view, however, participation in joint epistemic practices, partly constituted by recognition of these norms, facilitates the richer kind of freedom (doxastic autonomy) needed to pursue the sorts of intellectual projects characteristic of a good human life.

If that is on the right track, it encourages us to consider what socio-political conditions might facilitate more and less doxastic autonomy so conceived. This is in parallel to (though obviously also deeply intertwined with) ideas about how different kinds of socio-political arrangements make for more and less *practical* autonomy. For instance, within a society of people structured wholly as masters and slaves, the slaves almost completely lack autonomy over their actions. That is not to say that they do not exercise a kind of rational agency in acting in the ways that they act—maybe they are perfectly responsive to reasons—but since their actions are controlled by a master, we don't think of them as free agents, and it would be odd to expect them to act differently. Similarly, we might think that whenever some people in a community are wholly dominated in thought, e.g., through brainwashing or indoctrination, these people almost completely lack autonomy over their beliefs.[28] Again, that is not to say that such people do not exercise a kind of rational agency with respect to their beliefs—they may deliberate, weigh reasons, even adjust their understanding of the inferential and probabilistic relations between their beliefs—but, since all of this activity is ultimately controlled by other people, we don't regard them as free, and it would be odd to expect them to believe differently.

On the other extreme, if a group of people can treat each other in any way they please, each according to their individual and fleeting whims, complete anarchy would reign, and we shouldn't regard this as a society fostering the *practical* autonomy of its members over their individual actions. To be sure, people living in anarchy may possess more of the sort of "natural" freedoms Hobbes imagined we trade in for the security of civil society, but there wouldn't be the sort of practical autonomy that Rousseau argues results from participation in joint practices partly constituted by mutual recognition of the legitimacy of moral norms. Similarly, if a group of people do not mutually recognize epistemic norms, then something akin to cognitive anarchy would reign, and we shouldn't regard this as a society with enough shared understanding of what is the case to foster *doxastic* autonomy. Again, people living in intellectual anarchy may well have a lot of natural freedom to pass their mind from one "thought" to the next in whatever way strikes their fancy, but there would hardly be anything like autonomy in maintaining a system of beliefs.

This sketch of extremes is suggestive but obviously highly unrealistic, given strong evolutionary and social forces that seem to prevent complete domination or complete anarchy, in either the practical or doxastic realms. I hope, however, that the sketch can frame further investigation into the elements of a social arrangement that affect how much practical and doxastic autonomy we think there is among a group of people. Accordingly, the question about doxastic freedom that I think we should address isn't "Under what conditions are we free with respect to our actions and beliefs?" but rather "What social arrangements facilitate more and less autonomy with respect to our actions and beliefs?" Moreover, in order to understand the autonomous exercise of one's agency, I think we need to further explore the middle ground between domination and anarchy, in both the practical and doxastic realms, while conceiving of both of these realms as essentially social. My hunch is that we will find this middle ground by understanding the social arrangements that allow for nondominated participation in shared practical and intellectual practices.

To make this more vivid, consider practices such as the development and refinement of a scientific theory, the formation and updating of shared encyclopedia such as Wikipedia, or the generation and transmission of information about current events relevant to one's community. When these practices go well, they involve a kind of mutual recognition of fellow participants as having different experiences and only partially overlapping perspectives which need to be integrated into a more objective common perspective. That doesn't mean that "anything goes", intellectually. Rather, it is through mutual recognition of the legitimate evaluability of one's beliefs by epistemic norms that one achieves the sort of autonomy one can achieve by participating in these intellectual practices. And this sort of participation is what makes one epistemically responsible for those aspects of one's belief system that one brings to the table when one so participates.[29]

I've just mentioned some obviously collective, though by no means universal, epistemic pursuits (science, Wikipedia, news). However, I'm inclined to think the basic picture of autonomous belief works for more general (perhaps even universal) and socially distributed epistemic practices. Indeed, we might say that everyone engages in the social practice of *living together*, which involves the epistemic practice of *making sense of what is the case*. This practice requires understanding that different people have different experiences and so only partially overlapping perspectives on what is the case. Thus, a more intersubjective view of reality can come only from integrating these into a shared understanding of what is the case. Again, that doesn't mean anything goes. Integration of different perspectives requires the mutual recognition of the legitimacy of epistemic norms. In reality, this recognition probably comes in degrees and covers some, but not all, of any one individual's beliefs, which is why we can imagine someone being epistemically responsible to varying degrees for the different beliefs they bring to bear in the sharing of knowledge within their epistemic community. Then, the interesting theoretical question about doxastic freedom and epistemic responsibility becomes one about how to make this very abstract formulation of a collective moral and intellectual practice more precise for particular circumstances, so that we can identify particular autonomy-enhancing features of how we treat each other.

So, rather than try to give a metaphysical account of when an individual's belief is free, I want to suggest that believers are autonomous (to the degree that they are) in virtue of the way their beliefs contribute to a collective epistemic practice of making sense of what is the case. And participation in this project is partly constituted by implicit acceptance of the legitimacy of epistemic norms. The normative epistemological standards applying to belief on this picture are not prescriptions that could or should guide someone's *choice* of belief. They're standards we use to evaluate each other's beliefs when thinking about who knows what in our pursuit of wider integration of diverse subjective perspectives into a more objective view of what is the case.

We may not (usually) get to choose what we believe, but we do get to choose whether to testify to others, contribute what we believe to some group's overall understanding of an issue, check our beliefs against technological-*cum*-social repositories of collective knowledge, and appeal to others in appreciating the ideologies and biases influencing belief-formation and information-processing in ourselves and the institutions in which we have power. Those are the sorts of autonomous activities that don't even begin to make sense from the individualistic perspective, but which seem to me to be quite central to what it is to be someone who knows something—at least in most of the cases where it might make sense to care about whether someone believes as they ought to believe.

Notes

1. I have in mind literature such as Festinger and Maccoby (1964), Tversky and Kahneman (1973), Anderson (2012), Lepper, and Ross (1980), Gilbert, Krull, and Malone (1990), Evans and Over (1996), Sloman (1996), Stanovich (1999, 2011), Carruthers (2009a), Kahneman (2011), and Mercier and Sperber (2017).
2. Compare Bem (1970), Gopnik and Meltzoff (1994), Williamson (2000), Lycan (2008), Dretske (2004), and Carruthers (2009b) for various arguments against the idea that we can generally introspect what we believe.
3. This is a version of the argument which I partly defended against Rosenberg's criticisms in Chapter 5. Ultimately, however, that defense made reference to the sorts of interpersonal evaluations of reasonableness and reliability which I think demand social grounding.
4. Kornblith (1993) and Pappineau (1999, 2013) develop versions of this idea based on an agent's actual aims. Grimm (2009), Steglich-Peterson (2011, 2018), and Cowie (2014) develop versions of the idea based on the aims an agent should have, and Reisner (unpublished, ch. 2) develops a version of the idea based on an individual's wellbeing. See also Reisner (2018) and Maguire and Woods (2020) for discussion of various ways of grounding epistemic reasons in practical interests. Rinard's (2018, 2019) form of pragmatism moves away from conceiving of epistemic norms as truth-directed norms of reasonableness and reliability (she is skeptical of the idea that there are distinctively *epistemic* norms). However, I think her view can still be interpreted as a version of the general strategy of explaining the grip of claims about what we ought to believe in terms of individual believers' practical interests considered generally.
5. Compare Kelly (2003, 2007).
6. For reasons I will explain in the final section of this chapter, I think this intuition about the applicability of epistemic norms is different than the idea that we'd be right to criticize or blame someone for failing to comply with these norms.

7. Stich (1990, ch. 5) makes this point; see Kornblith (2002, ch. 5) for a response. See also Hoffman (2019) for extensive biological evidence for this claim.
8. Some philosophers argue that we should understand epistemic normativity in terms of what it takes for a belief to be fitting rather than valuable. The idea is that a belief is the correct response to that to which it responds (the facts) when it is true, and in this sense, truth is what it takes for a belief to be fitting. See Chappell (2012), McHugh (2014b), and others. This might provide an alternative version of the kind of view I am discussing at this point in the text, but I think the objection I go on to give applies just as much to this view.
9. For discussion of versions of this idea, see Wedgwood (2002), Boghossian (2003), Shah (2003), Engel (2004), Millar (2004), Gibbard (2005), Shah and Velleman (2005), Zangwill (2005), Whiting (2012), Littlejohn (2012, 2013), Wiland (2012, 117), and Nolfi (2015).
10. Compare Côté-Bouchard (2016, 3194–3195) for a related critique of constitutivism.
11. I think this idea can be developed as a form of constitutivism, as discussed in Côté-Bouchard (2016, 3187–3189), if one maintains that part of what it is to believe something is to exercise a cognitive capacity with this essential function. But, in my view, one needn't embrace the constitutivist claim about belief to embrace a good-functioning account of the source of epistemic normativity.
12. For views of epistemic normativity in the vicinity of this idea, see Plantinga (1993b), Kornblith (2002, ch. 5), Bird (2007, 94), Burge (2010), Graham (2010, 2012, 2014), Simion, Kelp, and Ghijsen (2016), Simion (2019, 2025). However, Burge, Graham, and Simion develop their ideas in ways that embed cognitive functions in social practices, which is similar to the sort of social grounding for epistemic normativity I pursue later.
13. For a related critique, see Papineau (2013).
14. Although I have not been discussing issues of responsibility and blame, I think this reference to the social need to maintain reputations as good testifiers is a good place to begin to look for a theory of epistemic blame. For congenial developments of this idea, see Kauppinen (2018), Jessica Brown (2020), and Boult (2020).
15. Goldman (1999, ch. 4), drawing on the idea articulated in Goldman (1979), argues that the processes relevant to a reliabilist account of doxastic justification for belief formed through testimony are those *internal* to an individual's mind. For important challenges to this assumption, see Goldberg (2010, chs 2, 4). For useful discussion, see also Fricker (1995), Lyons (1997), Rysiew (2000), Graham (2006, 2010), and Coady (2012, ch. 1).
16. Clifford captures this picturesquely, writing about someone who fails to believe in accordance with evidence, that "The danger to society is not merely that it should believe wrong things, though that is great enough; but that it should become credulous, and lose the habit of testing things and inquiring into them; for then it must sink back into savagery" (1877, 294)
17. Compare accounts of epistemic norms as social norms developed in Faulkner (2010), Graham (2015), Henderson and Graham (2017a, 2017b, 2019), and Reynolds (2017). Although they don't develop their ideas in explicitly Hobbesian terms, I think there are important commonalities. Moreover, insofar as the "notorious bullshitter" objection I go on to consider is a problem for the Hobbesian, it will be a problem for them too.

18. Of course, epistemic communities are more complicated than I have just made it sound. We often depend on different people for different kinds of testimonial support, and we often exchange knowledge with others whose reputations for reasonableness and reliability are not known to us. So, developing this account more fully would require an understanding of how each of us are members of various overlapping epistemic subcommunities, and how tacit recognition of the legitimacy of the relevant norms becomes a default background condition to most contexts of talking to people about what is the case.
19. Different views of joint action account for this kind of accountability in different ways. Gilbert (1990, 180–181; 1996, 184; 2008, 180, 2009) argues that joint action requires a mutual recognition of the participants' obligation to one another; see also Darwall's (2006) discussion of bi-polar obligations. By contrast, Bratman (1999, 2014) argues that the participants must each have a collective intention, which includes a commitment to "meshing" sub-plans for executing the intention, where this involves each person's plans putting normative constraints on the others; see also Roth (2003, 2004, 2015) for a related view that rejects Bratman's attempts to reduce this normative constraint to individualistic constraints on practical reasoning. Korsgaard (2009) argues that joint action requires recognizing each other's reasons as reasons.
20. Dyke (2021) argues that epistemic reasons are collective instrumental reasons, i.e., reasons that derive from what would best satisfy the aims of groups of people. This is similar to the idea I discuss in this section, but my concern is with explaining the grip epistemic norms have on individuals. So even if the reasons one has for believing various things derive from one's membership in a group which has aims that would be advanced by one's belief, I think that won't yet explain why people do and should care about these reasons. As with the essential function of one's reproductive organs (see section 7.2), there's no obvious reason people should care about the aims of any group of which they are a member. For example the United States may aim for the elimination of bitcoin, and maybe actions performed by certain citizens of the United States would advance this aim, but this doesn't explain why these people do or should care about doing things that would advance this aim.
21. See Gunn (2020) for a similar appeal to participation in joint epistemic practices as the foundation for epistemic community.
22. Millgram (2015, ch. 2) presents an especially pessimistic account of this. See Nguyen (2018) for a more hopeful response.
23. Of course, Robinson Crusoe was once a member of a society; so, it is plausible that he will have internalized many of the community-based reasons for caring about knowledge that I mentioned above. And we project the norms we tacitly accept onto his situation when thinking about his beliefs. So, it wouldn't be surprising if he goes about his solitary life, forming and maintaining beliefs in ways that look to be normatively evaluable very much like our beliefs are, which is gestured at in the fact that, by the end of the story, he meets Friday and engages in the sort of social epistemic interaction we'd expect from a member of human society.
24. Compare Chrisman (2020, 59–64).
25. I have subsequently developed this in Chrisman (2024).

26. Compare Nottlemann (2007, ch. 15) for discussion of doxastic autonomy conceived in normative rather than metaphysical terms.
27. This is related to the republican conception of freedom as nondomination (see especially Pettit 1997, ch. 2; Pettit 2012, ch. 1); however, I go on to suggest that one also lacks doxastic autonomy in an intellectual anarchy. Compare also Medina's (2013) appeal to the value of epistemic friction for resisting the threats of epistemic domination.
28. For some practical ideas about what facilitates this in the age of social media, see Chrisman and McColl (2021).

PART III
EPISTEMIC DISCOURSE

8
From Epistemic Contextualism to Epistemic Expressivism

8.1 Introduction

This book is about epistemic normativity. In Part I, I focused on the kind of agency we exercise with respect to our beliefs, because I think some sort of doxastic agency is presupposed by the normative evaluation of beliefs that is implicit in knowledge attributions. I argued that we exercise agency with respect to our beliefs not mainly in the formation of beliefs, nor in the state of belief itself, but in the activity of belief-system maintenance. In Part II, I focused on the nature of epistemic norms and values, seeking to explain the connection these have to truth. I suggested we understand epistemic 'ought to believe' claims as adverting to a state norm deriving from what is constitutive of the activity of belief-system maintenance and implying various normative conclusions about action involved in inquiry and instruction. Because of the way state norms can imply other-regarding action norms, this line of thought dovetails with a resolutely social account of the nature and grip of epistemic norms and values. The basic idea is that beliefs ought to be true, which implies that we ought to do things to help each other maintain systems of belief that are well grounded. In an epistemic community governed by such norms, we will value individual items of knowledge and expect each other to do so as well because of the stabilizing role knowledgeable belief plays in improving the way members of the epistemic community base their beliefs on reasons and so expand what is known. This fact, rather than anything about the supposed performance of believing or the individual achievement involved in knowing something, provides the basis I think we should use for addressing axiological puzzles about why knowledge seems more valuable than unknowledgeable belief.

At least that's my basic idea. But I haven't yet explained how I think epistemic rules and values are mobilized and transmitted within an epistemic community. In some sense, of course, this happens by *talking* about belief and knowledge, and the epistemic rules and values attaching to these. But I don't think we do this by making observation reports of epistemic rules of belief that we have somehow recognized "out there" in reality, or by describing some objective property—"epistemic value"—had by those beliefs we consider reasonable and reliable

Belief, Agency, and Knowledge: Essays on Epistemic Normativity. Matthew Chrisman, Oxford University Press.
© Matthew Chrisman 2022. DOI: 10.1093/oso/9780192898852.003.0008

enough to count as knowledge. Rather, I think we should understand the deontological and axiological commitments implicit in our epistemic claims as constitutive of the social practice of belief-system maintenance. This means we shouldn't assume that epistemic claims are straightforwardly *descriptive* of normative reality. Thus, I turn now, in Part III, to the task of developing a nondescriptivist account of epistemic discourse. To make things manageable, my focus will primarily be on knowledge attributions. However, I think most of what I say about knowledge attributions can be extended in fairly natural ways to other aspects of epistemic discourse, such as the evaluation of beliefs as reasonable, rational, justified, and "what one ought to believe".

This nondescriptivism is perhaps where my inspiration in Craig and Sellars (discussed in Chapter 1) will be most apparent. A key idea that they share is that knowledge is not a purely empirical phenomenon that we could somehow identify and study independently of our deeply social practices of attributing knowledge. However, they also think that those practices are ones that must fit within a broadly naturalistic conception of what is real. The lesson I draw from this, regarding the meaning of knowledge attributions, is that philosophers working at the interface of epistemology and the philosophy of language should do more than merely attempt to identify the truth conditions of knowledge attributions based on our intuitions about when the word 'knows' has application. It is imperative to think also about how knowledge attributions are used for normative rather than descriptive purposes. Or, more precisely, we should develop an account of the normative aspects of the *meaning* of knowledge attributions.

The most well-known nondescriptivist approach to the meaning of normative language is expressivism. Roughly speaking, this is the idea that the mental states expressed by sentences can be divided into cognitive attitudes that function to represent how reality is, and noncognitive attitudes that have the psychofunctional profile of desires, preferences, or intentions; and n*ormative* sentences have nondescriptive meaning because of how they primarily function to express noncognitive attitudes.[1] This seems to have been the dominant view about ethical discourse in philosophy from around the 1940s to the 1980s, and it has received several high-profile refinements and extensions in the past forty years, suggesting that it is still one of the main meta-ethical positions.[2] And those contemporary meta-ethicists who defend expressivism about ethical discourse have already noticed this possibility of extending expressivism into epistemic discourse.[3]

Until relatively recently, however, the idea that knowledge attributions might warrant an expressivist treatment has not been much discussed by epistemologists.[4] So, in this chapter, I will explain one way to motivate expressivism about epistemic discourse and especially about knowledge attributions. Because expressivism is relatively unfamiliar in epistemology, the argument I develop starts squarely within epistemological debates about whether 'knows' is context-sensitive rather than within broader meta-ethical debates about the difference between claims about how reality is and claims about what people ought to do, think, or feel.

I'll first present some familiar arguments for and against contextualism. Then I'll show how they are parallel to arguments for and against the view known as speaker-relativism in ethics. Ethical expressivism is often thought to carry the advantages of speaker-relativism while avoiding its problems, so I'll draw on a prominent version of ethical expressivism to explain how epistemic expressivism might also be thought to carry the advantages of contextualism while avoiding its problems. This isn't ultimately the view I favor, but developing it in this chapter is helpful for motivating the alternative nondescriptivist view about epistemic discourse I do favor, which is the project of Chapter 9.

8.2 Two Problems for Epistemic Contextualism

Traditional accounts of the meaning of knowledge attributions assume that they describe a complex property had by subjects. This property is presumed to be the same invariantly across the various linguistic contexts in which the claims might be made. That is to say, unlike the word 'tall', the word 'knows' doesn't vary in its applicability depending on who is using it or in what context. This idea is sometimes called "invariantism".

Skeptical paradoxes have been used to put some pressure on this assumption of invariantism. For example, consider the following form of Skeptical Argument:

(SA)   P1: S doesn't know that he's not a brain-in-a-vat,
       P2: If S doesn't know that he's not a brain-in-a-vat, then S doesn't know that-o [where o is any obvious proposition, knowledge of which we would ordinarily attribute to S],
       C: Thus, S doesn't know that-o.

For many instances of S and o, the premises seem true but the conclusion seems false, because it contradicts many ordinary knowledge attributions that seem patently true. In light of this, invariantists have three options, each of which seem problematic. They can deny P1 and argue that, despite appearances to the contrary, S really does have the property of knowing that S is not a brain-in-a-vat. Or they can deny P2 and argue that all of the plausible closure principles that seem to entail P2 are false. Or they can accept the skeptical conclusion C and argue that all of the ordinary attributions of knowledge to S which seem true are actually false.

All of these positions have been defended and there has been considerable debate about them. But it would be nice if there were a way to avoid the paradox altogether, by showing how to accept the premises while rejecting the conclusion of SA. That is one of the main things epistemic contextualism is designed to do.[5] There is now considerable debate about how contextualism is best formulated, tying into issues in the philosophy of language about how to articulate semantic content and think about the compositionality of meaning.[6] I don't want to get into the weeds of this issue here, since, for my purposes, it is good enough to focus on the thesis that sentences of the form,

(1) S knows that p,

are true just in case

(2) S's belief that p meets epistemic standards e,

where the value of e is thought to vary depending on the linguistic context in which (1) is used.

Contextualists argue that this idea allows for dissolution of the paradox generated by SA. For one can accept the soundness of the argument but deny that the conclusion actually contradicts ordinary knowledge claims that seem to be patently true. The now familiar idea is that, *in the context where the argument is given,* the relevant epistemic standards are higher, and it is plausible that S doesn't meet them, but, in most ordinary contexts, the relevant epistemic standards are lower, and so it is plausible that S does meet them.

Moreover, outside of any consideration of skeptical paradoxes, contextualism seems to be bolstered by reflection on ordinary epistemic discourse. It is fairly easy to imagine cases where attributing knowledge to someone in one context seems true, while attributing knowledge of the same proposition to the same person in another context seems false, despite the fact that all epistemically relevant features of the putative knower are held fixed (e.g., same belief, same degree of confidence, same reasons for believing). In Cohen's (1999) first airport case, a speaker attributes knowledge about a flight itinerary to someone who has been overheard discussing it, and this seems right given that the stakes are low for the speaker. But in the second airport case, which is otherwise identical except that the stakes are high for the speaker, it seems correct for them not to attribute knowledge.[7]

So, in addition to getting us out of one kind of skeptical paradox, contextualism vindicates and explains intuitions about cross-context variations in the attributability of knowledge. Nevertheless, further reflection on ordinary epistemic discourse raises two seemingly difficult problems for contextualism, which I will now outline briefly, and return to in some detail in the sections that follow.

The first problem is that contextualism seems to disrespect other equally strong intuitions about the dialectical connections between knowledge claims made in different contexts. To bring this problem into view, consider cases in which two tokens of a knowledge attribution uttered in different contexts seem to stand in agreement, despite the fact that contextualism entails that there are different epistemic standards operative in the two contexts. Similarly, we can consider cases in which a token affirmation and its apparent denial uttered in different contexts seem to stand in conflict, despite the fact that contextualism entails that there are different epistemic standards operative in the two contexts. For example, a knowledge claim that is intended to reaffirm or change one's view, expressed previously in a different context, about whether someone knows something.

To get such a case, imagine, first, a situation where Sharon and Chris are going to visit their son, Charlie, who is planning to pick them up at the airport. The day before the flight, the arrival time gets moved up by an hour, and Chris asks Sharon, "Does Charlie know when our flight is now supposed to arrive?" Sharon replies, "Yes,

(3) He knows,

I talked to him earlier and told him that we're supposed to arrive at 5:30 am." Assume first that nothing serious hangs on whether Charlie will pick them up on time. If he comes late, they could wait for him to show up, or take a taxi from the airport. Nevertheless, having recently talked to him and given him the arrival time details, Sharon takes him to know when the flight is supposed to arrive.

Now, let's imagine that, later, Chris takes a call from a business associate proposing an important conference call with a client. The call is at a time that Chris could make, but only if Charlie does pick them up from the airport. He tells Sharon about the proposal and continues, "Are you sure Charlie knows when we're supposed to arrive? Perhaps he'll look back at the itinerary I sent him before the flight time was changed." Then, Sharon might say, "I thought he knew, but I didn't explicitly note that it was a change. So, I guess it's possible he'll get confused by the old itinerary and

(4) He doesn't know.

So, you should give him a quick call to confirm before you schedule the conference call." Or she might say, "He promised to be there at 5:30 am, which is when the flight arrives, so I stand by what I said before:

(5) He knows.

Go ahead and schedule the conference call." According to contextualism, the standards for knowledge have plausibly changed between the context of Sharon's first knowledge claim and the context of her later knowledge claim—whichever way the case continues. And that is because the question of whether Charlie knows the arrival time becomes more important due to his father's proposed conference call.

In both continuations of the case, the later knowledge claim seems to manifest a "dialectical connection" to the earlier knowledge claim. After the conference call comes up, Sharon either wants to deny that Charlie knows the arrival time and thereby *retract* her earlier claim, or she wants to attribute knowledge and thereby *reaffirm* her earlier claim. According to contextualism, however, all of these knowledge claims are true or false, relative to the standards operative in the context in which they are uttered. Since the standards are different earlier (low) and later (high) in the cases, it is difficult to see how contextualism could capture these intuitive dialectical connections.[8]

To make this more explicit, consider the full truth conditions. It is as if Sharon first says:

(3*) Charlie's belief that our flight arrives at 5:30 am meets epistemic standards e1,

and then as if she says (in the first continuation):

(4*) Charlie's belief that our flight arrives at 5:30 am doesn't meet epistemic standards e2,

or (in the second continuation):

(5*) Charlie's belief that our flight arrives at 5:30 am does meet epistemic standards e2.

But (4*) is hardly a denial of (3*), and (5*) is hardly a reaffirmation of (3*).

So, the basic problem is that contextualism seems unable to capture the way in which the disattribution of knowledge (4) could express denial of a correlated affirmation of knowledge (3) uttered in a different context with different epistemic standards. And by the same token, contextualism seems unable to capture the way in which the attribution of knowledge (5) could express reaffirmation of a correlated affirmation of knowledge (3) uttered in a different context with different epistemic standards.[9] Let's call this the *dialectical intuitions problem*.

DeRose suggests that we shouldn't take intuitions of disagreement too seriously or think there is a major problem with contextualism if it disrespects them.[10] He writes:

> So far from that being obvious to me, I've always been fairly strongly inclined to think they do not contradict one another. But that's just me, and it is perhaps no accident that I became a contextualist. But when I have presented such cases to large enough groups of students, and then asked about whether the claims contradict one another, I have always found both positive and negative answers strongly represented. (2005, 194)

It's important to note, however, that the contextualist needs to explain away not only intuitions of dialectical conflict, but also the intuitions of dialectical support.

So, mere disagreement about whether there is *conflict* between (3) and (4) isn't going to tell us much about the (arguably much stronger) intuition in the alternative continuation of the case, namely, that (5) is a *reaffirmation* of the claim made by (3).

Also, contextualists can't make intuitions of conflict seem too weak and ephemeral. Otherwise, their diagnosis of the paradox in SA would fall apart. After all their diagnosis requires that the conclusion of this argument is, *despite years of it seeming otherwise to epistemologists*, consistent with all sorts of ordinary knowledge attributions made in nonskeptical contexts. Were the intuition of dialectical conflict between cross-context knowledge claims really as weak as DeRose suggests, no one would be very exercised about SA, and we certainly wouldn't be worried about skeptical "paradoxes".[11]

In response to this kind of objection, Cohen (1999, 77–78) argues that we would posit the same sort of semantic blindness to anyone who accepted that some road is flat and later accepted some table is not flat, but then got puzzled by the fact that the if the table is not flat then surely the road is not flat. He points out that, despite the fact that this can confuse people, most philosophers would have no problem with the idea that flatness attributions are context-sensitive.

For my part, however, I doubt that the semantic blindness here is as robust as the contextualist needs it to be in the case of 'knows'. This is the second major problem for contextualism revealed by reflection on ordinary epistemic discourse.[12] For it seems to me that if we were to explicitly accuse ordinary speakers of contradicting themselves in cross-context cases where they attribute flatness in one context but deny it in another context, they will quickly appeal to, or easily be led to, the *purpose*-relativity of the claims, as a way to dispel the appearance of contradiction. The same isn't true in the case of knowledge claims. Cohen (2004) acknowledges this difference and offers the following explanation: "We find [contextualism] much easier to accept in the case of flatness than knowledge, because ascriptions of flatness do not have the normative force that ascriptions of knowledge/justification do" (2004, 193).

I would of course agree that knowledge attributions are normative, unlike flatness attributions, but this does not yet explain why ordinary speakers are more hesitant to admit the context-sensitivity of 'knows' than they are of 'flat', *unless* we can say why context-sensitivity in normative terms is harder to admit than context-sensitivity in non-normative terms.[13] If Cohen's suggestion is that it is because we *value* knowledge, then I want to ask why that makes the crucial difference—after all, pool players value flatness, but they would presumably admit just as easily as anyone else that 'flat' is context-sensitive. For this reason, I think we will reach a more satisfactory explanation here only by spelling out, in a bit more detail, the normative nature of knowledge claims, in contrast to the non-normative nature of flatness claims.

More to the point, however, very few philosophers seriously think that the question of whether some surface is flat generates a perplexing philosophical puzzle, but many have seriously thought that SA or some variant generates a perplexing philosophical puzzle. This suggests that the semantic error theory required by contextualism entails attributing semantic blindness not just to ordinary speakers, but also to philosophers whose job it is to reflect carefully on things like the semantics of 'knows'. One might suggest that the disanalogy with 'flat' here is due to the fact that philosophers don't care about flatness as much as they care about knowledge. But precisely *because* knowledge is one of the traditional subjects of philosophic investigation, and philosophers tend to know more about meanings than ordinary speakers, I would have thought that if 'knows' is semantically context-sensitive in roughly the same way as 'flat', philosophers would have discovered this way out of the puzzles generated by SA a long time ago.

None of this is not a knockdown argument against contextualism, but I suspect that much of the intuitive resistance to contextualism on the part of philosophers comes from the fact that its answer to SA seems too easy. The differences between 'flat' and 'knows' reveal that contextualism turns not on the posit of a minor and easily explainable sort of semantic blindness to ordinary speakers; rather contextualism turns on the posit of a deep and hard-to-explain semantic blindness to anyone who resists contextualism about 'knows' or is perplexed by SA.[14] This makes the contextualist response to skeptical paradoxes such as SA seem unacceptably ad hoc, so let's call this the *ad hoc semantics problem*.

8.3 Ethical Speaker-Relativism and the Two Problems

The debate about epistemic contextualism sometimes seems to transpire without a clear recognition of the fact that a similar account of the meaning of ethical claims has long been defended in meta-ethics. This is ethical speaker-relativism, the thesis that the meaning of ethical claims is implicitly relative to features of the speaker. Dreier characterizes the general position as "the theory that the content of (what is expressed by) a sentence containing a moral term varies with (is a function of) the context in which it is used. The content of a moral term itself depends on the most salient moral system in the context of use" (1990, 6). Schematically, this is the thesis that a claim such as,

(6) Doing X is right,

has the truth conditions given by

(6*) Doing X is required by moral system M,

where the value of M is determined by the context in which (6) is used.

Proponents of this view argue that it has at least the following advantages.[15] First, it can answer error-theorists' skeptical worries about the existence of ethical facts in the natural world—one of the central challenges framing much of the debate in the last forty years of meta-ethics.[16] The relativist's idea is that ethical truths are not universal but relative to particular and variable moral communities, outlooks, or contexts, which makes it easier (albeit perhaps not perfectly easy) to see how there can be ethical truths in a natural world.[17] Second, the view has semantic resources for explaining linguistic data about people in different contexts who manifest a difference of opinion about some ethical matter, when this difference doesn't seem easily attributable to a deficiency in evidence or rationality on either side. In these cases, differences of opinion are not treated as *disagreement,* because the content of each sentence is implicitly relative to a different moral system.

These two advantages have been well enough presented by proponents of ethical speaker-relativism, so all I want to point out here is that they line up with the two advantages claimed earlier for epistemic contextualism. Skepticism about morality often construes ordinary ethical discourse as erroneously committed to objectively obtaining ethical facts, and ethical speaker-relativism offers a way to save ordinary discourse by reinterpreting the content of ethical claims. Likewise, skepticism about knowledge often construes ordinary epistemological discourse as erroneously committed to invariant knowledge, and contextualism offers a way to save ordinary discourse by reinterpreting the content of knowledge claims. In both cases, there seem to be deep differences of opinion that aren't easily attributed to a failure of rationality or evidence on one or the other side. Ethical speaker-relativism provides a way to explain these differences without attributing error to either side; likewise, epistemic contextualism provides a way to explain them without attributing error to either side.[18]

Perhaps unsurprisingly, then, the two problems with contextualism discussed in section 8.2 also threaten ethical speaker-relativism. It is a standard objection that the position cannot account for the intuition that two utterances of the same ethical sentence (or the utterance of an ethical sentence and its ostensible negation) can stand in agreement (or conflict), even when they are uttered in different situations or by different speakers. The speaker-relativist would have to say that their meanings are implicitly relativized to different moral systems, but that seems wrong. This is the analog of the dialectical intuitions problem that we saw threatening contextualism.

As with contextualism, the problem is not fatal. Defenders of the theory can try to strike a balance between downplaying the robustness of the intuitions and coming up with a plausible error theory for why we have the mistaken intuitions. However, the ethical speaker-relativist must, like the epistemic contextualist, admit that the intuitions are pretty strong. For the proposed answer to ethical skepticism hinges on treating skepticism about morality as being based on linguistic error about the correct account of the meaning of our ethical claims; however, ethical theorists would not find skeptical worries at all compelling or troubling were the intuition of genuine disagreement or agreement, even in cross-context cases, not fairly robust.

Some ethical speaker-relativists pursue a "partners-in-crime" response to this sort of worry, by arguing that the context-relativity of ethical claims is unobvious but unproblematic like the context-relativity of other context-sensitive claims such as those involving the term 'flat'. However, as before, the depth of philosophical perplexity generated by the skeptical worries that ethical speaker-relativism is designed (in part) to answer, belies close analogy with uncontroversially context-sensitive claims. Thus, the relativist's positing of semantic context-sensitivity for ethical claims looks like an ad hoc response to skepticism about morality. And this is just the analog of the ad hoc semantics problem that threatens contextualism.

The purpose of this section has not been to engage in any serious discussion of the viability of ethical speaker-relativism, which has been debated at length in meta-ethics. My point, rather, has been to show how ethical speaker-relativism is relevantly parallel to epistemic contextualism in its core thesis about the meaning of ethical claims.[19] And I have been concerned to highlight the way that two of the central motivations, and two of the central problems, for epistemic contextualism, have analogs in consideration of ethical speaker-relativism. In the next section, I shall explain how expressivism is sometimes thought to be a solution to these problems in the ethical case.

8.4 Ethical Expressivism and the Two Problems

We started with invariantism about knowledge attributions, which is the idea that the epistemic property described by a knowledge attribution doesn't vary across different contexts. This is parallel to a universalism in meta-ethics, which says that the moral properties described by ethical claims don't vary across different contexts. Epistemic contextualism and ethical speaker-relativism challenge the invariantist and universalist aspects of these respective positions, arguing that the properties described by epistemic and ethical claims vary in subtle ways depending on the contexts in which the claims are made. Relativizing to standards helps to dissolve various philosophical paradoxes and puzzles in epistemology and ethics, but we found this move to generate the dialectical intuitions problem and the ad hoc semantics problem for these positions. Because of this, we should consider rejecting the assumption shared by all of these positions, viz., that epistemic and ethical claims are straightforwardly descriptive.

Expressivism is a *nondescriptivist* alternative to universalist and relativist positions. It has already been pursued in some detail in meta-ethics, and I think we should explore the possibility of extending it to meta-epistemology. Expressivism is a family of related views and the focus of an ongoing research program in meta-ethics, so, perhaps not everyone who calls themselves an expressivist would endorse what I am about to say.[20] Still, for my purposes here, I am thinking of the view as one that encourages us to ask first not about the metaphysical nature of ethical values, but rather about the *communicative* role of ethical evaluations.[21] Expressivists do this because they think a proper understanding of ethical evaluations will reveal that they are not descriptions of ethically evaluative features of *reality*, but rather are expressions of *the speakers'* ethical values.

Expressivism then starts with the idea that we can explain a sentence's meaning in terms of the state of mind it is conventionally used to convey or express. On this approach, a declarative sentence such as "The cat is on the mat" is usually said to mean what it does because it expresses a descriptive belief about the cat being on the mat. The idea isn't that someone who makes an assertion with this sentence has to have that belief, but rather that the conventional linguistic function of the sentence is to convey such a belief. Someone insincerely asserting "The cat is on the mat" counts as abusing this convention. Expressivists then argue that, although ethical sentences also mean what they do because they express a state of mind, they express a different sort of state of mind.[22] Different expressivists have competing accounts of the relevant contrast, but typically the idea is to divide the mind into *descriptive beliefs* about how reality is, and *nondescriptive states*, such as preferences, desires, intentions, plans, or even normative beliefs about what people ought to do, think, and feel. These nondescriptive states are thought to have a different psychofunctional role in the way people are motivated to act, compared to descriptive beliefs.

One powerful and well-known version of this idea is due to Gibbard (1986, 1990), who characterizes the relevant state of mind conventionally expressed by normative sentences as a complex state of "norm-acceptance". Specifically, he argues that ethical sentences conventionally express the speaker's acceptance of a system N of norms, such that the speaker believes the subject of the sentence to be in circumstances in which N ethically permits or forbids something.[23] For example, on this view the sentence,

(7) I ought not vote for candidate X

will not be said to express a belief that

(7*) My voting for candidate X is forbidden by N,

but rather a complex state of mind composed of a belief with the content of (7*) and the acceptance of the system of norms N alluded to therein. So, the basic idea is that ethical claims conventionally express complex states of norm-acceptance rather than descriptive beliefs. This is why they are not descriptive of reality but connected to motivational states of mind.

So much for my thumbnail sketch of expressivism. Obviously much more would be required to adequately defend the position against natural worries, but this has been explored in detail by others. Here, the crucial point is the difference between ethical expressivism and ethical speaker-relativism in their respective explanations of the meaning of ethical sentences. The speaker-relativist treats ethical sentences as descriptive of a relative fact, while the expressivist treats ethical sentences as conventionally expressing a state of norm-acceptance which *contains* a relativized belief about what is permitted or forbidden by the relevant norms but is *overall* a nondescriptive attitude with the psychofunctional profile of a desire, preference, or intention. This allows the expressivist to avoid the two problems we saw facing speaker-relativism, without obviously losing the two advantages of that position.

One of the advantages of speaker-relativism was that it can easily explain why different people make apparently conflicting ethical claims even when there is no obvious way to attribute error to one or the other party. The explanation is that they aren't really disagreeing. However, this explanation is precisely what generated the dialectical intuitions problem, which stemmed from the fact that there is an intuitive dialectical connection between many pairs of ethical claims. For example, the pragmatic hawk says,

(8) War is morally obligatory,

and the idealistic dove says,

(9) War is morally wrong,

and they certainly seem to be opposing each other's views. Moreover, if an honorable Samurai says,

(10) War is morally obligatory,

it would seem that he has agreed with the hawk and disagreed with the dove. But because the speaker-relativist will construe the content of these claims as relative to the (different) moral systems determined by the speakers' (different) contexts, she must disrespect the intuition that these claims could be dialectically connected.

Arguably, expressivists can better capture the intuitive dialectical connections. For, they contend that the utterance of an ethical sentence expresses a complex state of mind, including two components: a belief about what a particular system of norms permits or forbids, and the acceptance of this system of norms. This gives them the resources to recognize *two* axes along which two ethical utterances may be in disagreement or agreement. That is, instead of only recognizing the possibility of disagreement or agreement in relativized factual belief as the ethical speaker-relativist does, the norm-expressivist can also recognize that different utterances can express the acceptance of opposing or concurring norms. Thus, as far as the norm-expressivist is concerned, two ethical claims *can* express genuine opposition or agreement even if they do not express *logically* contradictory or identical beliefs. This means that expressivists can avoid the dialectical connection problem threatening ethical speaker-relativism.[24]

The second problem facing speaker-relativism was the ad hoc semantics problem. This stemmed from the fact that speaker-relativists will want to explain away intuitions of disagreement as weak and unreliable. However, these intuitions cannot be *too* weak, otherwise it would be mysterious why the existence of ethical facts is philosophically puzzling. As we have just seen, expressivists can respect the intuitions of a dialectical connection between ethical claims,[25] so they don't have to deny the accuracy of these intuitions and thus aren't initially open to the ad hoc semantics problem.

In response, one might object that in its nondescriptivism expressivism requires positing a different but nonetheless problematic sort of semantic blindness. After all, don't we take ourselves to be expressing descriptive beliefs when we make ethical claims? Some philosophers might insist on this as a theoretical commitment, but I doubt that ordinary speakers have pre-theoretical intuitions about whether some range of sentences conveys a descriptive belief or another kind of mental state.[26] So, although expressivism might fairly be said to involve a controversial theory of the meaning of ethical claims, it is does not suffer the ad hoc semantics problem challenging speaker-relativism.

8.5 Epistemic Expressivism Solves the Two Problems

We can pursue a nondescriptivist view of epistemic discourse by developing a form of *epistemic* expressivism with the obvious analogy: ethical speaker-relativism is to ethical expressivism what epistemic contextualism is to epistemic expressivism. As we have seen, epistemic contextualism can be summed up as the thesis that sentences of the form

(11) *S* knows that *p*,

are true just in case

(11*) *S*'s true belief that *p* meets epistemic standards *e*,

where the value of *e* is determined by features of the linguistic context in which (11) is used. Rather than treating instances of (11) as the expression of a descriptive belief with relativized truth conditions given by (11*), as the contextualist does, epistemic expressivists could treat instances of (11) as expressions of states of epistemic norm-acceptance. It is *epistemic* norm-acceptance, in that the standards accepted as normative are epistemic ones. Nevertheless, on this view, norm-acceptance is still conceived as a complex state of mind consisting of a descriptive belief with (11*) as its truth conditions, *and* the acceptance of the epistemic norms alluded to therein. Epistemic expressivism combines the idea that epistemic discourse is normative together with the expressivist idea that normative claims are not (overall) descriptions of reality, but rather are expressions of states of mind with a different psycho-functional role to that of beliefs about reality. This is just a rough sketch of the position, but I think the upshot is that the resources to avoid the problems threatening contextualism fall directly out of the parallels between epistemic expressivism and ethical expressivism, without losing the advantages of contextualism.

One of the advantages of contextualism was supposed to be that it can explain the apparent cross-context variation in the attributability of knowledge. However, it seems to win this advantage at the cost of incurring the dialectical intuitions problem. This was because contextualism treats the claims as semantically relative to features of the speaker's context, and thereby eliminates any dialectical connections between claims made in contexts with different epistemic standards. However, just as the ethical expressivist explained the apparent variability of ethical claims by appeal to the fact that they are used to express states of norm-acceptance rather than descriptive beliefs, it looks like the epistemic expressivist has similar resources to explain cross-context variations. The basic idea is that, in some contexts, we accept epistemic norms that license S's belief that p—thus, we say that S knows that p—but, for other contexts, we accept different epistemic norms which do not license this belief—thus, we say that S doesn't know that p. By maintaining that knowledge claims express states of norm-acceptance rather than relativized descriptions of reality, the epistemic expressivist, like the ethical expressivist, gains a second axis of possible opposition or agreement.[27] That is, they can account for the intuition of cross-context conflict and agreement by claiming that the speakers are expressing pragmatically opposed or concurring states of norm-acceptance, rather than logically contradictory or identical descriptive beliefs.[28]

More intuitively, it is easy to see how the degree of a speaker's willingness to treat a subject as believing what they epistemically ought to believe might vary with the speaker's changing circumstances. If the level of epistemic scrutiny in my own circumstances is low, I will be perfectly willing to treat someone as believing as they ought, even if their belief is based on good but perhaps not terrific evidence; however, if the level of scrutiny in my circumstances goes up, and I suspect that the person doesn't have terrific evidence for their belief, I will be less willing to treat them as believing what they epistemically ought to believe. In this way, the norm-expressivist can explain the intuitive variations in the attributability of knowledge across conversational contexts, without losing dialectical connections via the semantic relativity.

Moreover, by locating the source of intuitive variations about the attributability of knowledge in the mental states *expressed* by knowledge attributions (rather than in the facts *described* by knowledge attributions), the expressivist avoids disrespecting the intuitions driving the dialectical intuitions problem and thus doesn't have to posit any implausible semantic blindness at this stage of the argument. As a result, it looks as if the epistemic expressivist can pursue a response to SA that is similar to the contextualist's response. There is a crucial difference, however. For the expressivist, the paradox is generated not by people mistaking the semantic content of the skeptical conclusion with the negation of many ordinary knowledge claims; instead, it is generated by people insisting that the epistemic norms acceptable in a discussion of skeptical scenarios are also acceptable in other contexts. For the expressivist, the skeptical conclusion *does* conflict with ordinary knowledge claims, but this is a conflict of epistemic standards, rather than a conflict between logically contradictory descriptions of reality. It's a conflict about whether we should trust or rely on S as to whether p. In the skeptical context, we accept standards as normative which tell us not to treat S as entitled to his belief that-o, while in the nonskeptical context we accept standards as normative that tell us to treat S as entitled to his belief that-o. We cannot comply with both norms simultaneously, but, just as we can drive on the right in one country and on the left in another, we can follow one epistemic norm in one context and another in another context.[29]

Does this expressivist response to the skeptical paradox generated by consideration of SA require the positing of inexplicable semantic blindness? Again, expressivism treats it as mistaken for anyone to think that their knowledge claims are purely descriptive, i.e., expressive of beliefs about the way reality is. And, although there are perhaps slightly more people who make this mistake than in the case of ethical claims, I suspect it is still restricted to philosophers who have a view about whether the conventional linguistic function of epistemic sentences is to convey a belief about reality. I doubt that ordinary speakers have opinions about the expressive force of their claims that are fine-grained enough to cut either for or against expressivism on this point.

So, if this line of argument is on the right track, epistemic expressivism would seem to promise the advantages of contextualism without suffering two of its main problems. Moreover, I think there's a further case to be made for an expressivist analysis of epistemic discourse, based in the way knowledge attributions function to regulate epistemic communities. In some contexts, we're concerned with whether someone might be a good informant about particular sorts of information. We say, e.g., "Geoff will know whether the 1977 BMW R1100 comes standard with disk brakes; he knows everything about that bike." In other contexts, we're concerned to get our audience to rely on us. We say, e.g., "I know that the bank will be open on Saturday, we can deposit our checks then." Sometimes we are closing off further inquiry. We say, e.g., "We now know that the butler committed the murder." And perhaps in other contexts, we are concerned with the comparative strength of the entitlement to our beliefs. We say, e.g., "Even if I don't know that I have hands, I know that I am thinking."

Unlike contextualists, however, epistemic expressivists will attribute this phenomenon not to variations in the descriptive truth-conditions of knowledge claims, but rather to cross-context differences in which epistemic standards are accepted by conversational participants as normative. These standards can in turn be explained in terms of contextual variations in why we evaluate whether or not a particular believer ought to have a particular belief.[30] If the argument of Chapter 7 is right, these sorts of evaluations get a grip on us due to our ongoing participation in an epistemic community, and what expressivism now adds is the idea that there is a variety of connected ways in which epistemic discourse functions to regulate our knowledge economy. Because of cross-context variations in access, skill, and storage that different people have in terms of knowledge, it's no wonder that we accept different epistemic norms in different contexts for keeping track of who can be trusted about which kinds of information and for what purposes.[31]

More specifically, different epistemic norms entitle beliefs for importantly different reasons. Reliabilist norms entitle beliefs formed by a reliable belief-forming process, and evidentialist norms entitle beliefs based on sufficient evidence. Intellectualist norms focus on a believer's ability to justify their belief, whereas psycho-neurological norms are concerned more with the immediate and good functioning of a believer's cognitive systems. Skeptical norms entitle belief only when very high standards are met, and anti-skeptical norms entitle belief when lower standards are met. So, in some ways, this proposal is neutral with respect to traditional epistemological debates about the nature of knowledge. In fact, I suspect that part of the reason why such traditional debates have seemed so intractable is that meta-epistemologists have succumbed to the dogma of descriptivism. In other words, they have taken it for granted that knowledge claims express a descriptive belief and thus have to be understood in terms of the attribution of some constellation of factual properties; this in turn encourages them to think that there is some bit of reality determining whether reliabilists or internalists are right about the nature of knowledge that p. I have tried to show that if we give up this assumption in epistemology, as the expressivist tradition has urged us to do in ethics, we gain the resources to explain *why* the differences seem intractable, while neither resolving them nor dismissing their importance.[32]

8.6 Conclusion

Throughout this book, I have been stressing the way in which knowledge attributions involve implicit normative evaluations of their subjects, and I have sought to make sense of the doxastic agency they presuppose, the grip they have on normal human life, and the values they manifest. One can embrace the views I defended about those topics while also embracing the typical assumption that epistemic discourse is descriptive of reality. However, because I think nondescriptivist views make the best sense of normative discourse in general, I think we should develop nondescriptivist views about epistemic discourse. When we survey recent epistemology, though, the most prominent debates simply assume that knowledge attributions are descriptive, and the main question they address is whether the content of those descriptions is relativized in some way. So, in this chapter, I used some well-known challenges to one prominent view in this debate, epistemic contextualism, to argue that epistemic expressivism is a viable nondescriptivist alternative, because it can retain the advantages of contextualism while avoiding two of its main problems.

This discussion was not meant as a full case for epistemic expressivism, but rather as an attempt to explain the view and some motivations for it from within recent debates in epistemology. I suspect that epistemologists have been reluctant to consider epistemic expressivism for one of two reasons. So, I want to conclude by mentioning these, providing brief responses on behalf of epistemic expressivism, but also conceding that further investigation is required.

The first reason is that many epistemologists regard it as obvious that knowledge attributions are truth-apt and, since expressivism is often understood as the view that normative claims are *not* truth-apt, one might think it's impossible to develop a viable form of epistemic expressivism. For anyone who has read much about expressivism in the past thirty years, this isn't by itself a worry, since contemporary versions of expressivism are almost invariably "quasi-realist", in that they embrace some non-correspondence theory of truth, in order to embrace the truth-aptness of normative claims while rejecting the idea that these claims *describe* reality.[33]

Perhaps, however, the deeper worry in this vicinity is that expressivists typically reject truth-conditionalist accounts of the compositional content of their target claims. This means that they face difficult problems explaining the meaning of claims that embed normative terms in various semantically complex contexts. This is a very general problem for expressivist views, related to the famous Frege-Geach problem.[34] When it comes to *ethical* terms, many philosophers seem convinced enough by the practical-motivational character of ethical discourse to at least explore expressivist responses to the Frege-Geach problem, in terms of a speculative "logic of attitudes". However, I suspect most epistemologists would be quick to deny that epistemic concepts are motivational in a similar way, and this probably makes expressivism about epistemic claims seem like a non-starter in the face of the Frege-Geach problem.

For my own part, I think there are options within this debate for making out an expressivist but still compositional account of normative language.[35] However, as I will explain in the following chapter, as long as the content of sentences (or the propositions assigned as their meanings) are explained in terms of the mental states conventionally expressed, and we posit a fundamental distinction between cognitive representations of reality and attitudinal pressures on action, there is going to be a regress problem for any view explaining the meaning of sentences in terms of mental states expressed. So, if epistemic expressivism is tied to this approach to the theory of meaning, I think it won't ultimately work as the best nondescriptivist account of epistemic claims.

The second reason that many epistemologists have been reluctant to consider epistemic expressivism is that they regard it as obvious that knowledge attributions express *cognitive* attitudes and, in particular, beliefs. After all, it certainly seems that one can know whether someone knows something, which would require a belief about whether someone knows something. However, expressivism is often understood as the view that normative claims express *noncognitive* attitudes *rather than beliefs*. Indeed, the version of expressivism I developed earlier was based on Gibbard's idea that normative claims express states of "norm-acceptance" that have something to do with the attitudinal regulation of behavior, and that this marks them off as different from ordinary beliefs.

Again, we should recognize that quasi-realists have developed versions of expressivism that attempt to earn for expressivists the right to speak of normative beliefs.[36] And, as a quasi-realist, Gibbard certainly wants to recognize a sense in which states of norm-acceptance are beliefs. He'll just say that they are normative beliefs (or, as he more commonly puts it, "plan-laden" beliefs) rather than "prosaically factual" beliefs. So, initially, this second objection seems to trade on an impoverished conception of what epistemic expressivists could say about the mental states expressed by knowledge attributions.

However, I would grant that there is a deeper worry in the vicinity. This is about the function of normative concepts. As a nondescriptivist view, expressivism is committed to the idea that the target predicates don't express concepts whose function is to pick out things that have some natural property. For instance, epistemic expressivism denies that the phrase 'knows that $2 + 2 = 4$' functions to describe subjects as knowing that $2 + 2 = 4$, where this is conceived as subjects having a natural property. The epistemic expressivist argues instead that this predicate functions to express an attitude of norm-acceptance toward subjects who believe that $2 + 2 = 4$. But, as I will explain in more detail in the following chapter, all concepts stand in inferential relations to other concepts, and these relations require explanation. And many philosophers believe this explanation should proceed through metaphysical relations to properties in reality. So, even if we are tempted by expressivism to a nondescriptivist alternative about epistemic concepts, we are going to need a more robust explanation of the logical and evidential relations between these concepts and other concepts than is typically provided by expressivism. For this reason, I develop an alternative to epistemic expressivism in the following chapter.

Notes

1. The word "primarily" here is especially important because it acknowledges the sorts of hybrid expressivist views that have been developed to suggest that ethical claims express both cognitive and noncognitive attitudes, but that the latter is somehow more fundamental. See especially Ridge (2006, 2014), Schroeder (2009), and Toppinen (2013, 2017).

2. For an overview of early emotivist versions of expressivism, see Chrisman (2013). For discussions of the history of expressivism and some recent developments, see Schroeder (2010), Chrisman (2011; 2017, ch. 3), and van Roojen (2015, ch. 8).
3. See especially Blackburn (1996, 87; 1998, 318), Gibbard (2003, 227), and Ridge (2007). I discuss the relationship between ethical expressivism and epistemic expressivism in more detail in Chrisman (2009). See also Chrisman (2012d) for an overview of arguments for epistemic expressivism.
4. A few notable exceptions are Heller (1999), Field (1998, 2000, 2009), Chrisman (2006), Kappel (2010a), Hazlett (2014), Beddor (2016, 2019), and D. Greco (2017). Some epistemologists have considered epistemic expressivism to dismiss it. See Cuneo (2007, chs 5–6) and Lynch (2009). In some cases, epistemic expressivism has been developed in response to these criticisms; see especially Kappel (2011), Carter and Chrisman (2012), Ahlstrom-Vij (2013), Kappel and Moeller (2014), and Grajner (2015). See Chrisman (2012d) for an overview.
5. This paradox and criticism of the invariantist responses is discussed in DeRose (1995). See Cohen (1988, 1999), DeRose (1995, 2009), Lewis (1996), and Neta (2003a, 2003b) for canonical statements of contextualism. For earlier articulations, see Stine (1976), Annis (1978), and Castañeda (1980).
6. Perhaps the main axis of this debate is between contextualism and subject-sensitive invariantism, i.e., the view that whether a subject knows that p can depend on the practical stakes *for the subject* of whether p is true. For articulations and defenses of this kind of view, see especially Fantl and McGrath (2007, 2009, 2012), Hawthorne (2003), and Stanley (2005). Contextualism is usefully contrasted with related semantic views such as contrastivism and relativism; see especially Schaffer (2004) and MacFarlane (2005). There has also been significant discussion of the difference between contextuality in knowledge itself and contextuality in the semantics of knowledge attributions, e.g., in Rieber (1998), M. Williams (2001), Rosenberg (2002), Feldman (2001, 2004), and Bach (2005). Various modifications to and new defenses of contextualism have also been debated. See especially J. Greco (2003b, 2008, 2010), Blome-Tillman (2009, 2014), DeRose (2009), McKenna (2013), Baumann (2016), Ichikawa (2017a), and the essays in Ichikawa (2017b). This is a huge area of literature that I won't discuss in much detail, as pretty much all of it assumes the main thing I want to challenge in this chapter, namely, that knowledge attributions have a primarily descriptive meaning.
7. This derives from Cohen (1988) and is closely related to DeRose's (1992) bank cases. The original cases were first-personal knowledge attributions, which collapsed the distinction between aspects of the speaker's linguistic context and the practical stakes for the putative knower. See Bach (2005), Jessica Brown (2006), and Chrisman (2007) for discussion of the drawbacks of focusing on first-personal cases; see also DeRose (2005, 181–183; 2009, 59–61) for relevant analysis of the distinction.
8. Intuitions about disagreement are notoriously complex, and there are surely cases where we think two people disagree in what they say, even though the propositions expressed by the sentences they utter aren't logically incompatible. There are the "disagreements in attitude" I'll discuss later in the chapter in connection with expressivism, but there are also the sort of meta-linguistic disagreements discussed by Plunkett and Sundell (2013), Barker (2013), Umbach (2016), and Sundell (2016). See also Finlay (2017) for discussion and other forms of practical disagreement.

9. It is perhaps worth mentioning that this point applies both to object-level knowledge claims and to evaluations of knowledge claims as true or false. Sharon could just as easily have said things like, "What I said earlier was false/true," but the contextualist would have the same problem capturing the dialectical connections. Often, contextualism's critics charge that contextualism cannot explain the typical way we evaluate knowledge claims made in different contexts as true or false—see, e.g., Rosenberg (2002, 164). However, I think that problem is only symptomatic of the deeper problem for contextualism of capturing the apparent dialectical connections between both object-level knowledge claims and meta-level evaluations of knowledge claims.
10. See Turri (2017) and Buckwalter (2017) for discussion of empirical evidence of speakers' intuitions about the sorts of cases used to motivate contextualism.
11. Compare Schiffer (1996).
12. Stanley (2004) argues that there are important syntactic differences between 'flat' and 'knows' that undermine Cohen's analogy. My argument here doesn't turn on these differences, and even though they seem real, I am unconvinced that they undermine anything more than a strong reading of early contextualist rhetoric to the effect that 'knows' is context-sensitive, like 'flat'. See DeRose (2005) for more discussion of Stanley's objection.
13. Maybe this is because 'flat' is not context-sensitive. See Unger (1975, 49) for discussion of absolute flatness and a comparison of this to knowledge. However, Cohen's point applies also to 'tall' and other more clearly context-sensitive terms.
14. See Rysiew (2001), Hofweber (1999), Hawthorne (2003), Conee (2005), and Williamson (2005b) for similar objections. Rysiew (2001) argues that contextualism requires thinking that ordinary speakers are ignorant of the sentence-meaning and speaker-meaning of knowledge claims. The former sort of error is not, in his view, implausible, but he finds "it manifestly implausible to suppose that speakers can be wrong about what it is they mean—about what their communicative intentions are—in uttering certain sentences" (2001, 483). I'm unsure whether this is always true, since if Cohen is right that we can "get competent speakers to question their everyday flatness ascriptions by implicitly raising the standards" (2004, 193), this would seem to be a case where ordinary speakers *are* ignorant of their (at least past) speaker intentions. Hofweber (1999) develops Schiffer's and Rysiew's objection further; but see also Neta (2003) for an independent argument that speakers can manifest other sorts of semantic ignorance besides ignorance of the sentence-meaning of their claims. It seems to me, however, that the deeper issue is not only about ordinary speakers but also about philosophers who are exercised by SA. It may be more plausible to think that speakers are making an error about the literal content of knowledge claims than about their communicative intentions in making them, but is it plausible to think that they're so mistaken about either that they would think that SA generates a paradox?
15. Dreier (1990) argues that his subjectivist version of the view also has the advantage that it can explain the truth in ethical internalism.
16. See Mackie (1977, ch. 1) and related discussion in Joyce (2001), Hussain (2004, 2010), Caruso (2012), Blackmore (2013), Olson (2011a, 2014), and Beckman (2018).

17. Mackie argues that our ordinary ethical claims are not relative in their semantics, but it would take me too far afield to enter into the debate between Mackie and relativists here.
18. However, see Wright (2005) for an argument that contextualism cannot really neutrally allow that skepticism and ordinary epistemological discourse are both correct in their own contexts. I think the contextualist might welcome this conclusion, while arguing that contextualism nonetheless better explains the pull of skepticism, but I won't go into this issue further here.
19. There are of course differences. One important one is the structure of ethical and epistemic standards appealed to by relativists and contextualists. Ethical standards are imagined to be relatively fixed within a community or at least within an individual, and they are unordered, whereas epistemic standards are imagined to change in a much more fluent way from context to context, and they are ordered from low to high. I think this difference doesn't affect the argument I made in this section, but it can be mobilized in an expressivist fashion to explain why the dialectical intuitions and ad hoc semantics problems are more pressing in the epistemic case and so provide stronger motivation for "going expressivist" about the relevant discourse. However, in the following chapter, I will also explain some reasons based on the motivational profile of epistemic attitudes for thinking the case for expressivism is considerably less strong in the epistemic case.
20. For example, several philosophers of language have recently articulated versions of expressivism in terms of the dynamic update potential of normative claims in an ongoing conversation, which needn't rely on any particular view about what mental state is expressed by these claims. See especially Yalcin (2012, 2018), Charlow (2015), and Pérez Carballo and Santorio (2016).
21. Compare Gibbard, who writes, "The expressivists' strategy is to change the question. Don't ask directly how to define 'good'...[rather] shift the question to focus on judgments: ask, say, what judging that [something] is good consists in" (2003, 6).
22. Sometimes, expressivism is characterized as the view that *identifies* the meaning of sentences with mental states and, more specifically, the meaning of normative sentences with noncognitive mental states. I think this is misleading in that it suggests that expressivists (and Lockeans more generally) don't think propositions are the meaning of declarative sentences, and it would seem to commit expressivists to the view that the compositional semantic content of normative sentences cannot be articulated by giving a functional articulation of their truth conditions. Elsewhere, I have argued at length that this is not the best way to understand the expressivist position, because it trades on an inaccurate interpretation of the project of compositional semantics pursued via articulations of truth conditions. See Chrisman (2016a, ch. 6; 2016b).
23. See Gibbard (1986, 479). To be precise, this is not exactly Gibbard's view. He argues that the emotions of guilt and resentment are intimately tied to specifically ethical norms, and at its core norm acceptance is about what is rational, and specifically ethical sentences express the speaker's acceptance of norms that permit or forbid guilt and resentment. This complication is both controversial and not relevant here, so I shall suppress it. He also develops a model-theoretic account of the semantic content of normative statements, which is an extension of the familiar possible worlds model for

descriptive statements. This is refined and expanded in Gibbard (2003) where the notion of accepting a norm is replaced with the notion of a judgment's being plan-laden. For more discussion of this, see Chrisman (2005).

24. Some may worry that expressivism cannot really capture the sense in which two ethical claims disagree because a *difference* in mental states expressed by an ethical claim and its negation is not *genuine disagreement*, unless these mental states are descriptive beliefs. But notice that the theoretical burden imposed by the dialectical intuitions problem is not to establish that accepting different norms is itself "genuine" disagreement—this would require establishing what genuine disagreement is—but rather to account for the intuition of dialectical connections between the claims. If the pragmatic opposition and agreement exhibited by expressions of states of norm-acceptance counts as genuine, then the norm-expressivist has the resources to *underwrite* these intuitions. But if the only "genuine" disagreement is logical contradiction, then the norm-expressivist will be happy to *explain away* these intuitions by recourse to the pragmatic opposition and agreement found in ethical expressions.

25. Or at least they have a better way to explain them away. See preceding note.

26. Notoriously, some versions of ethical expressivism say that ethical sentences are neither true nor false because they express noncognitive attitudes rather than beliefs, and this claim is surely at odds with pre-theoretical intuitions about ethical sentences. However, more recent and sophisticated forms of expressivism, such as Gibbard's, have modulated this extreme claim while still maintaining that the mental state expressed by ethical sentences is importantly different from the descriptive beliefs expressed by non-normative sentences. In Chapter 9.3 I go into some more detail about expressivists commitments in the theory of meaning and argue that there is possibly a more subtle way in which their view is ad hoc.

27. MacFarlane (2014, 192–193) argues that this is no advantage of epistemic expressivism over contextualism, as the contextualist can agree with the expressivist that knowledge attributions express the speaker's acceptance of an epistemic standard; for example, one could remain a contextualist and argue that knowledge claims implicate or presuppose that the speaker accepts a particular epistemic standard. MacFarlane thinks this means that the contextualist can offer the same explanation of apparent disagreement between knowledge claims made in different contexts. But he also thinks this isn't a satisfactory explanation of disagreement, since two speakers might agree that someone knows something even though they accept different standards, so a difference in the standards accepted doesn't explain disagreement. I think this is partly right, which is why I developed the dialectical intuitions problem as a challenge not merely to explain intuitions of disagreement, but also to explain the full range of apparent dialectical connections that are possible between knowledge claims made in different contexts. For this, I think the idea that knowledge claims implicate or presuppose that the speaker accepts a particular epistemic standard is not enough; we need the idea that claims function conventionally to convey this acceptance as applied to a true belief. This is the expressivist idea. But an expressivist also needs a fuller account of the dialectical relations between different epistemic standards. As mentioned, it seems possible to order epistemic standards from low to high (unlike ethical standards), and this means that a speaker who says a belief meets one standard will seem to be in agreement with a

speaker who thinks the same belief meets a different standard, when the first is conceived to be higher (more stringent) than the second. We will only get intuitions of disagreement or retraction when the relevant standards clash, as is the case when someone is said not to know that p relative to a high standard, but said to know that p relative to a low standard.

28. Again, one will wonder whether this is "genuine" disagreement and agreement, but there's no reason to think that this is a special problem for the epistemic expressivist. So insofar as the response to this worry was satisfactorily answered in the meta-ethical case, it is answered here too. See note 24.

29. Are there some contexts where we *have* to accept the skeptical norms—i.e., where SA is sound? On the expressivist account, it is intelligible that some people do (in some contexts) accept skeptical norms while others (in the same context) refuse to. This could explain the "endless" character of some epistemological debates, but it could also provide some traction for moving forward: the question becomes one of whether there are some contexts in which the information economy is best managed by following norms that would not count as trustworthy a person's belief that-*o* based on ordinary evidence. Maybe there are such contexts and maybe there aren't. The issue here is not to answer this normative epistemological question, but to frame it anew in light of the emerging meta-epistemological view.

30. An alternative way to go here is to follow Williamson (2013) in taking there to be a tight connection between thinking that S knows p and thinking that S is entitled to use p as a premise in their practical reasoning. Then, on the norm-expressivist view, knowledge claims could be used to regulate entitlements and obligations in the strictures of practical reasoning.

31. This is similar to the account pursued in Craig (1990); see especially pp. 11–17. See also Reynolds (2002), Dogramaci (2012), and Hannon (2019).

32. For an independent argument that at least some epistemological discourse is partially nonfactual, which is motivated by similar observations about the intractability of certain sorts of epistemological debates, see Field (1998, 2018). Sellars's (1956) claim that knowledge attributions place one in the "space of reasons" and thus cannot be analyzed in purely descriptive terms, without committing something like the "naturalistic fallacy", can also be interpreted as a denial of the factuality of knowledge claims, though I'll argue in the next chapter that his idea fits better with an inferentialist alternative to expressivism.

33. See especially Blackburn (1993), Timmons (1998), and Gibbard (2003).

34. For overview and discussion, see Schroeder (2008b), Charlow (2014), Woods (2017), and Chrisman (2017a, 45–57).

35. See for instance Ridge (2014, 124–134), Baker and Woods (2015), Chrisman (2016b), Anderson (2019), and James Brown (2020) for discussion.

36. See in particular Sinclair (2006; 2021, ch. 7), Ridge (2014), and Köhler (2017). It is less clear that they have a fully worked out account of normative knowledge; see Chrisman (2010d) for discussion.

9
From Epistemic Expressivism to Epistemic Inferentialism

9.1 Introduction

Epistemologists have been less concerned about meta-epistemological issues than ethicists have been about meta-ethical issues. However, epistemic norms do have a robust grip on us and we do value knowledge in a categorical way that extends beyond anything that might derive from our individual desires and interests or from naturally explicable function of individual belief systems (see Chapter 7). So, epistemic norms and values need explanation, and whatever naturalistic inclinations motivate concern about the integration of *ethical* norms and values into a scientific view of reality should also motivate the same concerns about *epistemic* norms and values. I think this motivates the view that epistemic normativity is not something we find already "out there" in reality waiting to be recognized and described in our epistemic practice, but rather something that is constructed by that practice. One might think this undermines the validity of epistemic discourse, but not every area of discourse purports to be fully descriptive of reality. As Hume taught us, there is an important difference between claims about how reality is and claims about how people ought to act and feel in light of how they take reality to be.

When it comes to ethical discourse, inspired by Hume, nondescriptivist views have typically been developed as forms of expressivism. The core idea is to treat ethical claims as the expression of attitudes that are action-directing rather than reality-representing. If correct, this vindicates ethical discourse while comporting with naturalism and fitting nicely with a popular account of ethical thought as internally connected to motivation. In the previous chapter, I showed how this idea can be extended to epistemic discourse. My goal was not to present a full defense of epistemic expressivism, but simply to get a recognizably nondescriptivist theory onto the menu of options considered by epistemologists developing accounts of the meaning and communicative function of *epistemic* discourse.

I concluded the chapter by pointing out that two of the main objections to expressivism in ethics are reflected in the initial reservations that epistemologists are likely to have about epistemic expressivism, and indeed that they appear more pressing. First, in light of the Frege-Geach problem, it is challenging for expressivists to explain the meaning of epistemic claims in a way that fits with a general account of sentence meaning that is capable of explaining the meaning of logically complex claims. Second, epistemic judgments are less plausibly argued to be desire-like in their psycho-functional connection to motivation than are ethical judgments (though this is highly controversial in ethics too).

There are responses to these objections available to the epistemic expressivist, but I don't find them completely satisfactory. Moreover, I think an alternative, inferentialist account provides a better nondescriptivist theory of normative claims in general, and on epistemic claims in particular. So, in this chapter, I want to explain why inferentialism, rather than expressivism, is my preferred framework for developing a nondescriptivist account of the meaning and function of epistemic claims. This won't constitute a full development of a version of epistemic inferentialism, but will hopefully convey enough of the approach that its attractions are clear.

9.2 What Is Epistemic Inferentialism?

To explain what epistemic inferentialism is and how it provides an alternative to epistemic expressivism, I find it helpful to start with a distinction between *Lockean* and *Peircean* accounts of meaning.[1] To explain linguistic meaningfulness, Lockeans focus on the phenomenon of a speaker intentionally expressing ideas, attitudes, or mental states to an audience by uttering words whose meaning depends in part on their conventionalized usability to get an audience to understand what the speaker is thinking or feeling.[2] On this approach, we try to explain why particular bits of language mean what they do primarily in terms of their contribution to the *expressive* function of conveying what's in the speaker's mind. By contrast, Peirceans focus on the phenomenon of a speaker vouching for some addition to what is mutually accepted in an ongoing conversation.[3] On this approach, we try to explain why particular bits of language mean what they do primarily in terms of their conventionalized usability to update the conversational common ground with the undertaking and acknowledgment of various commitments. In sum, Lockeans see *potential to express our minds to others* as the key to understanding meaning, whereas Peirceans see *potential to undertake mutually recognized discursive commitments* as the key to understanding meaning.[4]

In light of this distinction, as a general theory of meaning, inferentialism can be viewed as a version of the Peircean approach associated with philosophers such as Wilfrid Sellars (1954, 1974), Jay Rosenberg (1974, 1976), Robert Brandom (1994, 2008, 2013), and Michael Williams (1999, 2004, 2010, 2013). It offers a grounding explanation of the meaning of claims people make in conversation. The basic idea is to account for the meaning-determining discursive commitments undertaken by making a claim in terms of *inferential* responsibilities and entitlements. More specifically, a person who claims that *p* is understood to incur a defeasible responsibility for backing this claim up with reasons (the sorts of considerations from which one could infer *p*), should it later come into question. Furthermore, a person who makes a claim that *p* is understood to have acknowledged a defeasible collective entitlement to rely on this claim (as a consideration from which one could make further inferences) in reasoning about what to do, think, and feel.[5] At an abstract level, these inferential responsibilities and entitlements can be said to constitute the claim's *inferential role*, which is usually thought to be determined by the conventional rules implicit in linguistic practice.

Two clarifications are in order. First, I call this a "grounding explanation" of meaning because the version of inferentialism that I want to advance in this chapter is not intended as a compositional articulation of the semantic content of fragments of English, but rather as a meta-semantic view about what it is in virtue of which knowledge attributions have the semantic contents that they do.[6] As far as I am concerned, the semantic content of knowledge attributions can be said to be propositions (or, if one prefers, to be represented by sets of possible worlds posited as parts of a semantic model). Or, if we want to allow for context-sensitivity in knowledge attributions (which I do), then we can think of knowledge attributions as expressing incomplete propositions (or functions from contexts to worlds in a semantic model) that require the determination of a contextual parameter for truth; but epistemic inferentialism is also compatible with non-contextualist articulations of the propositional content of knowledge attributions. In any case, I'll assume that knowledge attributions express a (possibly incomplete) proposition of the form S knows that p, which could be modelled compositionally in terms of the semantic interaction of each of the words and the logical form of the sentence. However, the interesting meta-normative question about such sentences is not "What is their semantic content?" or "How can we model their propositional content compositionally?" but rather "Do they have this propositional content because they describe epistemic features of reality or for some other reason having to do with their expressive or commissive role in communication?"

Second, the notion of an inferential role is typically conceived by inferentialists as holistic in two senses. First, individual words don't have inferential roles on their own, but only in combination with other words in a whole sentence. So, inferentialists say that the meaning of individual words is grounded in their inferential *potential*: what they systematically contribute to the inferential role of all of the claims in which they figure. Second, one cannot usually infer much from individual sentences on their own. So, the inferential role of a sentence is usually conceived as a node in a whole web of inferential relations between possible sets of sentences. We could distinguish between narrower and wider conceptions of the inferential role, depending on how big the sets of sentences are whose semantic interrelations determine inferential role. However, nothing I argue for here depends on a particular view about this issue.

In spite of the two clarifications, one can be an inferentialist and still hold that all claims are descriptions of reality. However, most proponents of inferentialism also argue that some but not all areas of discourse have a nondescriptive inferential potential. For instance, many philosophers find inferentialism about logical vocabulary very plausible. The basic idea is that words such as 'not' and 'if-then' don't contribute to the descriptive content of the claims in which they figure, but rather provide a domain-neutral scaffolding to make logically complex claims. These complex claims may have parts whose inferential role is to undertake descriptive commitments about how reality is, but they could also have parts whose inferential role is to undertake nondescriptive commitments about what to do and feel. As a result, inferentialists hold that purely logical claims do not describe logical features of reality, but instead serve to regulate how we think (about how reality is but also about what to do and feel). This is borne out in the upstream and downstream inferential role of purely logical claims; when it comes to justifying a purely logical claim, one cannot do so by making descriptive claims, and part of what it is for a claim to be purely logical is precisely that nothing specific can be inferred from it about how reality is. This marks an important contrast with purely empirical claims, which many philosophers would regard as straightforwardly descriptive of reality.

Similarly, many inferentialists also argue that *normative* vocabulary is not primarily for making descriptive claims about reality's being a particular way, but rather for undertaking inferential commitments requiring justification by further normative premises, and licensing conclusions not mainly about how reality is normatively but about how to act and react.[7] So, given the fact that epistemic discourse is at least partly normative, it is not surprising that many proponents of an inferentialist theory of meaning at least hint at nondescriptivist inferentialism about epistemic discourse. I take this to be implicit in the famous quote from Sellars that, "in characterizing an episode or state as that of knowing, we are not giving an empirical description of that episode or state; we are placing it in the logical space of reasons, of justifying and being able to justify what one says" (1956, sec. 36). And all of the inferentialists mentioned earlier are heavily influenced by Sellars when they develop their epistemological ideas. Since these ideas are often developed in complex theoretical contexts which are not usually explicitly meta-epistemological, it will prove useful to work with a bare-bones form of epistemic inferentialism rather than any of their nuanced views. So, the Peircean inferentialist idea I want to develop in the rest of this chapter is that knowledge attributions get their meaning from their function of, at least in part, undertaking nondescriptive inferential commitments.

I say "at least in part" because, as I suggested in Chapter 8, we should treat '*S* knows that *p*' as a thick normative claim, one which carries descriptive content (that S believes that p), but which also carries normative content (that S ought to believe that p). Because of this, the version of epistemic inferentialism I have in mind will say that part of the meaning-constituting discursive role of epistemic vocabulary is to undertake justificatory responsibilities that cannot be met by *simply* giving descriptions of reality, and to grant inferential entitlements that extend *beyond* conclusions about how reality is into conclusions about how to act and react.

Later, I expand on this characterization of this basic form of epistemic inferentialism. But for now, the important point to note is how this view offers a different nondescriptivist account of knowledge attributions from the sort of epistemic expressivism discussed in Chapter 8. To appreciate this contrast, remember that inferentialists do not think of inferential commitments as a special kind of mental state. As Peirceans, they can accept that there are psychological presuppositions of the practice of undertaking inferential commitments, but they will insist that the notion of an *inferential commitment* belongs to the public domain of social standings, rather than to the psychological domain of particular persons' mental states.[8] In the following two sections, I use that contrast to argue that epistemic inferentialism is a better way to develop a nondescriptivist account of epistemic discourse than epistemic expressivism.

9.3 Epistemic Inferentialism Is Better than Epistemic Expressivism, Part 1

In the face of worries about locating robust epistemic norms and categorical epistemic values in the naturalistic worldview, both expressivism and inferentialism offer vindicating accounts of epistemic discourse: Because epistemic discourse gets its meaning from performing a communicative function other than describing normative features of reality, there is no pressure to locate epistemic norms and values in reality. The basic idea is that, epistemic discourse is more about what people ought to do, think, and feel than about how reality is.

This is the common ground between epistemic expressivism and epistemic inferentialism, but I think there are very general reasons to think inferentialism offers a better grounding explanation of meaning than does expressivism. Simply put, this is because its explanation is broader and deeper. Expressivists explain the meaning of normative language in terms of its contribution to expressing mental states with a psycho-functional role like desires or preferences, but that immediately raises questions about how to explain the meaning of *non*-normative language, such as logical, probabilistic, modal, and even empirical areas of discourse. An expressivist can say that some of this is covertly normative and so expresses practical attitudes, whereas the rest of it is descriptive and so expresses descriptive beliefs. But it is not clear to me why all areas of discourse have to fit into these two boxes. Inferentialism offers a broader and more flexible theoretical framework for capturing the meaning-relevant similarities and differences between these diverse areas of discourse. Moreover, even if we accept expressivists' explanatory strategy of explaining linguistic meaning in terms of mental state expressed, this immediately invites the further question of how to explain the meaning-like content of the *mental states* whose expression supposedly grounds linguistic meaning. In contrast, inferentialists deploy a deeper explanatory strategy which attempts to account for both linguistic meaning *and* the meaning-like content of mental states in terms of inferential roles.

I recognize, however, that this gesture at a grand argument is unlikely to convince those sympathetic to expressivism. They will object that inferentialism requires an explanation of what it is to be inferentially committed. They will suggest that, although being committed in this way may be a discursive social standing having to do with inferential responsibilities and entitlements, we must ultimately explain what it is to be so committed in Lockean terms by appeal to the attitudes individuals express when asserting these responsibilities and entitlements. I doubt that is correct, but I don't know how to adjudicate this dispute; at such an abstract level, it is perhaps fairest to accept that any complete theory of meaningfulness is going to include broadly Lockean-expressivist *and* Peircean-inferentialist elements.

Nevertheless, I think there are also some more concrete and specific reasons to favor my inferentialist account of epistemic claims over the expressivist account developed in the previous chapter. So, in the rest of this section and the next, I will delve in more detail into two of the main objections to epistemic expressivism and argue that epistemic inferentialism can avoid these objections. Hence, if we want a partly nondescriptivist account of epistemic discourse, I think we should embrace my form of epistemic inferentialism over the sort of epistemic expressivism developed in Chapter 8.

To bring the first objection into view, recall that, in the previous chapter, I briefly suggested that expressivists face a difficult problem integrating their specific account of the meaning of epistemic discourse within broader accounts of meaningfulness capable of covering all areas of discourse. Making epistemic claims is not an isolated language game that we play on islands disconnected to the rest of language; it is part and parcel of the fabric of assertoric practice. So, we need a way to integrate our theory of epistemic discourse into an overall theory of meaning capable of covering descriptive areas of discourse too.

To an extent, expressivism provides this if we understand it as founded on the Lockean idea that bits of language get their meaning from how they facilitate the expression of our minds to one another. This underwrites the expressivist-friendly idea that, while many claims facilitate the expression of beliefs about how reality is, knowledge attributions facilitate the expression of something a bit more complex: a state of norm acceptance. This psychological state includes the representation of a subject as believing a proposition, but it is partly nondescriptive because it also includes the attitude of accepting the set of epistemic norms which license the subject's belief as one they epistemically ought to have.

However, I think this move doesn't go far enough to integrate the expressivist theory of one area of discourse into a general theory of meaning, because it doesn't yet show how to explain the meaning of complex claims that mix ostensibly descriptive and nondescriptive parts. (This is an adaptation of an objection to expressivism that has been extensively discussed in meta-ethics.[9]) To appreciate the problem, consider the disjunctive claim, "René knows he has hands or he is psychologically unwell." If we think the first disjunct uttered by itself expresses a partly nondescriptive state of norm acceptance, and the second disjunct uttered by itself expresses a descriptive belief, then what do we say about the whole disjunctive claim? What is the meaning-determining expressive role of this claim, according to the expressivist?

As Schroeder (2008a, ch. 7) points out, in the descriptive case, this question becomes easy for Lockeans as soon as they hypothesize propositions as the semantic contents of sentences and the objects of descriptive beliefs. That allows them to say, for instance, that the claim, "Grass is green or snow is white" expresses a *belief* in the descriptive proposition that grass is green or snow is white. *Mutatis mutandis* for any other complex claim with entirely descriptive parts. But epistemic expressivists cannot say something so simple because they hold that there is no descriptive proposition of the form 'S knows that p', so there's no complex descriptive proposition that René knows he has hands or he is psychologically unwell.[10] So, what can expressivists say instead?

In meta-ethics, there have been several responses to this kind of objection, but most of them involve treating disjunctive claims with normative disjuncts in a fundamentally different way from disjunctive claims without normative disjuncts, which raises the worry that the overall account of meaning is ad hoc.[11] This is an especially big problem for epistemic expressivists, if one of the main arguments for the view is that it avoids the ad hoc semantics objection threatening contextualism (see Chapter 8.2).

Furthermore, disjunction is only a simple instance of a general challenge. We should also wonder what epistemic expressivists are going to say about the mental state expressed by mixed normative-descriptive conditionals (e.g., "If Kevin knows that he won't win, then he won't try"), probability operations on normative sentences (e.g., "It's probably the case that I know less than I think I do"), attitude ascriptions with normative parts (e.g., "Sally fears that she knows less than she thinks"), etc.[12] The challenge isn't to say something expressivist-friendly about each of these cases, one by one. The challenge is to provide a general recipe that parallels the simple and elegant idea that a logically complex statement expresses a logically complex belief with identical logically complex propositional content. It is not always easy to classify a statement as epistemic or non-epistemic, but if your

Lockean theory of meaning explains the meaning of epistemic claims by appealing to a fundamentally different kind of mental state than it appeals to in explaining the meaning of non-epistemic claims, it is going to face a difficult question about how to explain the meaning of logically mixed epistemic-non-epistemic claims.

I think epistemic inferentialists can avoid this first line of objection. They do so by shifting the focus from mental states expressed by the relevant claims to the inferential commitments undertaken by someone making the claims, and by using the notion of inferential commitments to develop an account of propositional content which doesn't assume that propositions are intrinsically representational of reality. This is possible because inferentialism begins as a general theory of the meaning of all claims. It says that every claim should be viewed as a proposed addition to the conversational common ground, which we can initially (and blandly) characterize as committing the speaker to the truth of the proposition expressed by the claim. Then, inferentialists will explain a *discursive commitment to the truth of a proposition* in terms of the intersection of, on the one hand, the speaker's defeasible responsibility to justify acceptance of the proposition and, on the other, the defeasible entitlement of all participants to the conversation to treat the proposition as a premise in further collective reasoning.

I think inferentialists can presume this much structure to discursive practice without any particular account of how propositions or beliefs relate to reality. And, by doing so, they avoid the expressivist's problem of how to account for the mental state expressed by logically complex claims that mix epistemic and non-epistemic parts. Although inferentialists do not rely on psychological notions in their theory of meaning, they can easily allow that every claim expresses a belief in the truth of a proposition (whether or not these propositions include nondescriptive vocabulary). So, inferentialists can accept the easy explanation unavailable to expressivists that these claims express beliefs in logically complex propositions. For example, the inferentialist will say that the disjunctive claim, "René knows he has hands or he is psychologically unwell" undertakes a commitment to the truth of the disjunctive proposition that René knows he has hands or he is psychologically unwell, and so this claim can be used to express the belief that René knows he has hands or he is psychologically unwell.

Within this structure, we may want to go on to hypothesize a domain of purely descriptive claims whose justification requires *only* appeal to further premises mobilizing exclusively empirical vocabulary, and which entitle further conclusions about how reality is.[13] If we do so, however, I think the inferentialist will insist that most logically complex claims aren't like that, since they mobilize connectives and operators whose discursive function isn't to track features of reality but to allow us to undertake more complex inferential commitments having to do with the rational connections between more basic pieces of content, both descriptive and nondescriptive. For example, it is notoriously difficult to say what features of reality are represented by an indicative conditional claim with a necessarily false antecedent. It's also tricky to say what bits of reality are described by a negative existential claim.

We shouldn't, however, take any of this to mean logically complex claims cannot carry *any* descriptive content. If a claim commits one to the truth of a complex proposition, and this entitles us to draw simple conclusions that are articulable in purely descriptive terms, then we can view these conclusions as expressing propositions that articulate the descriptive commitments carried by the more complex claims. Moreover, often, a commitment to the truth of a proposition does not entitle us to make any particular statement about how reality is, but it will do so in conjunction with other propositions whose truth we might already acknowledge. In this way, I would suggest that a complex statement, such as, "If Kevin knows that he won't win, then he won't try" doesn't describe reality all by itself, but it can entitle us to draw a conclusion about how reality is if we are *also* assuming the truth of the epistemic proposition embedded as the antecedent of this conditional.

Hence, by starting with the general notion of an inferential commitment, conceived as a social discursive status that one acquires in making a claim in ordinary conversation, epistemic inferentialism provides a way to avoid the first objection to epistemic expressivism. And it does so while retaining the ability to treat epistemic claims as partially nondescriptive, thereby offering a non-expressivist way to make sense of epistemic discourse as partly nondescriptive in the face of naturalistic worries about the objective reality of robust epistemic norms and categorical epistemic values.

9.4 Epistemic Inferentialism Is Better than Epistemic Expressivism, Part 2

Turning to the second objection. Many philosophers have been persuaded that there is a special "internal" connection between ethical judgments and motivation to action. Roughly speaking, what this means is that someone who sincerely and comprehendingly makes an ethical claim will have at least some motivation to act in predictable ways. For example, if someone sincerely claims that lying is morally wrong, but they are not at all motivated to avoid or condemn lying, then we should wonder if they really know what the term 'morally wrong' means, or we should look for some special psychiatric explanation for their failure of motivation, such as deep depression or wholesale akrasia. When this internalist idea is combined with a standard belief–desire account of human motivation, it leads many meta-ethicists to accept the conclusion that there must be something special about the psycho-functional role of the mental state expressed by moral claims. The core idea is that these mental states (what are sometimes called "ethical judgments") seem capable of playing the desire role in a belief–desire explanation of why someone is motivated to act in particular ways.[14]

In light of this line of thought in meta-ethics, an epistemic expressivist might suggest that there is also an internal connection between sincerely claiming to know that p and motivations to perform specific actions, such as calling an end to an inquiry into whether p, testifying to others that p, or appealing to p in certain kinds of reasoning. And if that is right, then perhaps it funds an extension to epistemic expressivism of the argument from the internal connection between ethical thought and motivation for ethical expressivism. Even if there is a connection between sincerely making epistemic claims and being motivated to perform specific actions, however, this fact doesn't seem to distinguish epistemic thought and discourse from any other area of thought and discourse. One who simply *believes* that p will surely also be motivated to do things such as stopping inquiring into whether p, testifying to others that p, and appealing to p in certain kinds of reasoning.

Furthermore, if we focus on the core normative concept of 'ought', there is an important difference between paradigm uses of this concept in ethics and epistemology. In ethics, although we apply 'ought' in other ways, the driving question is about what someone ought to *do*. Because of this, there is considerable plausibility in the idea that competence with practical 'ought' requires that people are at least somewhat motivated to do what they think they morally ought to do. By contrast, in epistemology, the driving question is about what someone ought to *believe*, and as we have seen throughout this book, believing isn't a form of acting. Indeed, it isn't even something one can be motivated to *do* because it is a way one *is* rather than something one *does*. Of course, I've suggested that there are doings (including some actions) closely connected to belief, but as long as we think of knowledge attributions as normative mainly because of how they evaluate their subject's belief, it is going to be considerably less plausible that competence with epistemic concepts requires being motivated to do particular things when one makes epistemic claims.[15] To be clear, the objection to epistemic expressivism here is not that knowledge attributions and epistemic ought-claims *lack* the internal connection to motivation claimed by the expressivist. Rather my point is that the existence of such a connection is not intuitive data to be explained in the epistemic case like it arguably is in the ethical case. Hence, we should worry that one influential argument in favor of expressivist forms of nondescriptivism about an area of discourse doesn't extend cleanly from the ethical case to the epistemic case.

Epistemic inferentialism avoids this worry by stressing the distinctive *inferential* relations between epistemic claims/beliefs and actions and attitudes, rather than any supposedly psychological connection between the mental states expressed by these claims and motivations. But are there good reasons to suppose that epistemic claims have a similar inferential role to other normative claims? To use the supposed normative character of epistemic concepts to motivate a nondescriptivist form of inferentialism for epistemic discourse, we need positive reasons to think that epistemic claims require normative premises as justification, and that they justify conclusions not just about how reality is, but also about how to act and react to how we take reality to be. There are two kinds of reasons to think this is the case.

First, as I suggested in Part II, we make claims about what people ought to believe and these claims carry the same sort of robust normative force that ethical ought-claims carry. I argued for a particular social understanding of the source of this robust normativity, because I think we can't find it in some feature of reality conceived as facts about what is the case. But as long as one accepts the more general claim that robust normativity can't be found in reality (considered in abstraction from the plans and projects agents bring to bear on the world as they understand it), then there is reason to think epistemic concepts involving 'ought to believe' have the inferential role I've claimed earlier (section 9.2) for other normative concepts. Second, many epistemologists have argued that epistemic concepts play a distinctive justificatory role in the articulation of norms of action. I have in mind currently popular ideas about knowledge being a "norm of assertion" and a "norm of practical reasoning".[16] Maybe it is some other epistemic concept which plays that role, such as 'justified belief'. But the important point here is simply that all of these views focus on the role of epistemic claims in *justifying* action (rather than motivating action). The version of epistemic inferentialism I have been introducing in this chapter can incorporate that idea directly into an account of the inferential role of epistemic claims. This in turn is treated as the foundation of an account of that in virtue of which sentences using epistemic terms have the meanings (propositional contents) that they do.

Because inferentialists offer a general theory of propositional content applying to all claims, they can hold that knowledge attributions have the standard propositional contents of the form *S knows that p*. And they can allow that the full meta-semantic explanation of the propositional content of knowledge attributions may carry descriptive content *and* express beliefs. For example, I have suggested that knowledge attributions are "thick" normative claims, which means that they represent their subjects as having a true belief; and I have allowed that knowledge attributions express a normative belief, generically the belief that *S knows that p*. However, inferentialists will want to incorporate these descriptivist and expressivist elements of any full account of the meaning of knowledge attributions into a story about inferential role. More specifically, in order to remain nondescriptivists about epistemic discourse, inferentialists will want to explain why the inferential role of knowledge attributions is disanalogous to the inferential role of straightforwardly descriptive claims.

Perhaps there are other ways to capture this, but I find it illuminating to think of knowledge attributions as including an evaluation of the subject's belief as a belief which they *ought* to have, where this 'ought' is conceived as both epistemic and robustly normative. If this is right and nondescriptivist inferentialism is right about robustly normative ought-claims, then claims of the form "S knows that p" shouldn't be justifiable by descriptive claims alone. I think this is borne out in the data usually used to motivate contextualism: for any purely descriptive account of most circumstances where someone has a true belief, we can imagine two parallel cases where we will be inclined to attribute knowledge in one and to deny knowledge in the other (see discussion of cases often mobilized in favor of contextualism in Chapter 8.2). This reflects the fact that knowledge attributions have further normative claims upstream in their inferential role. And looking downstream, if knowledge attributions can play the distinctive role of other normative claims in justifying actions and feelings, then that is a further reason to think that their inferential role is not purely descriptive.

There are many details that remain to be developed, but my goal here has not been to offer a full version of epistemic inferentialism. Rather, I have merely tried to explain how it is different from epistemic expressivism and to explain why I think it offers a better starting point for developing a nondescriptivist account of epistemic discourse.

9.5 Epistemic Inferentialism Fits Well with Social Accounts of Epistemic Normativity

So far in this chapter, I have argued that epistemic inferentialism is superior to epistemic expressivism as an account of the meaning and communicative role of epistemic discourse. This argument has been based mainly on considerations within internecine debates around nondescriptivist accounts of epistemic discourse. But the reasons I like epistemic inferentialism are not limited to a comparative theoretical cost–benefit analysis with expressivism. I think the inferentialist account of the meaning and communicative function of epistemic claims also fits well with the argument for social foundations of epistemic normativity that I presented in Chapter 7. So, in this penultimate section, I seek to tie several themes of this book together by explaining that connection.

Austin claims that "when I say 'I know,' I give others my word" (1979, 99), which is sometimes thought to suggest that knowledge attributions, at least in the first-person, are performative rather than assertoric speech acts. And in a related vein, Rorty (1979, 1995) argues that epistemic terms are primarily terms of praise and don't have objective purport. According to him, we make claims about whose beliefs are justified and we keep track of who knows what; we do this not as some objective description of epistemic reality, but as a way of developing and maintaining relationships of solidarity within particular epistemic communities. Such relationships are important for holding those communities together and can be useful for advancing causes of social justice. This allows Rorty to cast the endless debate about the nature of knowledge as one that stems from a failure to recognize that 'knows', like 'good', is not a word that picks out something with an objective nature.

Although I don't want to endorse Austin's and Rorty's specific claims, I like how these pragmatist ideas provide social-epistemological traction on some of the axiological puzzles that have animated recent work on epistemic normativity. Rather than investigate the distinctive value of knowledge conceived as an evaluative property attaching objectively to knowledge, these pragmatists encourage us to think about why we value knowledge more than unknowledgeable true belief. I think it is right that the explanation of the distinctive axiological features of knowledge will lie with us who value knowledge, rather than with some supposedly objective evaluative property of knowledge.

The pragmatist approaches of philosophers such as Austin and Rorty have met significant resistance, due to the impression that they imply that there aren't any objectively correct answers about who knows what or which beliefs people really ought, epistemically, to have. Indeed, in this vein, some epistemologists have also objected more recently to epistemic expressivism on the grounds that it is subtly incoherent to view epistemic claims as expressing desire-like attitudes rather than beliefs about reality.[17] The basic idea in these objections is that any theory about something, including a theory about the meaning and communicative function of epistemic discourse, requires implicit commitment to the objectivity of epistemic values such as truth and knowledge. So, if a view, such as that of Austin, Rorty, or epistemic expressivists, denies that the target evaluative claims describe some objective feature of reality, then it does so in contradiction with an implicit commitment in any kind of theory-building.

Despite this kind of worry, I think it would be wrong to doubt that epistemic terms are often used to do things such as assure, praise, and express evaluative attitudes; it's just that they seem to do more, and because of this, a pragmatist theory of epistemic discourse needs to be grounded in something more general than these ideas. This is why I have been developing an inferentialist framework for thinking about the social function of epistemic discourse. And my core inspiration in doing so has not been the pragmatist ideas mentioned earlier, but rather the more constructivist and universalist ideas suggested by Craig's (1990) view of what the practical role of the knowledge concept has become, along with Sellars's (1956) reasons-based view of the practice of attributing knowledge.

Craig argues—rightly, in my view—that the need to keep track of reliable informants is not restricted to the need to get information about particular topics, but is rather a general interest that we have with each other in epistemic community. In his view, this means that we need a concept of knowledge that is better than a merely expressive tag with local significance. We need a general concept of knowledge, and this concept will have to allow for generalized application based on universal standards for knowledge. Craig makes some plausible claims about the extension of this concept, and he suggests a provocative genealogy of how it might have gotten to be that way; however, he doesn't provide an account of what grounds its being that way *now*. For this, I think we need a meta-semantic account of the propositional content of knowledge claims, and epistemic inferentialism—as an application of nondescriptivist inferentialism applied to the specific case of epistemic discourse—is intended to provide this.

In this way, I see the account of epistemic discourse introduced in this chapter as a continuation of the Craigian project. It comports with the idea that epistemic claims aim to be objectively correct, even while it underwrites this by appealing to the robust norms one commits to when attributing knowledge, rather than to objective epistemic features of reality. (Compare: an inferentialist about logical concepts usually holds that logical claims aim to be objectively correct, even if reality doesn't contain objective logical relations.)

In contrast to expressivists, inferentialists do not view knowledge attributions as conceptualizing their subjects (i.e., believers and their beliefs) in terms of the speaker's affective reactions to them, but rather in terms of the speaker's normative expectation that these subjects base their beliefs on good reasons. This is what I take to be the main import of Sellars's pragmatist idea that knowledge attributions place a person's mental state "in the logical space of reasons" (1956, sec. 36). The objectivity involved in this kind of "placing" is not the objectivity found by comparing our use of epistemic concepts to the way reality is. Rather, it's the kind of objectivity sought by reflecting on the robust normative commitments presupposed by thinking of someone's mental state as a belief, a mental state with objective purport because of how it ought to be held for truth-connected reasons.

At the beginning of this book, I highlighted the axiological and deontological dimensions of philosophical puzzles about epistemic normativity. Why is it that we regard knowledge as something with a distinctive kind of value generating a kind of categorical normative pull on us? How come we assume people's beliefs are answerable to seemingly robust and agency-implicating epistemic norms, even though beliefs fall outside of the sort of voluntary control typical of action? I don't take myself to have provided full answers to these questions, but I think that conceiving of knowledge attributions as normative claims, and situating the use of these claims in broader social conceptual practices wherein we do many other things besides describe reality, provides a rich nondescriptivist framework for thinking about these questions in a different way to how they are often approached in epistemology. The best explanations of knowledge's distinctive value will, in my opinion, appeal to the individual and social epistemological import of complying with robust epistemic norms of belief, rather than to the evaluative properties of knowledge, conceived as objective features of reality. And the best explanation of the way in which epistemic claims adverting to these norms implicate agency will, in my view, appeal to the distinctive inferential role of knowledge attributions, conceived as normative claims with a partly nondescriptive function in our overall conceptual and discursive practices.

9.6 Conclusion

In this book, I have sought to make sense of the robust kinds of epistemic norms that apply to our beliefs and to identify the distinctive sort of agency we exercise with respect to our beliefs. Because belief is a state of mind, and states are neither dynamic nor telic, I argued that epistemic norms of belief must be different from the sorts of norms that apply to actions (and other performances) that pursue some goal. Although there are individualistic reasons to comply with epistemic norms, I argued that our reasons to care about knowledge lie in our membership in epistemic communities, the sorts of social associations which require mutual regulation of our reputations as knowers for the purpose of engaging in joint epistemic practices.

This idea is supported by an account of epistemic discourse as undertaking commitments not mainly about how reality is, but rather about how to act and react, given how we presume reality to be. If claiming that someone knows something involves undertaking a commitment to do, think, and feel certain things that are crucial for sustaining and perpetuating our communal epistemic practice, it should be unsurprising that the reasons for valuing knowledge often transcend the instrumental benefits to individual knowers of having what they want (even when what they want is to have specific pieces of knowledge). Moreover, I argued that a person's maintaining their status as a knower often involves a kind of holistic exercise of agency in the always tacitly ongoing activity of maintaining a system of beliefs. Although I explained this activity in terms of the always ongoing activity of basing one's beliefs on reasons, and I allowed that there is a sense in which all believers engage in this activity to some degree, I argued that interaction with other people is required for us to conceptualize those reasons as binding for what we normal humans ought to believe. Further, and finally, I argued that it is by using a kind of discourse whose meaning is determined by its role in undertaking and acknowledging normative inferential commitments in collective discursive practice that we are able to pursue the practice of belief-system maintenance together in epistemic community.

Notes

1. It is not always easy to draw a line in recent meta-ethics between expressivism and inferentialism. Inferentialists sometimes describe themselves as defending an expressivist rather than a representationalist account of certain terms, such as logical connectives and the truth predicate; see Brandom (2000, ch. 1), M. Williams (2010, 2013), Price (2013). And expressivists often seem very sympathetic to the idea that normative claims have a distinctively practical inferential role, which is a key part of their argument that these claims do not function to describe reality. See, for instance, Ridge (2014, ch. 8),

Köhler (2017), and James Brown (2019, 2020). So, from a high enough vantage point, this might seem like an intramural debate. See Capps (2018) for useful discussion. However, by the end of this chapter, I want to have suggested not only that the approach I describe as expressivist should be replaced with an inferentialist alternative, but also that we'd profit from downplaying the notion of expression in favor of the notion of inference when we think about why epistemic claims are different from paradigmatically descriptive claims.

2. Locke wrote, "words in their primary or immediate signification signify nothing but the ideas in the mind of him that uses them" (1690/1979, III.2.2.), capturing one natural intuition about the centrality of expressing our minds to linguistic communication. For a robust defense of a Lockean approach to meaning, see Davis (2003).

3. Peirce wrote, "an act of assertion supposes that, a proposition being formulated, a person performs an act which renders him liable to the penalties of the social law (or, at any rate, those of the moral law) in case it should not be true, unless he has a definite and sufficient excuse" (1931–1958, 2.315), capturing another natural intuition about the centrality of the commitments undertaken to linguistic communication. For defense of a Peircean approach to metaethical questions about the meaning of normative terms, see Chrisman (2023).

4. What about the ideas of reference and representation, which many philosophers and linguists have taken to be central to meaning? One might countenance a "Fregean" approach focused in these notions, but I think we should understand the Lockean and Peircean approaches as attempting to answer a different question to the Fregean. The Lockeans and Peirceans want to explain, in part, why some words refer to things in reality and how some sentences represent ways reality could be, and they do this in contrasting terms: expressive potential or commissive function. So, I think both of these approaches can embrace the idea that a core function of meaningful speech is to refer to things in reality and represent how they are. However, they will both insist that this is not the only meaning-constituting function of language.

5. However, the label "inferentialism" shouldn't be thought to commit these philosophers to the idea that all rationally defensible attitudes and actions are the result of an inference, conceived as a reason-guided movement of the mind from premises to conclusion. The relevant sort of "inferential support" may be available only post hoc or to third-personal observers of the action/attitude, and it would still count as "inferential" on this broad way of thinking about reasoned support for actions and attitudes.

6. Correcting the account given in Chrisman (2010b), in Chrisman (2016a, ch. 6; 2016b), I explain in more detail the idea that inferentialism (and expressivism) should be viewed as meta-semantic theories providing grounding explanations, rather than as attempts to model the compositional semantic content of their target claims.

7. In Chrisman (2012b, 2016a), I develop a nondescriptivist inferentialist account of the meaning of 'ought', and the inferentialist account of knowledge attributions developed here can be seen as an application of that general view. However, even if one rejects my overall view of ought-claims, I think inferentialism about knowledge attributions could still provide an illuminating way to make sense of their normative character. For initial discussion, see Chrisman (2010e). For helpful discussion of inferentialism in metaethics, see Tiefensee (2016).

8. Blackburn (1988) develops a commitment-based account of logically complex statements with normative parts. But in doing so, he conceives of *being committed* as a special kind of mental state that is expressed by the logically complex sentence. Similarly, Horgan and Timmons (2006) develop a version of expressivism according to which there are two fundamentally different kinds of belief, which they characterize in terms of the difference between "is-commitments" and "ought-commitments", treating these as kinds of mental states. These are not versions of inferentialism as I understand it. However, inferentialists recognize psychological presuppositions in thinking of someone as discursively committed in some way. Perhaps one must believe what one says in order to count as sincere in undertaking an inferential commitment, and perhaps one must have various psychological dispositions to act and react in accord with what one says to count as capable of undertaking inferential commitments in the first place. However, discursive inferential commitments themselves are understood as public standings rather than psychological states.
9. It is one way to understand the Frege-Geach problem; see Geach (1965) and Searle (1962). For helpful further discussion, see Schroeder (2008b), and for a contrasting account of the challenge, see Woods (2017). See Warren (2015) for an argument that the Frege-Geach problem favors inferentialism over expressivism in the ethical case.
10. In response, one might suggest that the mixed disjunctive claim expresses a belief in a descriptive proposition and a state of norm acceptance, but one doesn't have to have the mental state expressed by either side of a disjunction in order to accept it as true. Moreover, if someone is convinced of the descriptive proposition that René is psychologically unwell, they can say this sentence without expressing the acceptance of any epistemic norms.
11. In my view, the most promising expressivist responses to this challenge come from hybrid views that treat normative statements as expressing practical/evaluative orientations *plus* connected representational beliefs, and so-called dynamic expressivist views that treat normative statements as proposed conversational updates designed for coordinating on shared practical attitudes. For the former, see Ridge (2014), Toppinen (2013), and Schroeder (2013). For the latter, Charlow (2015) and Willer (2017). Both research programs take seriously the challenge to give a general recipe for predicting the semantic contents of complex statements embedding normative parts. Ultimately, I suspect that hybrid expressivists don't take this seriously enough, unless they hold that purely descriptive sentences also express practical/evaluative orientations and representational beliefs. For otherwise they need to posit ambiguities in the semantic operation of basic logical words such as 'or'. And I'm not sure we should classify dynamic approaches to the meaning of normative claims as forms of expressivism, since they explain semantic contents in terms of update potentials rather than in terms of mental state expressed.
12. See Schroeder (2008a, part III) for discussion of these problems and a proposal for addressing them. His proposal requires that expressivists treat all statements, both normative and descriptive, as expressing states of *being for* something. According to him, this is the most constructive way for the expressivist to provide a unified and systematic semantics for semantically complex statements involving both normative and descriptive parts. However, it requires reconstructing the idea that descriptive

statements express representational beliefs in terms of the idea of *being for proceeding as if* they are true. And, to my mind, this raises the question of why parity of reasoning wouldn't require us to treat normative statements as also expressing states of being for proceeding as if they are true, and if we do that, we lose the contrast between normative statements and descriptive statements, which expressivists were supposed to explain.

13. Some of the inferentialist philosophers mentioned (especially Williams and Brandom) often seem to reject the idea that there could be any "purely" descriptive vocabulary. This is part of why they get described as "left-wing" Sellarsians, in contrast to "right-wing" Sellarsians inspired by his scientific realism, such as Ruth Millikan and Jay Rosenberg. These philosophers follow Sellars in holding out hope for a refined scientific language with the sophistication to picture reality, which we might think of as purely descriptive. For discussion, see Millikan (1984), Rosenberg (2007), O'Shea (2010), and Sicha (2014).

14. For useful general discussion see Björklund et al. (2012). In relation to expressivism, see also Blackburn (1988, 1998, chs 3–4), Gibbard (2003, ch. 7; 2012, appendix 2), Toppinen (2013), Ridge (2014, chs 2 and 5), Baker and Woods (2015), Zangwill (2011, 2021), and Sinclair (2017, 2021, chs 2 and 5). But see also Bar-On and Chrisman (2009) for an alternative "neo-expressivist" way of explaining this phenomenon without committing to a view about the psychofunctional role of moral judgments.

15. For a recent attempt to overcome this prima facie hurdle to epistemic versions of expressivism, see Ridge (2018), who appeals to the phenomenon of pragmatic encroachment to argue that epistemic claims do have the motivational profile expressivists typically attribute to practical claims. See also Gibbard (2012) for a book-length development of the idea that claims about meaning are normative for belief, and an expressivist account of claims about meaning.

16. See for instance Pollock and Cruz (1999: ch. 5), Williamson (2005), Stanley (2005a), Hawthorne and Stanley (2008), Neta (2008a), Jessica Brown (2008), and essays in Littlejohn and Turri (2013).

17. Kvanvig (2003a), Cuneo (2007), and Lynch (2009) have made versions of this argument. See Carter and Chrisman (2012) for an explanation of how their argument conflates commitment to valuing things epistemically with commitment to the reality of epistemic values.

Bibliography

Adler, Jonathan. 2002. *Belief's Own Ethics*. Cambridge, MA: MIT Press.

Ahlstrom-Vij, Kristoffer. 2013. "Moderate Epistemic Expressivism." *Philosophical Studies* 163 (2): pp. 337–357.

Alston, William. 1988. "The Deontological Conception of Epistemic Justification." *Philosophical Perspectives* 2 (Epistemology): pp. 257–299.

Alston, William. 1989. *Epistemic Justification*. Ithaca, NY: Cornell University Press.

Alston, William. 2005. *Beyond Justification: Dimensions of Epistemic Evaluation*. Ithaca, NY: Cornell University Press.

Altschul, Jon. 2014. "Epistemic Deontologism and Role-Oughts." *Logos & Episteme* V (3): pp. 245–263.

Anderson, Craig, Mark Lepper, and Lee Ross. 1980. "Perseverance of Social Theories: The Role of Explanation in the Persistence of Discredited Information." *Journal of Personality and Social Psychology* 39 (6): pp. 1037–1049.

Anderson, Elizabeth. 2012. "Epistemic Justice as a Virtue of Social Institutions." *Social Epistemology* 26 (2): pp. 631–673.

Anderson, Richard. 2019. "The Frege-Geach Problem for Normative Propositions." PhD Dissertation, University of Connecticut.

Annis, David. 1978. "A Contextualist Theory of Epistemic Justification." *American Philosophical Quarterly* 15 (3): pp. 213–219.

Anscombe, G. E. M. 1957. *Intention*. Oxford: Basil Blackwell.

Aristotle. 1924. *Metaphysics*, W. D. Ross (trans.) Oxford: Clarendon Press.

Armstrong, David. 1973. *Belief, Truth and Knowledge*. Cambridge: Cambridge University Press.

Audi, Robert. 1994. "Dispositional Beliefs and Dispositions to Believe." *Noûs* 28 (4): pp. 419–434.

Audi, Robert. 2001. "Doxastic Voluntarism and the Ethics of Belief." In *Knowledge, Truth, and Duty*, edited by Matthias Steup, pp. 93–113. New York: Oxford University Press.

Austin, J. L. 1979. *Philosophical Papers*. Oxford: Oxford University Press.

Bach, Kent. 1981. "An Analysis of Self-Deception." *Philosophy and Phenomenological Research* 41 (3): pp. 351–370.

Bach, Kent. 2005. "The Emperor's New 'Knows'." In *Contextualism in Philosophy: Knowledge, Meaning, and Truth*, edited by Gerhard Preyer and Georg Peter, pp. 51–89. Oxford: Oxford University Press.

Baker, Derek, and Jack Woods. 2015. "How Expressivists Can and Should Explain Inconsistency." *Ethics* 125 (2): pp. 391–424.

Bar-On, Dorit, and Matthew Chrisman. 2009. "Ethical Neo-Expressivism." In *Oxford Studies in Metaethics, Volume 4*, edited by Russ Shafer-Landau, pp. 133–165. Oxford: Oxford University Press.

Baracan Marcus, Ruth. 1990. "Some Revisionary Proposals about Belief and Believing." *Philosophy and Phenomenological Research* 50: pp. 133–153.

Barbey, Arron, and Steven Sloman. 2007. "Base-Rate Respect: From Ecological Validity to Dual Processes." *Behavioral and Brain Sciences* 30: pp. 241–297.

Barker, Chris. 2013. "Negotiating Taste." *Inquiry: An Interdisciplinary Journal of Philosophy* 56 (2–3): pp. 240–257.

Baumann, Peter. 2016. *Epistemic Contextualism: A Defense*. New York: Oxford University Press.

Bayne, Tim, and Elisabeth Pacherie. 2005. "In Defence of the Doxastic Conception of Delusion." *Mind & Language* 20 (2): pp. 163–188.

Beckermann, Ansgar. 2001. "Wissen und Wahre Meinung." In *Das weite Spektrum der Analytischen Philosophie: Festschrift für Franz Von Kutschera*, edited by Wolfgang Lenzen, pp. 24–43. Berlin: De Gruyter.

Beckman, Emma. 2018. "Mistaken Morality?: An Essay on Moral Error Theory." PhD Thesis, Umeå University.

Beddor, Bob. 2016. "Reduction in Epistemology." PhD Thesis, Rutgers University.

Beddor, Bob. 2019. "Noncognitivism and Epistemic Evaluations." *Philosophers' Imprint* 19: pp. 1–27.

Bem, Daryl. 1970. *Beliefs, Attitudes, and Human Affairs*. Belmont, CA: Brooks/Cole.

Bennett, Jonathan. 1990. "Why Is Belief Involuntary?" *Analysis* 1 (2): pp. 87–107.

Berker, Selim. 2013. "Epistemic Teleology and the Separateness of Propositions." *Philosophical Review* 122 (3): pp. 337–393.

Berrios, G. E. 1991. "Delusions as 'Wrong Beliefs': A Conceptual History." *British Journal of Psychiatry*, 159 (suppl. 14): pp. 6–13.

Bird, Alexander. 2007. "Justified Judging." *Philosophy and Phenomenological Research*, 74 (1): pp. 81–110.

Björklund, Fredrik, Gunnar Björnsson, John Eriksson, Ragnar Francén, and Caj Strandberg. 2012. "Recent Work on Motivational Internalism." *Analysis* 72 (1): pp. 124–137.

Blackburn, Simon. 1988. "Attitudes and Contents." *Ethics* 98 (3): pp. 501–517.

Blackburn, Simon. 1993. *Essays in Quasi-Realism*. Oxford: Oxford University Press.

Blackburn, Simon. 1996. "Securing the Nots: Moral Epistemology for the Quasi-Realist." In *Moral Knowledge? New Readings in Moral Epistemology*, edited by Walter Sinnott-Armstrong and Mark Timmons, pp. 82–100. Oxford: Oxford University Press.

Blackburn, Simon. 1998. *Ruling Passions: A Theory of Practical Reasoning*. Oxford: Clarendon Press.

Blackmore, Susan. 2013. "Living without Free Will." In *Exploring the Illusion of Free Will and Moral Responsibility*, edited by Gregg Caruso, pp. 161–176. Lanham, MD: Lexington Books.

Blome-Tillmann, Michael. 2009. "Knowledge and Presuppositions." *Mind* 118 (470): pp. 241–294.

Blome-Tillmann, Michael. 2014. *Knowledge and Presuppositions*. Oxford: Oxford University Press.

Boghossian, Paul. 2003. "The Normativity of Content." *Philosophical Issues* 13 (1): pp. 31–45.

BonJour, Laurence. 1980. "Externalist Theories of Empirical Knowledge." *Midwest Studies in Philosophy* 5 (1): pp. 53–73.

BonJour, Laurence. 1985. *The Structure of Empirical Knowledge*. Cambridge, MA: Harvard University Press.

Booth, Anthony. 2014. "On Some Recent Moves in Defence of Doxastic Compatibilism." *Synthese* 191 (8): pp. 1–14.

Bortolotti, Lisa. 2009. *Delusions and Other Irrational Beliefs*. Oxford: Oxford University Press.

Boult, Cameron. 2020. "There Is a Distinctively Epistemic Kind of Blame." *Philosophy and Phenomenological Research.* doi:10.1111/phpr.12726.

Boult, Cameron, and Sebastian Köhler. 2020. "Epistemic Judgement and Motivation." *Philosophical Quarterly* 70 (281): 738–758.

Boyd, Zelda, and Julian Boyd. 1977. "To Lose the Name of Action: The Semantics of Action and Motion in Tennyson's Poetry." *PTL: A Journal for Descriptive Poetics and the Theory of Literature* 2.

Boyle, Matthew. 2009. "Active Belief." *Canadian Journal of Philosophy* 39 (Sup. 1): pp. 119–147.

Boyle, Matthew. 2011. "'Making up Your Mind' and the Activity of Reason." *Philosophers' Imprint* 11 (17): pp. 1–24.

Braithwaite, R. B. 1933. "The Nature of Believing." *Proceedings of the Aristotelian Society* 33 (1): pp. 129–146.

Brandom, Robert. 1994. *Making It Explicit: Reasoning, Representing, and Discursive Commitment.* Cambridge, MA: Harvard University Press.

Brandom, Robert. 2000. *Articulating Reasons: An Introduction to Inferentialism.* Cambridge, MA: Harvard University Press.

Brandom, Robert. 2008. *Between Saying and Doing: Towards an Analytic Pragmatism.* Oxford: Oxford University Press.

Brandom, Robert. 2013. "Global Anti-Representationalism." In *Expressivism, Pragmatism and Representationalism*, edited by Huw Price, pp. 85–111. Cambridge: Cambridge University Press.

Bratman, Michael. 2014. *Shared Agency: A Planning Theory of Acting Together.* Oxford: Oxford University Press.

Brinton, Laurel. 2009. *The Development of English Aspectual Systems: Aspectualizers and Post-Verbal Particles.* Cambridge: Cambridge University Press.

Brown, James. 2019. "Expressivism and Cognitive Propositions." *Journal of the American Philosophical Association* 5 (3): pp. 371–387.

Brown, James. 2020. "Expressivism, Content, and Normative Propositions." PhD Thesis, University of Edinburgh.

Brown, Jessica. 2006. "Contextualism and Warranted Assertibility Manoeuvres." *Philosophical Studies* 130: pp. 407–435.

Brown, Jessica. 2008. "'Subject-Sensitive Invariantism' and the Knowledge Norm of Practical Reasoning." *Noûs* 42: 167–189.

Brown, Jessica. 2020. "What Is Epistemic Blame?" *Noûs* 54 (2): pp. 389–407.

Buckwalter, Wesley. 2017. "Epistemic Contextualism and Linguistic Behavior." In *The Routledge Handbook of Epistemic Contextualism*, edited by Jonathan Jenkins Ichikawa, pp. 44–56. New York: Routledge.

Burge, Tyler. 1997. "Interlocution, Perception, and Memory." *Philosophical Studies* 86: pp. 21–47.

Burge, Tyler. 2010. *Origins of Objectivity.* New York: Oxford University Press.

Capps, John. 2018. "From Global Expressivism to Global Pragmatism." *Metaphilosophy* 49 (1–2): pp. 71–89.

Carr, Jennifer. 2015. "Don't Stop Believing." *Canadian Journal of Philosophy* 45 (5): pp. 744–766.

Carruthers, Peter. 2009a. "An Architecture for Dual Reasoning." In *In Two Minds: Dual Processes and Beyond*, edited by Jonathan Evans and Keith Frankish, pp. 109–127. Oxford: Oxford University Press.

Carruthers, Peter. 2009b. "How We Know Our Own Minds: The Relationship between Mindreading and Metacognition." *Behavioral and Brain Sciences* 32: pp. 121–182.

Carter, J. Adam. 2022. "Collective (Telic) Virtue Epistemology." In *Social Virtue Epistemology*, edited by Mark Alfano, Jeroen De Ridder, and Colin Klein. London: Routledge.

Carter, J. Adam, and Matthew Chrisman. 2012. "Is Epistemic Expressivism Incompatible with Inquiry?" *Philosophical Studies* 159 (3): pp. 323–339.

Caruso, Gregg. 2012. *Free Will and Consciousness: A Determinist Account of the Illusion of Free Will*. Lanham, MD: Lexington Books.

Cassam, Quassim. 2010. "Judging, Believing and Thinking." *Philosophical Issues* 20 (1): pp. 80–95.

Cassam, Quassim. 2019. *Vices of the Mind: From the Intellectual to the Political*. Oxford: Oxford University Press.

Castañeda, Hector-Neri. 1980. "The Theory of Questions, Epistemic Powers, and the Indexical Theory of Knowledge." *Midwest Studies in Philosophy* 5 (1): pp. 193–238.

Chakravartty, Anjan. 2017. *Scientific Ontology: Integrating Naturalized Metaphysics and Voluntarist Epistemology*. Oxford: Oxford University Press.

Chappell, Richard Yetter. 2012. "Fittingness: The Sole Normative Primitive." *Philosophical Quarterly* 62 (249): pp. 684–704.

Charlow, Nate. 2014. "The Problem with the Frege-Geach Problem." *Philosophical Studies* 167 (3): pp. 635–665.

Charlow, Nate. 2015. "Prospects for an Expressivist Theory of Meaning." *Philosophers' Imprint* 15: pp. 1–43.

Chisholm, Roderick. 1966. *Theory of Knowledge*. Englewood Cliffs, NJ: Prentice-Hall.

Chisholm, Roderick. 1991. "Firth and the Ethics of Belief." *Philosophy and Phenomenological Research* 51 (1): pp. 119–128.

Chrisman, Matthew. 2005. "Review of Allan Gibbard's *Thinking How to Live*." *Ethics* 115: pp. 406–412.

Chrisman, Matthew. 2006. "Epistemic and Ethical Expressions." PhD Thesis, University of North Carolina at Chapel Hill.

Chrisman, Matthew. 2007. "From Epistemic Contextualism to Epistemic Expressivism." *Philosophical Studies* 135: pp. 225–254.

Chrisman, Matthew. 2008. "Ought to Believe." *Journal of Philosophy* 105 (7): pp. 346–70.

Chrisman, Matthew. 2009. "Expressivism, Truth, and (Self-)Knowledge." *Philosophers' Imprint* 9 (3): pp. 1–26.

Chrisman, Matthew. 2010a. "The Aim of Belief and the Goal of Truth." In *Self, Language, and World: Problems from Kant, Sellars, and Rosenberg*, edited by Jim O'Shea and Eric Rubenstein, pp. 188–208. Atascadero, CA: Ridgeview Publishing Co.

Chrisman, Matthew. 2010b. "Expressivism, Inferentialism, and the Theory of Meaning." In *New Waves in Metaethics*, edited by Michael Brady, pp. 103–125. Houndmills: Palgrave-Macmillan.

Chrisman, Matthew. 2010c. "From Epistemic Contextualism to Epistemic Inferentialism." In *Social Epistemology*, edited by Adrian Haddock, Alan Millar, and Duncan Pritchard, pp. 112–128. Oxford: Oxford University Press.

Chrisman, Matthew. 2010d. "Constructivism, Expressivism and Ethical Knowledge." *International Journal of Philosophical Studies* 18 (3): pp. 331–353.

Chrisman, Matthew. 2010e. "From Epistemic Expressivism to Epistemic Inferentialism." In *Social Epistemology*, edited by Adrian Haddock, Duncan Pritchard, and Alan Millar, pp. 112–128. Oxford: Oxford University Press.

Chrisman, Matthew. 2011. "Ethical Expressivism." In *The Continuum Companion to Ethics*, edited by Christian Miller, pp. 29–54. London: Continuum.
Chrisman, Matthew. 2012a. "The Normative Evaluation of Belief and the Aspectual Classification of Belief and Knowledge Attributions." *Journal of Philosophy* 109 (10): pp. 588–612.
Chrisman, Matthew. 2012b. "On the Meaning of 'Ought'." In *Oxford Studies in Metaethics, vol. 7*, edited by Russ Shafer-Landau, pp. 304–332. New York: Oxford University Press.
Chrisman, Matthew. 2012d. "Epistemic Expressivism." *Philosophy Compass* 7 (2): pp. 118–126.
Chrisman, Matthew. 2013. "Emotivism." In *The International Encyclopedia of Ethics*, edited by Hugh LaFollette, pp. 1–6. Oxford: Wiley-Blackwell.
Chrisman, Matthew. 2016a. *The Meaning of 'Ought': Beyond Descriptivism and Expressivism in Metaethics*. Oxford: Oxford University Press.
Chrisman, Matthew. 2016b. "Metanormative Theory and the Meaning of Deontic Modals." In *Deontic Modality*, edited by Nate Charlow and Matthew Chrisman, pp. 395–424. New York: Oxford University Press.
Chrisman, Matthew. 2017a. *What Is This Thing Called Metaethics?* London: Routledge.
Chrisman, Matthew. 2017b. "Performance Normativity and Here-and-Now Doxastic Agency." *Synthese*: pp. 1–9.
Chrisman, Matthew. 2018a. "Epistemic Normativity and Cognitive Agency." *Noûs* 52 (3): pp. 508–529.
Chrisman, Matthew. 2018b. "Two Nondescriptivist Views of Normative and Evaluative Statements." *Canadian Journal of Philosophy* 48 (3–4): pp. 1–20.
Chrisman, Matthew. 2020. "Believing as We Ought and the Democratic Route to Knowledge." In *The Ethics of Belief and Beyond: Understanding Mental Normativity*, edited by Sebastian Schmidt and Gerhard Ernst, pp. 47–70. New York: Routledge.
Chrisman, Matthew. 2023. "Inferentialism as an Alternative to Expressivism." In Russ Shafer-Landau (ed.), *Oxford Studies in Metaethics Volume 18*. New York: Oxford University Press: pp. 47–72.
Chrisman, Matthew. 2024. "Freedom of Thought." *Philosophical Issues* 34 (1): 196–212.
Chrisman, Matthew. Forthcoming. "A Peircean Inferentialist Alternative to Expressivism." In *Oxford Studies in Metaethics*, vol. 17, edited by Russ Shafer-Landau. Oxford: Oxford University Press.
Chrisman, Matthew and Berislav Marušić. Forthcoming. "Transparency, Self-Knowledge, and the Sociality of Belief." *The Journal of Philosophy*.
Chrisman, Matthew and Graham Hubbs. Forthcoming. "Epistemic Normativity as Autotelic: Why Suspension and Judgment Aren't Like Archery." *Philosophical Studies*.
Chrisman, Matthew and Peter McColl. 2021. "Social Media and Responsible Debate." In *Charter for Responsible Debate: Discussing Contentious Issues with Common Purpose*, edited by Matthew Chrisman, Alice König, Peter McColl, and John O'Connor, pp. 20–23. Edinburgh: The Young Academy of Scotland.
Chuard, Philippe, and Nicholas Southwood. 2009. "Epistemic Norms without Voluntary Control." *Noûs* 43 (4): pp. 599–632.
Churchland, Paul. 1981. "Eliminative Materialism and the Propositional Attitudes." *Journal of Philosophy* 78: pp. 67–90.
Clarke, Murray. 1986. "Doxastic Voluntarism and Forced Belief." *Philosophical Studies* 50 (1): pp. 39–51.
Clifford, William. 1877. "The Ethics of Belief." *Contemporary Review* 29: pp. 290–309.

Coady, David. 2012. *What to Believe Now: Applying Epistemology to Contemporary Issues.* Oxford: Wiley-Blackwell.
Cohen, Jonathan. 1992. *An Essay on Belief and Acceptance.* New York: Oxford University Press.
Cohen, Stewart. 1988. "How to Be a Fallibilist." *Philosophical Perspectives* 2: pp. 91–123.
Cohen, Stewart. 1999. "Contextualism, Skepticism, and the Structure of Reasons." *Philosophical Perspectives* 13: pp. 57–89.
Cohen, Stewart. 2004. "Contextualism and Unhappy-Face Solutions." *Philosophical Studies* 119: pp. 185–197.
Comrie, Bernard. 1976. *Aspect: An Introduction to the Study of Verbal Aspect and Related Problems.* New York: Cambridge University Press.
Conee, Earl. 2005. "Contextualism Contested." In *Contemporary Debates in Epistemology*, edited by Ernest Sosa and Matthias Steup, pp. 47–56. Oxford: Blackwell.
Côté-Bouchard, Charles. 2016. "Can the Aim of Belief Ground Epistemic Normativity?" *Philosophical Studies* 173: pp. 3181–3198.
Côté-Bouchard, Charles. 2017. "Belief's Own Metaethics? A Case against Epistemic Normativity." PhD Dissertation, King's College London.
Cowie, Christopher. 2014. "In Defence of Instrumentalism about Epistemic Normativity." *Synthese* 191: pp. 4003–4017.
Craig, Edward. 1990. *Knowledge and the State of Nature: An Essay in Conceptual Synthesis.* Oxford: Clarendon Press.
Crane, Tim. 2013. "Unconscious Belief and Conscious Thought." In *Phenomenal Intentionality*, edited by Uriah Kriegel, pp. 156–173. Oxford: Oxford University Press.
Cuneo, Terence. 2007. *The Normative Web: An Argument for Moral Realism.* Oxford: Oxford University Press.
Currie, Gregory, and Jon Jureidini. 2001. "Delusion, Rationality, Empathy." *Philosophy, Psychiatry, and Psychology* 8 (2–3): pp. 159–62.
Darwall, Stephen. 2006. The Second Person Standpoint: Morality, Respect, and Accountability. Cambridge, MA: Harvard University Press.
Davidson, Donald. 2000. "Truth Rehabilitated." In *Rorty and his Critics*, edited by Robert Brandom, pp. 65–73. Oxford: Blackwell Publishing.
Davis, Wayne. 2003 *Meaning, Expression, and Thought.* Cambridge: Cambridge University Press.
Della Roca, Michael. 2006. "Judgment and Will." In *The Blackwell Guide to Descartes' Meditations*, edited by Gaukroger, Stephen. Oxford: Wiley-Blackwell, pp. 143–159.
Dennett, Daniel. 1969. *Content and Consciousness: An Analysis of Mental Phenomena.* New York: Routledge.
Dennett, Daniel. 1987. *The Intentional Stance.* Cambridge, MA: MIT Press.
Dennett, Daniel. 1991. "Real Patterns." *Journal of Philosophy* 88 (1): pp. 27–51.
DePaul, Michael. 2001. "Value Monism in Epistemology." In *Knowledge, Truth, and Duty*, edited by Matthais Steup, pp. 170–182. Oxford: Oxford University Press.
DeRose, Keith 2005. "The Ordinary Language Basis for Contextualism." *Philosophical Quarterly* 55: pp. 172–198.
DeRose, Keith. 1992. "Contextualism and Knowledge Attributions." *Philosophy and Phenomenological Research* 52: pp. 913–929.
DeRose, Keith. 1995. "Solving the Skeptical Puzzle." *Philosophical Review* 104: pp. 1–52.
DeRose, Keith. 2005. "The Ordinary Language Basis for Contextualism, and the New Invariantism." *Philosophical Quarterly* 55 (219):172–198.

DeRose, Keith. 2009. *The Case for Contextualism: Knowledge, Skepticism, and Context*. Oxford: Oxford University Press.
Descartes, René. (1641/2006). *Meditations on First Philosophy*, edited and translated by Roger Ariew and Donald Cress, Indianapolis, IN: Hackett Publishing Company.
DeVries, Willem. 2005. *Wilfrid Sellars*. New York: Acumen.
Dogramaci, Sinan. 2012. "Reverse Engineering Epistemic Evaluations." *Philosophy and Phenomenological Research* 84 (3): pp. 513–530.
Dogramaci, Sinan. 2015. "Forget and Forgive: A Practical Approach to Forgotten Evidence." *Ergo: An Open Access Journal of Philosophy* 2 (26): pp. 645–677.
Dowty, David. 1979. *Word Meaning and Montague Grammar: The Semantics of Verbs and Times in Generative Semantics and in Montague's PTQ*. Norwell, MA: Kluwer Academic Publishers.
Dreier, James. 1990. "Internalism and Speaker Relativism." *Ethics* 101: pp. 6–26.
Dretske, Fred. 1988. *Explaining Behavior: Reasons in a World of Causes*. Cambridge, MA: MIT Press.
Dretske, Fred. 1995. *Naturalizing the Mind*. Cambridge, MA: MIT Press.
Dretske, Fred. 2004. "Knowing What You Think vs. Knowing That You Think It." In *The Externalist Challenge*, edited by Richard Schantz, pp. 389–399. Berlin: De Gruyter.
Dummett, Michael. 1993. "Testimony and Memory." In *Seas of Language*, pp. 411–428. Oxford: Oxford University Press.
Dyke, Michelle. 2021. "Could our Epistemic Reasons Be Collective Practical Reasons?" *Noûs* 55 (4): pp. 842–862. https://doi-org.ezproxy.is.ed.ac.uk/10.1111/nous.12335.
Egan, Andy. 2009. "Imagination, Delusion, and Self-Deception." In *Delusions, Self-Deception, and Affective Influences on Belief-formation*, edited by Tim Bayne and Jordi Fernandez, pp. 263–280. Hove: Psychology Press.
Engel, Pascal. 2004. "Truth and the Aim of Belief." In *Laws and Models in Science*, edited by D. Gillies, pp. 77–97. London: King's College Publications.
Engel, Pascal. 2013. "Doxastic Correctness." *Aristotelian Society Supplementary Volume*, 87 (1): pp. 199–216.
Evans, Jonathan. 2008. "Dual-Processing Accounts of Reasoning, Judgment, and Social Cognition." *Annual Review of Psychology* 59: pp. 255–278.
Evans, Jonathan, and David Over. 1996. *Rationality and Reasoning*. Hove: Psychology Press.
Everson, Stephen. 1988. "The Difference between Feeling and Thinking." *Mind* 97 (387): pp. 401–413.
Fairweather, Abrol, and Carlos Montemayor. 2017. *Knowledge, Dexterity, and Attention: A Theory of Epistemic Agency*. Cambridge: Cambridge University Press.
Fantl, Jeremy. 2007. "Review of *Thinking about Knowing*." *Philosophy and Phenomenological Research* 17 (1): pp. 228–231.
Fantl, Jeremy, and Matthew McGrath. 2007. "On Pragmatic Encroachment in Epistemology." *Philosophy and Phenomenological Research* 75 (3): 558–589.
Fantl, Jeremy, and Matthew McGrath. 2009. *Knowledge in an Uncertain World*. Oxford: Oxford University Press.
Fantl, Jeremy, and Matthew McGrath. 2012. "Contextualism and Subject-Sensitivity." *Philosophy and Phenomenological Research* 84 (3): pp. 693–702.
Fassio, Davide. 2011. "Belief, Correctness and Normativity." *Logique et Analyse* 54 (216): pp. 471–486.
Fassio, Davide. 2015. "Belief, Aim of." *Internet Encyclopedia of Philosophy*, URL: https://iep.utm.edu/beli-aim/#SH1a, accessed October 28, 2020.

Faulkner, Paul. 2010. "Norms of Trust." In *Social Epistemology*, edited by Adrian Haddock, Alan Millar, and Duncan Pritchard, pp. 129–147. Oxford: Oxford University Press.
Feldman, Richard. 2000. "The Ethics of Belief." *Philosophy and Phenomenological Research* 60 (3): pp. 667–95.
Feldman, Richard. 2001. "Skeptical Problems, Contextualist Solutions." *Philosophical Studies* 103 (1): pp. 61–85.
Feldman, Richard. 2004. "Comments on DeRose's "Single Scoreboard Semantics"." *Philosophical Studies* 119 (1–2): pp. 23–33.
Feldman, Richard. 2008. "Modest Deontologism in Epistemology." *Synthese* 161 (3): pp. 339–355.
Fernandez, Miguel Ángel Fernández (ed.). 2016. *Performance Epistemology*. Oxford: Oxford University Press.
Festinger, Leon, and Nathan Maccoby. 1964. "On Resistance to Persuasive Communication." *Journal of Abnormal and Social Psychology* 68 (4): pp. 359–366.
Field, Hartry. 1998. "Epistemological Nonfactualism and the a Prioricity of Logic." *Philosophical Studies* 92: pp. 1–24.
Field, Hartry. 2000. "A Priority as an Evaluative Notion." In *New Essays on the a Priori*, edited by Paul Boghossian and Christopher Peacocke, pp. 117–149. Oxford: Oxford University Press.
Field, Hartry. 2009. "Epistemology without Metaphysics." *Philosophical Studies* 143 (2): pp. 249–290.
Field, Hartry. 2018. "Epistemology from an Evaluativist Perspective." *Philosophers' Imprint* 18 (12): pp. 1–23.
Finlay, Stephen. 2017. "Disagreement Lost and Found." In *Oxford Studies in Metaethics, vol. 12*, edited by Russ Shafer-Landau, pp. 187–205. Oxford: Oxford University Press.
Fischer, John Martin, and Mark Ravizza. 1998. *Responsibility and Control: A Theory of Moral Responsibility*. Cambridge: Cambridge University Press.
Fodor, Jerry. 1975. *The Language of Thought*. Cambridge, MA: Harvard University Press.
Fodor, Jerry. 1981. *Representations: Philosophical Essays on the Foundations of Cognitive Science*. Cambridge, MA: MIT Press.
Fodor, Jerry. 1990. *A Theory of Content and Other Essays*. Cambridge, MA: MIT Press.
Foley, Richard. 1987. *The Theory of Rationality*. Cambridge, MA: Harvard University Press.
Frankish, Keith. 2004. *Mind and Supermind*. Cambridge: Cambridge University Press.
Frankish, Keith. 2007. "Deciding to Believe Again." *Mind* 116 (463): pp. 523–547.
Frankish, Keith. 2009. "Systems and Levels: Dual System Theories and the Personal-Subpersonal Distinction." In *Two Minds: Dual Processes and Beyond*, edited by Jonathan Evans and Keith Frankish, pp. 89–107. Oxford: Oxford University Press.
Frankish, Keith. 2012. "Dual Systems and Dual Attitudes." *Mind and Society* 11 (1): pp. 41–51.
Fricker, Elizabeth. 1995. "Critical Notice: Telling and Trusting: Reductionism and Anti-Reductionism in the Epistemology of Testimony." *Mind* 104 (414): pp. 393–411.
Friedman, Jane. 2013. "Rational Agnosticism and Degrees of Belief." In *Oxford Studies in Epistemology, vol. 4*, edited by Tamar Szabó Gendler and John Hawthorne. New York: Oxford University Press.
Geach, P. T. 1965. "Assertion." *The Philosophical Review* 74: pp. 449–465.
Gendler, Tamar. 2008a. "Alief and Belief." *Journal of Philosophy* 105 (10): pp. 634–663.
Gendler, Tamar. 2008b. "Alief in Action (and Reaction)." *Mind and Language* 23 (5): pp. 552–585.
Gettier, Edmund. 1963. "Is Justified True Belief Knowledge?" *Analysis* 23 (6): pp. 121–123.

Gibbard, Allan. 1986. "An Expressivist Theory of Normative Discourse." *Ethics* 96: pp. 472–485.
Gibbard, Allan. 1990. *Wise Choices, Apt Feelings: A Theory of Normative Judgment*. Cambridge, MA: Harvard University Press.
Gibbard, Allan. 2003 *Thinking How to Live*. Cambridge, MA: Harvard University Press.
Gibbard, Allan. 2005. "Truth and Correct Belief." *Philosophical Issues* 15 (1): pp. 338–350.
Gibbard, Allan. 2012. *Meaning and Normativity*. Oxford: Oxford University Press.
Gilbert, Daniel. 1991. "How Mental Systems Believe." *American Psychologist* 46 (2): pp. 107–119.
Gilbert, Daniel, Douglas Krull, and Patrick Malone. 1990. "Unbelieving the Unbelievable: Some Problems in the Rejection of False Information." *Journal of Personality and Social Psychology* 59 (4): pp. 601–613.
Gilbert, Margaret. 1990. "Walking Together: A Paradigmatic Social Phenomenon." *Midwest Studies in Philosophy* 15 (1): pp. 1–14.
Gilbert, Margaret. 1996. *Living Together*. Lanham, MD: Rowman & Littlefield.
Gilbert, Margaret. 2008. "Two Approaches to Shared Intention: An Essay in the Philosophy of Social Phenomena." *Analyse & Kritik* 30 (2): pp. 483–514.
Gilbert, Margaret. 2009. "Shared Intention and Personal Intentions." *Philosophical Studies* 144 (1): pp. 167–187.
Ginet, Carl. 1985. "Contra Reliabilism." *Philosophical Studies* 68 (2): pp. 175–187.
Ginet, Carl. 2001. "Deciding to Believe." In *Knowledge, Truth, and Duty: Essays on Epistemic Justification, Responsibility, and Virtue*, edited by Matthias Steup, pp. 63–76. New York: Oxford University Press.
Glüer, Katherin, and Åsa Wikforss. 2009. "Against Content Normativity." *Mind* 118 (469): pp. 31–70.
Glüer, Katherin, and Åsa Wikforss. 2013. "Against Belief Normativity." In *The Aim of Belief*, edited by Timothy Chan, pp. 81–101. Oxford: Oxford University Press.
Goldberg, Sanford. 2010. *Relying on Others: An Essay in Epistemology*. Oxford: Oxford University Press.
Goldman, Alvin. 1976. "Discrimination and Perceptual Knowledge." *Journal of Philosophy* 73: pp. 771–791.
Goldman, Alvin. 1979. "What Is Justified Belief." In *Justification and Knowledge*, edited by George Pappas, pp. 1–25. Boston: D. Reidel.
Goldman, Alvin. 1986. *Epistemology and Cognition*. Cambridge, MA: Harvard University Press.
Goldman, Alvin. 1999. *Knowledge in a Social World*. Oxford: Oxford University Press.
Goldman, Alvin. 2009. "Internalism, Externalism, and the Architecture of Justification." *Journal of Philosophy* 106: pp. 309–338.
Goldman, Alvin I. 2011. "Toward a Synthesis of Reliabilism and Evidentialism? Or: Evidentialism's Troubles, Teliabilism's Rescue Package." In *Evidentialism and its Discontents*, edited by Trent Dougherty, pp. 255–283. New York: Oxford University Press.
Goldsmith, John, and Erich Woisetschlaeger. 1982. "The Logic of the English Progressive." *Linguistic Inquiry*, 13 (1): pp. 79–89.
Gopnik, Alison, and Andrew Meltzoff. 1994. "Minds, Bodies and Persons: Young Children's Understanding of the Self and Others as Reflected in Imitation and 'Theory of Mind' Research." In *Self-Awareness in Animals and Humans*, edited by Sue Taylor Parker, Robert Mitchell, and Maria Boccia, pp. 166–186. New York: Cambridge University Press.

Graham, Peter. 2006. "Liberal Fundamentalism and its Rivals." In *The Epistemology of Testimony*, edited by Jennifer Lackey and Ernest Sosa, pp. 93–115. Oxford: Oxford University Press.
Graham, Peter. 2010. "Testimonial Entitlement and the Function of Comprehension." In *Social Epistemology*, edited by Duncan Pritchard, Alan Millar, and Adrian Haddock, pp. 148–174. Oxford: Oxford University Press.
Graham, Peter. 2011. "Perceptual Entitlement and Basic Beliefs." *Philosophical Studies* 153 (3): pp. 467–475.
Graham, Peter. 2012. "Epistemic Entitlement." *Noûs* 46 (3): pp. 449–482.
Graham, Peter. 2014. "Warrant, Functions, History." In *Naturalizing Epistemic Virtue*, edited by Abrol Fairweather and Owen Flanagan, pp. 15–35. Cambridge: Cambridge University Press.
Graham, Peter. 2015. "Epistemic Normativity and Social Norms." In *Epistemic Evaluation*, edited by David Henderson and John Greco, pp. 247–273. Oxford: Oxford University Press.
Grajner, Martin. 2015. "Hybrid Expressivism and Epistemic Justification." *Philosophical Studies* 172 (9): pp. 2349–2369.
Greco, Daniel. 2017. "Cognitive Mobile Homes." *Mind* 126 (501): pp. 93–121.
Greco, John. 2003a. "Knowledge as Credit for True Belief." In *Intellectual Virtue: Perspectives from Ethics and Epistemology*, edited by Michael DePaul and Linda Zagzebski, pp. 111–134. Oxford: Oxford University Press.
Greco, John. 2003b. "Putting Skeptics in their Place: The Nature of Skeptical Arguments and their Role in Philosophical Inquiry." *Philosophy and Phenomenological Research* 66 (2): pp. 432–436.
Greco, John. 2008. "What's Wrong with Contextualism?" *Philosophical Quarterly* 58 (232): pp. 416–436.
Greco, John. 2009a. "Knowledge and Success from Ability." *Philosophical Studies* 142: pp. 17–26.
Greco, John. 2009b. "The Value Problem." In *Epistemic Value*, edited by Adrian Haddock, Alan Millar, and Duncan Pritchard, pp. 313–322. Oxford: Oxford University Press.
Greco, John. 2010. *Achieving Knowledge: A Virtue Theoretic Account of Epistemic Normativity*. Cambridge: Cambridge University Press.
Govier, Trudy. 1976. "Belief, Values, and the Will." *Dialogue* 15: pp. 642–663.
Grimm, Stephen. 2009. "Epistemic Normativity." In *Epistemic Value*, edited by Adrian Haddock, Alan Millar, and Duncan Pritchard, pp. 243–264. Oxford: Oxford University Press.
Gunn, Hanna Kiri. 2020. "How Should We Build Epistemic Community?" *Journal of Speculative Philosophy* 34 (4): pp. 561–581.
Haack, Susan. 1998. *Manifesto of a Passionate Moderate*. Chicago, IL: University of Chicago Press.
Hannon, Michael. 2019. *What's the Point of Knowledge?: A Function-First Epistemology*. New York: Oxford University Press.
Hardwig, John. 1985. "Epistemic Dependence." *Journal of Philosophy* 82 (7): pp. 335–349.
Harman, Gilbert. 1973. "Review of *The Significance of Sense: Meaning Modality, and Morality*." *Philosophical Review* 82 (2): pp. 235–239.
Harman, Gilbert. 1986. *Change in View*. Cambridge, MA: MIT Press.
Hawthorne, John. 2003. *Knowledge and Lotteries*. Oxford: Oxford University Press.
Hawthorne, John, and Jason Stanley. 2008. "Knowledge and Action." *Journal of Philosophy* 105: pp. 571–590.

Hazlett, Allan. 2013. *A Luxury of the Understanding: On the Value of True Belief.* Oxford: Oxford University Press.
Hazlett, Allan. 2014. "Expressivism and Convention-Relativism about Epistemic Discourse." In *Naturalizing Epistemic Virtue*, edited by Abrol Fairweather and Owen Flanagan, pp. 223–246. Cambridge: Cambridge University Press.
Hedden, Brian. 2015. "Time-Slice Rationality." *Mind* 124 (494): pp. 449–491.
Heil, John. 1983. "Doxastic Agency." *Philosophical Studies* 43 (3): pp. 355–364.
Heller, Mark. 1999. "The Proper Role for Contextualism in an Anti-Luck Epistemology." *Noûs* 33 (13): pp. 115–129.
Heller, Mark. 2000. "Hobartian Voluntarism: Grounding a Deontological Conception of Epistemic Justification." *Pacific Philosophical Quarterly* 81 (2): pp. 130–141.
Henderson, David. 2009. "Motivated Contextualism." *Philosophical Studies* 142 (1): pp. 119–131.
Henderson, David. 2011. "Gate-Keeping Contextualism." *Episteme* 8 (1): pp. 83–98.
Henderson, David, and Peter Graham. 2017a. "Epistemic Norms and the 'Epistemic Game' They Regulate: The Basic Structured Epistemic Costs and Benefits." *American Philosophical Quarterly* 54 (4): pp. 367–382.
Henderson, David, and Peter Graham. 2017b. "A Refined Account of the 'Epistemic Game': Epistemic Norms, Temptations, and Epistemic Cooperation." *American Philosophical Quarterly* 54 (4): pp. 383–396.
Henderson, David, and Peter Graham. 2019. "Epistemic Norms as Social Norms." In *The Routledge Handbook of Social Epistemology*, edited by Miranda Fricker, Peter Graham, David Henderson, and Nikolaj Jang Lee Linding Pedersen, pp. 425–436. New York: Routledge.
Henderson, David, and John Greco. 2015. "Introduction." In *Epistemic Evaluation: Purposeful Epistemology*, edited by David Henderson and John Greco, pp. 1–28. Oxford: Oxford University Press.
Hetherington, Stephen. 2012. "Knowledge and Knowing: Ability and Manifestation." In *Conceptions of Knowledge*, edited by Stefan Tolksdorf, pp. 73–99. Berlin: De Gruyter.
Hieronymi, Pamela. 2009. "Believing at Will." *Canadian Journal of Philosophy, Supplementary Volume* 35 (suppl.): pp. 149–187.
Higginbotham, James. 2004. "The English Progressive." In *The Syntax of Time*, edited by Jacqueline Guéron and Jacqueline Lecarme, pp. 329–358. Cambridge, MA: MIT Press.
Hobbes, Thomas. 1651/2016. *Leviathan*, edited by Marshall Missner. New York: Routledge.
Hoffman, Donald. 2019. *The Case against Reality: How Evolution Hid the Truth from our Eyes*. Penguin Books.
Hofmann, Frank. 2005. "Epistemic Means and Ends: In Defense of Some Sartwellian Insights." *Synthese* 146: pp. 357–359.
Hofweber, Thomas. 1999. "Contextualism and the Meaning-Intention Problem." In *Cognition, Agency and Rationality*, edited by Kepa Korta, Ernest Sosa, and Xabier Arrazola, pp. 93–104. Kluwer: Kluwer Academic Publishers.
Horgan, Terry, and Mark Timmons. 2006. "Cognitivist Expressivism." In *Metaethics after Moore*, edited by Terry Horgan and Mark Timmons, pp. 255–298. Oxford University Press.
Hornsby, Jennifer. 2000. "Personal and Sub-Personal: A Defence of Dennett's Early Distinction." *Philosophical Explorations* 3 (1): pp. 6–24.
Holyer, Robert. 1983. "Belief and Will Revisited." *Dialogue* 22 (2): pp. 273–290.
Hubbs, Graham. 2013. "Alief and Explanation." *Metaphilosophy* 44 (5): pp. 604–620.

Huemer, Michael. 1999. "The Problem of Memory Knowledge." *Pacific Philosophical Quarterly* 80 (4): pp. 346–357.

Humberstone, I. L. 1971. "Two Sorts of 'Ought's." *Analysis* 32 (1): pp. 8–11.

Hunter, David. 2001. "Mind-Brain Identity and the Nature of States." *Australasian Journal of Philosophy* 79 (3): pp. 366–376.

Hussain, Nadeem. 2004. "The Return of Moral Fictionalism." *Philosophical Perspectives* 18 (1): pp. 149–188.

Hussain, Nadeem. 2010. "Error Theory and Fictionalism." In *The Routledge Companion to Ethics*, edited by John Skorupski, pp. 345–345. London: Routledge.

Ichikawa, Jonathan Jenkins. 2017a. *Contextualising Knowledge: Epistemology and Semantics*. Oxford: Oxford University Press.

Ichikawa, Jonathan Jenkins (ed.). 2017b. *The Routledge Handbook of Epistemic Contextualism*. London: Routledge.

Jackson, Alexander. 2011. "Appearances, Rationality, and Justified Belief." *Philosophy and Phenomenological Research* 82: pp. 564–593.

Jenkins, David. 2018. "The Role of Judgment in Doxastic Agency." *Thought: A Journal of Philosophy* 7 (1): pp. 12–19.

Jenson, J. Christopher. 2016. "The Belief Illusion." *British Journal for the Philosophy of Science* 67 (4): pp. 965–995.

Joyce, Richard. 2001. *The Myth of Morality*. Cambridge: Cambridge University Press.

Kahneman, Daniel. 2011. *Thinking, Fast and Slow*. New York: Allen Lane.

Kahneman, Daniel, and Shane Frederick. 2002. "Representativeness Revisited: Attribute Substitution in Intuitive Judgement." In *Heuristics and Biases: The Psychology of Intuitive Judgment*, edited by Thomas Gilovich, Dale Griffin, and Daniel Kahneman, pp. 49–81. Cambridge: Cambridge University Press.

Kappel, Klemens. 2010a. "Expressivism about Knowledge and the Value of Knowledge." *Acta Analytica* 25 (2): pp. 175–194.

Kappel, Klemens. 2010b. "On Saying that Someone Knows: Themes from Craig." In *Social Epistemology*, edited by Adrian Haddock, Alan Millar, and Duncan Pritchard, pp. 71–89. Oxford: Oxford University Press.

Kappel, Klemens. 2011. "Is Epistemic Expressivism Dialectically Incoherent?" *Dialectica* 65 (1): pp. 49–69.

Kappel, Klemens, and Emil Moeller. 2014. "Epistemic Expressivism and the Argument from Motivation." *Synthese* 191 (7): pp. 1–19.

Kauppinen, Antti. 2018. "Epistemic Norms and Epistemic Accountability." *Philosophers' Imprint* 18 (8): pp. 1–16.

Keeling, Sophie. 2023. "Accounting for Doxastic Agency: Mental Action and Self-Awareness." *Synthese* 201(6): 1–24.

Keeling, Sophie. 2021. "Knowing our Reasons: Distinctive Self-Knowledge of Why We Hold our Attitudes and Perform Actions." *Philosophy and Phenomenological Research* 102 (2): pp. 318–341.

Kelly, Thomas. 2003. "Epistemic Rationality as Instrumental Rationality: A Critique." *Philosophy and Phenomenological Research* 66 (3): pp. 612–640.

Kelly, Thomas. 2007. "Evidence and Normativity: Reply to Leite." *Philosophy and Phenomenological Research* 75: pp. 465–474.

Kelly, Thomas. 2016. "Historical Versus Current Time Slice Theories in Epistemology." In *Goldman and his Critics*, edited by Hillary Kornblith and Brian McLaughlin, pp. 43–65. Walden, MA: Blackwell.

Kelp, Christoph. 2018. *Good Thinking: A Knowledge First Virtue Epistemology*. London: Routledge.
Kelp, Christoph, and Jon Greco (eds.). 2020. *Virtue Theoretic Epistemology: New Methods and Approaches*. Cambridge: Cambridge University Press.
Kenny, Anthony. 1963. *Action, Emotion, and Will*. London: Routledge and Kegan Paul.
Köhler, Sebastian. 2017. "Expressivism, Belief, and All That." *Journal of Philosophy* 114 (4): pp. 189–207.
Kornblith, Hilary. 1982. "The Psychological Turn." *Australasian Journal of Philosophy* 60 (3): pp. 238–253.
Kornblith, Hilary. 1993. "Epistemic Normativity." *Synthese* 94: pp. 357–376.
Kornblith, Hilary. 1995. "Naturalistic Epistemology and its Critics." *Philosophical Topics* 23 (1): pp. 237–255.
Kornblith, Hilary. 2001. "Epistemic Obligation and the Possibility of Internalism." In *Virtue Epistemology: Essays on Epistemic Virtue and Responsibility*, edited by Abrol Fairweather and Linda Zagzebski, pp. 231–248. New York: Oxford University Press.
Kornblith, Hilary. 2002. *Knowledge and its Place in Nature*. New York: Oxford University Press.
Korsgaard, Christine. 2003. "Realism and Constructivism in Twentieth-Century Moral Philosophy." *Journal of Philosophical Research* 28 (Supplement): pp. 99–122.
Korsgaard, Christine. 2009. *Self-Constitution: Agency, Identity, and Integrity*. Oxford: Oxford University Press.
Koziolek, Nicholas. 2018. "Belief as an Act of Reason." *Manuscrito* 41 (4): pp. 287–318.
Kusch, Martin. 2009. "Testimony and the Value of Knowledge." In *Epistemic Value*, edited by Duncan Pritchard, Adrian Haddock, and Alan Millar, pp. 60–94. Oxford: Oxford University Press.
Kvanvig, Jonathan. 2003a. *The Value of Knowledge and the Pursuit of Understanding*. Cambridge: Cambridge University Press.
Kvanvig, Jonathan. 2003b. "Simple Reliabilism and Agent Reliabilism." *Philosophy and Phenomenological Research* 66 (2): pp. 451–456.
Kvanvig, Jonathan. 2005. "Truth Is Not the Primary Epistemic Goal." In *Contemporary Debates in Epistemology*, edited by Matthais Steup and Ernest Sosa, pp. 285–295. Oxford: Blackwell Publishing.
Lackey, Jennifer. 2007. "Why We Don't Deserve Credit for Everything We Know." *Synthese* 158 (3): pp. 345–361.
Lackey, Jennifer. 2008. *Learning from Words: Testimony as a Source of Knowledge*. Oxford: Oxford University Press.
Landman, Fred. 1992. "The Progressive." *Natural Language Semantics* 1 (1): pp. 1–32.
Lasonen-Aarnio, Maria. 2010. "Unreasonable Knowledge." *Philosophical Perspectives* 24 (1): pp. 1–21.
Lehrer, Keith. 1990. *Theory of Knowledge*. New York: Routledge.
Leitgeb, Hannes. 2017. *The Stability of Belief: How Rational Belief Coheres with Probability*. Oxford: Oxford University Press.
Leon, Mark. 2002. "Responsible Believer." *The Monist* 85 (3): pp. 421–435.
Levy, Neil. 2007. "Doxastic Responsibility." *Synthese* 155 (1): pp. 127–155.
Lewis, David. 1996. "Elusive Knowledge." *Australasian Journal of Philosophy* 74: pp. 549–567.
Littlejohn, Clayton. 2012. *Justification and the Truth-Connection*. Cambridge: Cambridge University Press.

Littlejohn, Clayton. 2013. "The Russellian Retreat." *Proceedings of the Aristotelian Society* 113 (3pt3): pp. 293–320.

Littlejohn, Clayton, and Turri, John (eds). 2013. *Epistemic Norms: New Essays on Action, Belief, and Assertion*. Oxford: Oxford University Press.

Loar, Brian. 1981. *Mind and Meaning*. Cambridge: Cambridge University Press.

Locke, John. 1690/1979. *An Essay Concerning Human Understanding*, edited by Peter Nidditch. Oxford: Clarendon.

Lockie, Robert. 2018. *Free Will and Epistemology: A Defence of the Transcendental Argument for Freedom*. London: Bloomsbury Academic.

Loeb, Louis. 2002. *Stability and Justification in Hume's Treatise*. Oxford: Oxford University Press.

Lord, Errol. 2020. "Suspension of Judgment, Rationality's Competition, and the Reach of the Epistemic." In *The Ethics of Belief and Beyond: Understanding Mental Normativity*, edited by Sebastian Schmidt and Gerhard Ernst, pp. 126–145. Abingdon: Routledge.

Lycan, William. 1986. "Tacit Beliefs." In *Belief: Form, Content, and Function*, edited by Radu Bogdan, pp. 61–82. Oxford: Oxford University Press.

Lycan, William. 2008. "Phenomenal Intentionalities." *American Philosophical Quarterly* 45 (3): pp. 233–252.

Lynch, Michael. 2004. *True to Life: Why Truth Matters*. Cambridge, MA: MIT Press.

Lynch, Michael. 2009 "Truth, Value and Epistemic Expressivism." *Philosophy and Phenomenological Research* 79: pp. 76–97.

Lynch, Michael. 2013. "The Truth of Values and the Values of Truth." In *Epistemic Value*, edited by Duncan Pritchard. Oxford: Oxford University Press, ch. 10.

Lyons, Jack. 1997. "Testimony, Induction and Folk Psychology." *Australasian Journal of Philosophy* 75 (2): pp. 163–178.

MacFarlane, John. 2005. "The Assessment Sensitivity of Knowledge Attributions." In *Oxford Studies in Epistemology, vol 1*. edited by Tamar Szabo Gendler and John Hawthorne, pp. 197–234. Oxford: Oxford University Press.

MacFarlane, John. 2014. *Assessment Sensitivity: Relative Truth and its Applications*. Oxford: Clarendon Press.

Mackie, J. L. 1977. *Ethics: Inventing Right and Wrong*. Harmondsworth: Penguin Books.

MacNabb, D. G. C. 1951. *David Hume: His Theory of Knowledge and Morality*. Oxford: Blackwell.

Maffie, James. 1990. "Naturalism and the Normativity of Epistemology." *Philosophical Studies* 59 (3): pp. 333–349.

Maguire, Barry, and Jack Woods. 2020. "The Game of Belief." *Philosophical Review* 129 (2): pp. 211–249.

Mandelbaum, Eric. 2010. "The Architecture of Belief: An Essay on the Unbearable Automaticity of Believing." PhD Thesis, University of North Carolina, Chapel Hill.

Mandelbaum, Eric. 2013. "Against Alief." *Philosophical Studies* 165 (1): pp. 197–211.

Mandelbaum, Eric. 2014. "Thinking is Believing." *Inquiry: An Interdisciplinary Journal of Philosophy* 57 (1): pp. 55–96.

Mandelbaum, Eric. 2016. "Attitude, Inference, Association: On the Propositional Structure of Implicit Bias." *Noûs* 50 (3): pp. 629–658.

Martin, M. G. F. 2002. "The Transparency of Experience." *Mind and Language* 17: pp. 476–425.

Martin, M. G. F. 2004. "The Limits of Self-Awareness." *Philosophical Studies* 120: pp. 37–89.

Marušić, Berislav. 2015. *Evidence and Agency: Norms of Belief for Promising and Resolving*. Oxford: Oxford University Press.

Marušić, Jennifer Smalligan. 2010. "Does Hume Hold a Dispositional Account of Belief?" *Canadian Journal of Philosophy* 40 (2): pp. 155–183.
McCormick, Miriam. 2011. "Taking Control of Belief." *Philosophical Explorations* 142: pp. 169–183.
McCormick, Miriam. 2014. *Believing against the Evidence: Agency and the Ethics of Belief.* New York: Routledge.
McDowell, John. 1982. "Criteria, Defeasibility, and Knowledge." *Studies in the Philosophy of Logic and Knowledge* 68: pp. 455–479.
McDowell, John. 1986. "Singular Thought and the Extent of Inner Space." In *Subject, Thought, and Context*, edited by John McDowell and Philip Petit. Oxford: Clarendon Press, ch. 5.
McDowell, John. 2009. *Having the World in View: Essays on Kant, Hegel, and Sellars.* Cambridge, MA: Harvard University Press.
McGrath, Matthew. 2020. "Being Neutral: Suspension of Judgement, Agnosticism and Inquiry." *Noûs*, online first.
McHugh, Connor. 2012. "The Truth Norm of Belief." *Pacific Philosophical Quarterly* 93 (1): pp. 8–30.
McHugh, Conor. 2013. "Epistemic Responsibility and Doxastic Agency." *Philosophical Issues* 23 (1): pp. 132–157.
McHugh, Conor. 2014a. "Exercising Doxastic Freedom." *Philosophy and Phenomenological Research* 88 (1): pp. 1–37.
McHugh, Conor. 2014b. "Fitting Belief." *Proceedings of the Aristotelian Society* 114 (2pt2): pp. 167–187.
McHugh, Conor and Daniel Whiting. 2014. "The Normativity of Belief." *Analysis* 74 (4): pp. 698–713.
McKenna, Robin. 2013. "Epistemic Contextualism: A Normative Approach." *Pacific Philosophical Quarterly*, 94 (1): pp. 101–123.
McNamara, Paul. 2006. "Deontic Logic." In *The Stanford Encyclopedia of Philosophy (Spring 2006 Edition)*, edited by Edward Zalta, URL: http://plato.stanford.edu/archives/spr2006/entries/logic-deontic/, accessed October 18, 2016.
Medina, José. 2013. *The Epistemology of Resistance.* Oxford: Oxford University Press.
Mercier, Hugo, and Dan Sperber. 2017. *The Enigma of Reason: A New Theory of Human Understanding.* Cambridge, MA: Harvard University Press.
Meylan, Anne. 2013. "The Value Problem of Knowledge." *Res Philosophica* 90 (2): pp. 261–275.
Meylan, Anne. 2015. "The Legitimacy of Intellectual Praise and Blame." *Journal of Philosophical Research* 40: pp. 189–203.
Meylan, Anne. 2017. "The Consequential Conception of Doxastic Responsibility." *Theoria* 83 (1): pp. 4–28.
Meylan, Anne. 2020. "Knowledge Is Extrinsically Apt Belief: Virtue-Epistemology and the Temporal Objection." In *Virtue Theoretic Epistemology: New Methods and Approaches*, edited by Christoph Kelp and John Greco, pp. 166–180. Cambridge: Cambridge University Press.
Millar, Alan. 2004. *Understanding People: Normativity and Rationalizing Explanation.* New York: Oxford University Press.
Millar, Alan. 2007. "What the Disjunctivist Is Right About." *Philosophy and Phenomenological Research* 74 (1): pp. 176–198.

Millar, Alan. 2008. "Perceptual-recognitional Abilities and Perceptual Knowledge." In *Disjunctivism: Perception, Action, Knowledge*, edited by Adrian Haddock and Fiona Macpherson, pp. 330–347. Oxford: Oxford University Press.

Millgram, Elijah. 2015. *The Great Endarkenment: Philosophy for an Age of Hyperspecialization*. Oxford: Oxford University Press.

Millikan, Ruth G. 1984. *Language, Thought, and Other Biological Categories*. Cambridge, MA: MIT Press.

Miracchi, Lisa. 2015. "Competence to Know." *Philosophical Studies* 172 (1): pp. 29–56.

Mittwoch, Anita. 1988. "Aspects of English Aspect: On the Interaction of Perfect, Progressive and Durational Phrases." *Linguistics and Philosophy* 11 (2): pp. 203–254.

Moore, G. E. 1903. *Principia Ethica*. Cambridge: University Press.

Moran, Richard. 2004. "Anscombe on 'Practical Knowledge'." *Royal Institute of Philosophy Supplement* 55: pp. 43–68.

Moran, Richard. 2012. "Self-Knowledge, 'Transparency,' and the Forms of Activity." In *Introspection and Consciousness*, edited by Declan Smithies and Daniel Stoljar, pp. 211–236. Oxford: Oxford University Press.

Moser, Paul. 1985. *Empirical Justification*. Dordrecht, The Netherlands: Reidel.

Moss, Sarah. 2015. "Time-Slice Epistemology and Action under Indeterminacy." In *Oxford Studies in Epistemology, vol. 5*, edited by Tamar Szabó Gendler and John Hawthorne, pp. 172–194. Oxford: Oxford University Press.

Mourelatos, Alexander. 1978. "Events, Processes, and States." *Linguistics and Philosophy* 2 (3): pp. 415–434.

Mourelatos, Alexander. 1993. "Aristotle's Kinêsis/Energeia Distinction: A Marginal Note on Kathleen Gill's Paper." *Canadian Journal of Philosophy* 23 (3): pp. 385–388.

Nelson, Alan. 1997. "Descartes's Ontology of Thought." *Topoi* 16 (2): pp. 163–178.

Neta, Ram. 2003a. "Contextualism and the Problem of the External World." *Philosophy and Phenomenological Research* 66: pp. 1–31.

Neta, Ram. 2003b. "Skepticism, Contextualism, and Semantic Self-knowledge." *Philosophy and Phenomenological Research* 67 (2): pp. 396–411.

Neta, Ram. 2008a "Anti-Intellectualism and the Knowledge-Action Principle." *Philosophy and Phenomenological Research* 75: pp. 180–187.

Neta, Ram. 2008b. "In Defense of Disjunctivism." In *Disjunctivism: Perception, Action, Knowledge*, edited by Fiona Macpherson and Adrian Haddock, pp. 311–329. Oxford: Oxford University Press.

Neta, Ram. 2019. "The Basing Relation." *Philosophical Review* 128 (2): pp. 179–217.

Newman, Lex, and Alan Nelson. 1999. "Circumventing Cartesian Circles." *Noûs* 33 (3): pp. 370–404.

Nguyen, C. Thi. 2018. "Expertise and the Fragmentation of Intellectual Autonomy." *Philosophical Inquiries* 6 (2): pp. 107–124.

Nolfi, Kate. 2014. "Why Is Epistemic Evaluation Prescriptive?" *Inquiry: An Interdisciplinary Journal of Philosophy* 57 (1): pp. 97–121.

Nolfi, Kate. 2015. "How to be a Normativist about the Nature of Belief." *Pacific Philosophical Quarterly* 96 (2): pp. 181–204.

Nolfi, Kate. 2018. "Moral Agency in Believing." *Philosophical Topics* 46 (1): pp. 53–74.

Nottelmann, Nikolaj. 2007. *Blameworthy Belief: A Study in Epistemic Deontologism*. Dordrecht, The Netherlands: Springer.

Nottelmann, Nikolaj. 2017. "Against a Descriptive Vindication of Doxastic Voluntarism." *Synthese* 194 (8): pp. 2721–2744.

O'Hear, Anthony. 1972. "Belief and the Will." *Philosophy* 47 (180): pp. 95–112.

O'Shea, James. 2007. *Wilfrid Sellars: Naturalism with a Normative Turn.* Malden, MA: Polity.

O'Shea, James. 2010. "Normativity and Scientific Naturalism in Sellars' 'Janus-Faced' Space of Reasons." *International Journal of Philosophical Studies* 18 (3): pp. 459–471.

O'Shaughnessy, Brian. 2000. *Consciousness and the World.* Oxford: Oxford University Press.

Olson, Jonas. 2011a. "Error Theory and Reasons for Belief." In *Reasons for Belief*, edited by Andrew Reisner and Asbjørn Steglich-Petersen. Cambridge: Cambridge University Press, pp. 75–93.

Olson, Jonas. 2011b. "In Defense of Moral Error Theory." In *New Waves in Metaethics*, edited by Michael Brady. New York: Palgrave-Macmillan.

Olson, Jonas. 2014. *Moral Error Theory: History, Critique, Defence.* Oxford: Oxford University Press.

Owens, David. 2000. *Reason without Freedom: The Problem of Epistemic Normativity.* New York: Routledge.

Papineau, David. 1999. "Normativity and Judgment." *Proceedings of the Aristotelian Society* 22: pp. 17–41.

Papineau, David. 2013. "There Are No Norms of Belief." In *The Aim of Belief*, edited by Timothy Chan, pp. 64–79. Oxford: Oxford University Press.

Parsons, Terence. 1989. "The Progressive in English: Events, States and Processes." *Linguistics and Philosophy* 12 (2): pp. 213–241.

Peacocke, Christopher. 2009. "Mental Action and Self-Awareness: Epistemology." In *Mental Actions*, edited by Lucy O'Brien and Matthew Soteriou. Oxford: Oxford University Press, pp. 192–214.

Peels, Rik. 2016. *Responsible Belief: A Theory in Ethics and Epistemology.* Oxford: Oxford University Press.

Peirce, Charles. 1877. "The Fixation of Belief." *Popular Science Monthly* 12: pp. 1–15.

Peirce, Charles. 1931–1958. *Collected Papers of Charles Sanders Peirce*, edited by Charles Hartshorne, Paul Weiss, and Arthur W. Burks. Cambridge, MA: Harvard University Press.

Percival, Philip. 2003. "The Pursuit of Epistemic Good." *Metaphilosophy* 34 (1–2): pp. 29–47.

Pérez Carballo, Alejandro, and Paolo Santorio. 2016. "Communication for Expressivists." *Ethics* 126 (3): pp. 607–635.

Perrine, Timothy. 2017. "Epistemic Value and Accurate Representation." PhD Dissertation, Indiana University.

Pettit, Philip. 1997. *Republicanism: A Theory of Freedom and Government.* Oxford: Oxford University Press.

Pettit, Philip. 2012. *On the People's Terms: A Republican Theory and Model of Democracy.* Cambridge: Cambridge University Press.

Phillips, John. 2020. "Belief and Cognitive Agency: Making Room for Epistemic Normativity." PhD Dissertation, University of North Carolina at Chapel Hill.

Plantinga, Alvin. 1993a. *Warrant: The Current Debate.* New York: Oxford.

Plantinga, Alvin. 1993b. *Warrant and Proper Function.* New York: Oxford University Press.

Plunkett, David, and Timothy Sundell. 2013. "Disagreement and the Semantics of Normative and Evaluative Terms." *Philosophers' Imprint* 13 (23): pp. 1–37.

Pollock, John. 1995. *Cognitive Carpentry: A Blueprint for How to Build a Person.* Cambridge, MA: MIT Press.

Pollock, John, and Joseph Cruz. 1999. *Contemporary Theories of Knowledge*. Lanham, MD: Rowman & Littlefield Publishers.
Price, H. H. 1954. "Belief and Will." *Aristotelian Society Supplementary* 28 (1): pp. 1–26.
Price, H. H. 1969. *Belief*. London: Routledge.
Price, Huw. 2004. "Naturalism without Representationalism." In *Naturalism in Question*, edited by David Macarthur and Mario de Caro, pp. 71–88. Cambridge, MA: Harvard University Press.
Price, Huw. 2013. "Prospects for Global Expressivism." in *Expressivism, Pragmatism and Representationalism*, edited by Huw Price, pp. 147–194. Cambridge: Cambridge University Press.
Price, Huw, and David Mcarthur. 2007. "Pragmatism, Quasi-Realism, and the Global Challenge." In *New Pragmatists*, edited by Cheryl Misak, pp. 91–121. Oxford: Oxford University Press.
Pritchard, Duncan. 2007. "Recent Work on Epistemic Value." *American Philosophical Quarterly* 44 (2): pp. 85–110.
Pritchard, Duncan. 2008. "McDowellian Neo-Mooreanism." In *Disjunctivism: Perception, Action, Knowledge*, edited by Fiona Macpherson and Adrian Haddock, pp. 283–310. Oxford: Oxford University Press.
Pritchard, Duncan. 2009. "Apt Performance and Epistemic Value." *Philosophical Studies* 143 (3): pp. 407–416.
Pritchard, Duncan. 2010. "The Value of Knowledge." In *The Nature and Value of Knowledge*, by Adrian Haddock, Alan Millar, and Duncan Pritchard, pp. 6–26. Oxford: Oxford University Press.
Pritchard, Duncan. 2012. *Epistemological Disjunctivism*. Oxford: Oxford University Press.
Putnam, Hilary. 1975. *Mind, Language, and Reality*. Cambridge: Cambridge University Press.
Quine, W. V. 1969. "Epistemology Naturalized." In *Ontological Relativity and Other Essays*. New York: Columbia University Press.
Quine, W. V. 1986. "Reply to Morton White." In *The Philosophy of W. V. Quine*, edited by L. E. Hahn and P. A. Schilpp, pp. 663–665. La Salle, IL: Open Court.
Queloz, Matthieu. 2021. *The Practical Origins of Ideas: Genealogy as Conceptual Reverse-Engineering*. Oxford: Oxford University Press.
Radcliffe, Dana. 1997. "Scott-Kakures on Believing at Will." *Philosophy and Phenomenological Research* 57 (1): pp. 145–151.
Raz, Joseph. 1997. "When We Are Ourselves: The Active and the Passive." *Supplement to Proceedings of the Aristotelian Society* 71: pp. 211–227.
Reisner, Andrew. 2018. "Pragmatic Reasons for Belief." In *The Oxford Handbook of Reasons and Normativity*, edited by Daniel Star, pp. 705–729. Oxford: Oxford University Press.
Reisner, Andrew. Unpublished. *The Pragmatic Foundations of Theoretical Reason*.
Reynolds, Steven. 2002. "Testimony, Knowledge, and Epistemic Goals." *Philosophical Studies* 110 (2): pp. 139–161.
Reynolds, Steven. 2017. *Knowledge as Acceptable Testimony*. New York: Cambridge University Press.
Ridge, Michael. 2006. "Ecumenical Expressivism: Finessing Frege." *Ethics* 116 (2): pp. 302–336.
Ridge, Michael. 2007. "Epistemology for Ecumenical Expressivists." *Aristotelian Society Supplementary* 81 (1): pp. 83–108.
Ridge, Michael. 2014. *Impassioned Belief*. Oxford: Oxford University Press.

Ridge, Michael. 2018. "How to Be an Epistemic Expressivist." In *Metaepistemology*, edited by Conor McHugh, Jonathan Way, and Daniel Whiting, pp.141–158. Oxford: Oxford University Press.
Rieber, Steven. 1998. "Skepticism and Contrastive Explanation." *Noûs* 32 (2): pp. 189–204
Riggs, Wayne. 2002a. "Beyond Truth and Falsehood: The Real Value of Knowing That P." *Philosophical Studies* 107 (1): pp. 87–108.
Riggs, Wayne. 2002b. "Reliability and the Value of Knowledge." *Philosophy and Phenomenological Research* 64 (1): pp. 79–96.
Riggs, Wayne. 2003. "Balancing our Epistemic Ends." *Noûs* 37 (2): pp. 342–352.
Riggs, Wayne. 2007. "The Value Turn in Epistemology." In *New Waves in Epistemology*, edited by Vincent Hendricks and Duncan Pritchard, pp. 300--323. London: Palgrave Macmillan.
Rinard, Susanna. 2018. "Believing for Practical Reasons." *Noûs* 53 (4): pp. 763–784.
Rinard, Susanna. 2019. "Equal Treatment for Belief," *Philosophical Studies* 176 (7): pp. 1923–1950.
Rohrbaugh, Guy. 2015. "Inner Achievements." *Erkenntnis* 80 (6): pp. 1191–1204.
Rorty, Richard. 1979. *Philosophy and the Mirror of Nature*. Princeton, NJ: Princeton University Press.
Rorty, Richard. 1995 "Is Truth a Goal of Enquiry? Davidson vs. Wright." *Philosophical Quarterly* 45: pp. 281–300.
Rosenberg, Jay. 1974. *Linguistic Representation*. Dordrecht: D. Reidel.
Rosenberg, Jay. 1976. "The Concept of Linguistic Correctness." *Philosophical Studies: An International Journal for Philosophy in the Analytic Tradition* 30 (3): pp. 171–184.
Rosenberg, Jay. 2002. *Thinking about Knowing*. Oxford: Clarendon Press.
Rosenberg, Jay. 2007. *Wilfrid Sellars: Fusing the Images*. Oxford: Oxford University Press.
Roth, Abraham. 2003. "Practical Intersubjectivity." In *Socializing Metaphysics: The Nature of Social Reality*, edited by Frederick Schmitt, pp. 65–91. Oxford: Rowman & Littlefield.
Roth, Abraham. 2004. "Shared Agency and Contralateral Commitments." *Philosophical Review* 113 (3): pp. 359–410.
Roth, Abraham. 2015. "Practical Intersubjectivity and Normative Guidance: Bratman on Shared Agency." *Journal of Social Ontology* 1 (1): pp. 39–48.
Rothstein, Susan. 2004. *Structuring Events*. Oxford: Blackwell.
Rousseau, Jean-Jacques. 1762/2002. *The Social Contract*, edited by Susan Dunn. New Haven, CT: Yale University Press.
Rowland, Richard. 2013. "Moral Error Theory and the Argument from Epistemic Reasons." *Journal of Ethics and Social Philosophy* 7 (1): pp. 1–24.
Ryan, Sharon. 2003. "Doxastic Compatibilism and the Ethics of Belief." *Philosophical Studies* 114 (1–2): pp. 47–79.
Rysiew, Patrick. 2000. "Testimony, Simulation, and the Limits of Inductivism." *Australasian Journal of Philosophy* 78 (2): pp. 269–274.
Rysiew, Patrick. 2001. "The Context-Sensitivity of Knowledge Attributions." *Noûs* 35: pp. 477–514.
Sartwell, Crispin. 1992. "Why Knowledge Is Merely True Belief." *The Journal of Philosophy* 89: pp. 167–180.
Schaffer, Jonathan. 2004. "From Contextualism to Contrastivism." *Philosophical Studies* 119 (1–2): pp. 73–104.
Schiffer, Stephen. 1996. "Contextualist Solutions to Skepticism." *Proceedings of the Aristotelian Society* 96: pp. 317–333.

Schroeder, Mark. 2008a. *Being For: Evaluating the Semantic Program of Expressivism.* New York: Oxford University Press.

Schroeder, Mark. 2008b. "What Is the Frege-Geach Problem?" *Philosophy Compass* 3 (4): pp. 703–720.

Schroeder, Mark. 2009. "Hybrid Expressivism: Virtues and Vices." *Ethics* 119 (2): pp. 257–309.

Schroeder, Mark. 2010. *Noncognitivism in Ethics.* London: Routledge.

Schroeder, Mark. 2011. "Ought, Agents, and Actions." *Philosophical Review* 120 (1): pp. 1–41.

Schroeder, Mark. 2013. "Tempered Expressivism." In *Oxford Studies in Metaethics, vol. 8*, edited by Russ Shafer-Landau, pp. 283–313. Oxford: Oxford University Press.

Schwitzgebel, Eric. 2002. "A Phenomenal, Dispositional Account of Belief." *Noûs* 36 (2): pp. 249–275.

Schwitzgebel, Eric. 2012. "Mad Belief." *Neuroethics* 5 (1): pp. 13–17.

Scott-Kakures, Dion. 1993. "On Belief and the Captivity of the Will." *Philosophy and Phenomenological Research* 54 (4): pp. 77–103.

Searle, John. 1962. "Meaning and Speech Acts." *Philosophical Review* 71 (4): pp. 423–432.

Sellars, Wilfrid. 1953. "Inference and Meaning." *Mind* 62 (247): pp. 313–338.

Sellars, Wilfrid. 1954. "Some Reflections on Language Games." *Philosophy of Science* 21 (3): pp. 204–228.

Sellars, Wilfrid. 1956 "Empiricism and the Philosophy of Mind." In *Minnesota Studies in the Philosophy of Science, vol. 1*, edited by Herbert Feigl and Michael Scriven, pp. 253–329. Minneapolis, MN: University of Minnesota Press.

Sellars, Wilfrid. 1963. "Philosophy and the Scientific Image of Man." In *Science, Perception, and Reality*, pp. 35–78. Atascadero, CA: Ridgeview.

Sellars, Wilfrid. 1963. "Philosophy and the Scientific Image of Man," in *Science, Perception and Reality*, Atascadero, CA: Ridgeview Publishing Company, pp. 8–41.

Sellars, Wilfrid. 1969. "Language as Thought and as Communication." *Philosophy and Phenomenological Research* 24 (4): pp. 506–527.

Sellars, Wilfrid. 1971. "Science, Sense Impressions, and Sensa: A Reply to Cornman." *Review of Metaphysics* 25: pp. 391–447.

Sellars, Wilfrid. 1974. "Meaning as Functional Classification." *Synthese* 27 (3–4): pp. 417–437.

Setiya, Kieran. 2008. "Believing at Will." *Midwest Studies in Philosophy* 32 (1): pp. 36–52.

Setiya, Kieran. 2013. "Epistemic Agency: Some Doubts." *Philosophical Issues* 23 (1): pp. 179–198.

Shah, Nishi. 2003. "How Truth Governs Belief." *The Philosophical Review* 112 (4): pp. 447–482.

Shah, Nishi, and David Velleman. 2005. "Doxastic Deliberation." *The Philosophical Review* 114 (4): pp. 497–534.

Sicha, Jeffrey. 2014. "Defending the Unpopular Sellars: Picturing and 'The Descriptive'." *Journal of Philosophical Research* 39: pp. 127–163.

Sidgwick, Henry. 1874/1907. *The Methods of Ethics, 7th edition,* London: Macmillan.

Simion, Mona. 2019. "Knowledge-First Functionalism." *Philosophical Issues* 29 (1): pp. 254–267.

Simion, Mona. 2025. *Knowledge-First Epistemology: A Defence.* Cambridge: Cambridge University Press.

Simion, Mona, Christoph Kelp, and Harmen Ghijsen. 2016. "Norms of Belief." *Philosophical Issues* 26 (1): pp. 374–392.

Sinclair, Neil. 2006. "The Moral Belief Problem." *Ratio* 19 (2): pp. 249–260.

Sinclair, Neil. 2017. "Reasons Internalism and the Function of Normative Reasons." *Dialectica* 71 (2): pp. 209–229.
Sinclair, Neil. 2021. *Practical Expressivism*. Oxford: Oxford University Press.
Sinnott-Armstrong, Walter. 1984. "'Ought' Conversationally Implies 'Can'." *The Philosophical Review* 93 (2): pp. 249–261.
Sloman, Steven. 1996. "The Empirical Case for Two Systems of Reasoning." *Psychological Bulletin*, 119: pp. 3–22.
Smith, Angela. 2005. "Responsibility for Attitudes: Activity and Passivity in Mental Life." *Ethics* 115 (2): pp. 236–271.
Sosa, Ernest. 2003. "Beyond Internal Foundations to External Virtues." In *Epistemic Justification: Internalism vs. Externalism, Foundations vs. Virtues*, by Laurence BonJour and Ernest Sosa, pp. 97–170. Malden, MA: Blackwell.
Sosa, Ernest. 2007. *A Virtue Epistemology: Apt Belief and Reflective Knowledge, vol. 1*. New York: Oxford University Press.
Sosa, Ernest. 2010. "How Competence Matters in Epistemology." *Philosophical Perspectives* 24: pp. 465–476.
Sosa, Ernest. 2011a. *Knowing Full Well*. Princeton, NJ: Princeton University Press.
Sosa, Ernest. 2011b. "Value Matters in Epistemology." *Journal of Philosophy* 108 (4): pp. 167–190
Sosa, Ernest. 2015. *Judgment and Agency*. Oxford: Oxford University Press.
Sosa, Ernest. 2016. "Process Reliabilism and Virtue Epistemology." In *Goldman and his Critics*, edited by Hilary Kornblith and Brian McLaughlin, pp. 125–148. Walden, MA: Blackwell.
Sosa, Ernest. 2019. "Animal versus Reflective Orders of Epistemic Competence." In *Thinking about Oneself*, edited by Luca Tateo and Waldomiro Silva-Filho, pp. 21–32. Cham, Switzerland: Springer Verlag.
Soteriou, Matthew. 2005. "Mental Action and the Epistemology of Mind." *Noûs* 39 (1): pp. 83–105.
Soteriou, Matthew. 2013. *The Mind's Construction: The Ontology of Mind and Mental Action*. Oxford: Oxford University Press.
Srinivasan, Amia. 2020. "Radical Externalism." *Philosophical Review* 129 (3): pp. 395–431.
Stanley, Jason. 2004. "On the Linguistic Basis for Contextualism." *Philosophical Studies* 119: pp. 119–146.
Stanley, Jason. 2005. *Knowledge and Practical Interests*. Oxford: Oxford University Press.
Stanovich, Keith. 1999. *Who Is Rational? Studies of Individual Differences in Reasoning*. Mahwah, NJ: Erlbaum.
Stanovich, Keith. 2011. *Rationality and the Reflective Mind*. New York: Oxford University Press.
Stanovich, Keith, and Richard West. 2000. "Individual Differences in Reasoning: Implications for the Rationality Debate." *Behavioral and Brain Sciences* 23: pp. 645–726.
Steglich-Petersen, Asbjørn. 2006. "No Norm Needed: On the Aim of Belief." *Philosophical Quarterly* 56 (225): pp. 499–516.
Steglich-Petersen, Asbjørn. 2011. "How to Be a Teleologist about Epistemic Reasons." In *Reasons for Belief*, edited by Asbjørn Steglich-Petersen and Andrew Reisner, pp. 13–33. Cambridge: Cambridge University Press.
Steglich-Petersen, Asbjørn. 2018. "Epistemic Instrumentalism, Permission, and Reasons for Belief." In *Normativity: Epistemic and Practical*, edited by Conor McHugh, Jonathan Way, and Daniel Whiting, pp. 260–280. Oxford: Oxford University Press.

Steup, Matthais. 2000. "Doxastic Voluntarism and Epistemic Deontology." *Acta Analytica*, 15 (24): pp. 25–56.
Steup, Matthais. 2008. "Doxastic Freedom." *Synthese* 161 (3): pp. 375–392.
Steup, Matthias. 2017. "Believing Intentionally." *Synthese* 194 (8): pp. 2673–2694.
Steup, Matthias. 2012. "Belief Control and Intentionality." *Synthese* 188 (2): pp. 145–163.
Steward, Helen. 1997. *The Ontology of Mind: Events, Processes, and States*. Oxford: Oxford University Press.
Stich, Stephen. 1990. *The Fragmentation of Reason: Preface to a Pragmatic Theory of Cognitive Evaluation*. Cambridge, MA: MIT Press.
Stine, Gail. 1976. "Skepticism, Relevant Alternatives, and Deductive Closure." *Philosophical Studies* 29 (4): pp. 249–261.
Stocker, Michael. 1971. "'Ought' and 'Can'." *Australasian Journal of Philosophy* 44 (3): pp. 313–317.
Strawson, Galen. 2003. "Mental Ballistics or the Involuntariness of Spontaneity." *Proceedings of the Aristotelian Society* 103 (3): pp. 227–256.
Street, Sharon. 2010. "What Is Constructivism in Ethics and Metaethics?" *Philosophy Compass* 5 (5): pp. 363–384.
Stroud, Barry. 1977. *Hume*. London: Routledge.
Sullivan-Bissett, Ema. 2017. "Biological Function and Epistemic Normativity." *Philosophical Explorations* 20 (1): pp. 94–110.
Tang, Weng Hong. 2016. "Reliabilism and the Suspension of Belief." *Australasian Journal of Philosophy* 94 (2): pp. 362–377.
Teichmann, Roger. 2015. "Why 'Why?'? Action, Reasons and Language." *Philosophical Investigations* 38 (1–2): pp. 115–132.
Thompson, Michael. 2008. "Naive Action Theory." In *Life and Action*. Cambridge, MA: Harvard University Press.
Tiefensee, Christine. 2016. "Inferentialist Metaethics, Bifurcations and Ontological Commitment." *Philosophical Studies* 173 (9): pp. 2437–2459.
Timmons, Mark. 1999. *Morality without Foundations: A Defense of Ethical Contextualism*. Oxford: Oxford University Press.
Toppinen, Teemu. 2013. "Believing in Expressivism." *Oxford Studies in Metaethics, vol. 8*, edited by Russ Shafer-Landau, pp. 253–283. Oxford: Oxford University Press.
Toppinen, Teemu. 2017. "Hybrid Accounts of Ethical Thought and Talk." In *The Routledge Handbook of Metaethics*, edited by Tristram McPherson and David Plunkett, pp. 243–259. London: Routledge.
Turner, Piers. 2004. "Epistemic Deontology and the Consequentialist Consensus." M.A. Thesis, University of North Carolina, at Chapel Hill.
Turri, John. 2011. "Manifest Failure: The Gettier Problem Solved." *Philosophers' Imprint* 11 (8): pp. 1–11.
Turri, John. 2017. "Epistemic Contextualism: An Idle Hypothesis." *Australasian Journal of Philosophy* 95 (1): pp. 141–156.
Tversky, Amos, and Daniel Kahneman. 1973. "Availability: A Heuristic for Judging Frequency and Probability." *Cognitive Psychology* 5 (2): pp. 207–232.
Umbach, Carla. 2016. "Evaluative Propositions and Subjective Judgments." In *Subjective Meaning: Alternatives to Relativism*, edited by Cécile Meier and Janneke van Wijnbergen-Huitink, pp. 127–168. Berlin: De Gruyter.
Unger, Peter. 1975. *Ignorance: A Case for Scepticism*. Oxford: Oxford University Press.
Vahid, Hamid. 2009. *The Epistemology of Belief*. London: Palgrave Macmillan.
van Roojen, Mark. 2015. *Metaethics: A Contemporary Introduction*. London: Routledge.

van Voorst, Jan. 1992. "The Aspectual Semantics of Psychological Verbs." *Linguistics and Philosophy* 15 (1): pp. 65–92.
Velleman, David. 2000. "On the Aim of Belief." In *The Possibility of Practical Reason* pp. 123–143. New York: Oxford University Press.
Vendler, Zeno. 1957. "Verbs and Times." *Philosophical Review* 66 (2): pp. 143–160.
Vierkant, Tillman. 2022. *The Tinkering Mind*. Oxford: Oxford University Press.
Warren, Mark. 2015. "Moral Inferentialism and the Frege-Geach Problem." *Philosophical Studies* 172 (11): pp. 2859–2885.
Watson, Gary. 1996. "Two Faces of Responsibility." *Philosophical Topics* 24 (2): pp. 227–248.
Weatherson, Brian. 2008. "Deontology and Descartes's Demon." *Journal of Philosophy* 105 (9): pp. 540–569.
Wedgwood, Ralph. 2002. "The Aim of Belief." *Philosophical Perspectives* 16 (16): pp. 267–297.
Wedgwood, Ralph. 2007. *The Nature of Normativity*. Oxford: Oxford University Press.
Whiting, Daniel. 2012. "Does Belief Aim (Only) at the Truth?" *Pacific Philosophical Quarterly* 93 (2): pp. 279–300.
Wiland, Eric. 2012. *Reasons*. Vancouver: Continuum.
Wilkinson, Sam. 2013. "The Status of Delusion in the Light of Marcus's Revisionary Proposals." *Theoria: An International Journal for Theory, History and Foundations of Science* 2 8(3): pp. 421–436.
Wilkinson, Sam. 2014. "Levels and Kinds of Explanation: Lessons from Neuropsychiatry." *Frontiers in Psychology* 5: pp. 1–9.
Willer, Malte. 2017. "Advice for Noncognitivists." *Pacific Philosophical Quarterly* 98 (S1): 174–207.
Williams, Bernard. 1973. "Deciding to Believe." In *Problems of the Self: Philosophical Papers, 1956–1972*, pp. 136–151. Cambridge: Cambridge University Press.
Williams, Bernard. 1981. "Ought and Obligation." In *Moral Luck*, pp. 114–123. Oxford: Oxford University Press.
Williams, Bernard. 2002. *Truth and Truthfulness: An Essay in Genealogy*. Princeton, NJ: Princeton University Press.
Williams, Michael. 1999. "Meaning and Deflationary Truth." *The Journal of Philosophy* 96 (11): pp. 545–564.
Williams, Michael. 2001. *Problems of Knowledge: A Critical Introduction to Epistemology*. Oxford: Oxford University Press.
Williams, Michael. 2004. "Context, Meaning, and Truth." *Philosophical Studies: An International Journal for Philosophy in the Analytic Tradition* 117 (1–2): pp. 107–30.
Williams, Michael. 2010. "Pragmatism, Minimalism, Expressivism." *International Journal of Philosophical Studies* 18 (3): pp. 317–330.
Williams, Michael. 2013. "How Pragmatists Can Be Local Expressivists." In *Expressivism, Pragmatism and Representationalism*, edited by Huw Price, pp. 128–144. Cambridge: Cambridge University Press.
Williamson, Timothy. 2000. *Knowledge and its Limits*. Oxford: Oxford University Press.
Williamson, Timothy. 2005a. "Contextualism, Subject-Sensitive Invariantism, and Knowledge of Knowledge." *Philosophical Quarterly* 55 (219): pp. 213–235.
Williamson, Timothy. 2005b. "Knowledge, Context, and the Agent's Point of View." In *Contextualism in Philosophy*, edited by Gerhard Preyer and Georg Peter, pp. 91–114. Oxford: Oxford University Press.

Woods, Jack. 2017. "The Frege-Geach Problem." In *The Routledge Handbook of Metaethics*, edited by Tristram McPherson and David Plunkett, pp. 226–242. London: Routledge.

Wrenn, Chase. 2006. "Epistemology as Engineering?" *Theoria* 72 (1): pp. 60–79.

Wright, Crispin. 2005. "Contextualism and Scepticism: Even-Handedness, Factivity and Surreptitiously Raising the Standards." *Philosophical Quarterly* 55: pp. 236–262.

Yalcin, Seth. 2012. "Bayesian Expressivism." *Proceedings of the Aristotelian Society* 112 (2pt2): pp. 123–160.

Yalcin, Seth. 2018. "Expressivism by Force." In *New Work on Speech Acts*, edited by D. Fogal, D. Harris, and M. Moss, pp. 401–430. Oxford: Oxford University Press.

Young, Iris Marion. 1990. *Justice and the Politics of Difference*. Princeton, NJ: Princeton University Press.

Young, Iris Marion. 2006. "Responsibility and Global Justice: A Social Connection Model." *Social Philosophy and Policy* 23: pp. 102–130

Zagzebski, Linda. 2003. "The Search for the Source of Epistemic Good." *Metaphilosophy* 34 (1–2): pp. 12–28.

Zagzebski, Linda. 1996. *Virtues of the Mind: An Inquiry Into the Nature of Virtue and the Ethical Foundations of Knowledge*, Cambridge: Cambridge University Press.

Zangwill, Nick. 2005. "The Normativity of the Mental." *Philosophical Explorations* 8 (1): pp. 1–19.

Zangwill, Nick. 2011. "Noncognitivism and Consistency." *Zeitschrift für Philosophische Forschung* 65 (4): pp. 465–484.

Zangwill, Nick. 2021. "Expressivism, Inferentialism and the Simulation Game." *Philosophy and Phenomenological Research*.

Zimmerman, Aaron. 2018. *Belief: A Pragmatic Picture*. New York: Oxford University Press.

Index

For the benefit of digital users, indexed terms that span two pages (e.g., 52–53) may, on occasion, appear on only one of those pages.

achievement, *see* Vendler–Kenny typology
action norms 10, 99n.11, 100n.12, 102, 105–6, 110–13, 149
   conditional view of 107
   existential view of 107
   material implications of 106–7
   universal view of 107
   see also state norms
activities 2–3, 8–10, 25, 29–32, 38, 48–9, 56–7, 61–3, 69, 71–2, 83, 90, 93–5, 124; *see also* aspectual classification of verb phrases; belief system maintenance
active states 58–63, 65, 69, 71, 113
addiction, state of 60, 69
aim of belief 9–10, 32–4, 64, 66, 81–2, 98
   radical argument against truth as 82–92
   truth as constitutive of 93–5, 97, 124–5
   vs. end of belief 90, 92
   vs. regulative goal of belief 89, 91–2, 120
Alston, William 39–40, 101, 104
antirepresentationalism, *see* nondescriptivism
Anscombe, G. E. M. 57, 73n.1
anxiety, state of 60, 69
aptness, *see* performance normativity
archery 22, 27
aspectual classification of verb phrases 24–6, 32, 38, 48, 61–3, 67, 112
axiological dimensions of epistemic normativity, *see* epistemic normativity

barn façade case 45–7; *see also* belief-formation
basing 67–9, 76n.26, 93, 119, 121, 133, 186
Bayesian updating; *see* cognitive processes
belief-desire rationalization of action 46, 56, 64–7, 135–6
belief-formation 8–9, 33–4, 38–49, 63, 67–8, 101, 115n.1, 118n.20, 119–20, 149; *see also* inquiry; deliberation
belief-system maintenance 65–72, 93–8, 109–13, 119–20, 135–40, 149–50
   as atelic 8–11, 29–32, 48, 53n.29, 67–71, 92; *see also* activities; aim of belief
   as involving basing on other beliefs, *see* basing

dispositional aspect of 8–11, 46–7, 67, 72; *see also* dispositional belief
interpersonal aspects of 9–11, 65–7, 97, 149–50
role of memory in 8–9, 42, 45, 48; *see also* cognitive processes
sustaining processes in 41–2, 48–9, 67, 120–1
BonJour, Laurence 81–2
Boyle, Matthew 56–60, 63, 113
brain-in-a-vat 137–8, 151
Brandom, Robert 173–4

Cartesian tradition 11, 21, 55, 113
categorical normative force, *see* epistemic norms
Clifford, W. K. 128, 132–3, 138
cognitive performances in belief-formation, *see* cognitive processes
cognitive and noncognitive attitudes 150, 165–6; *see also* expressivism
cognitive processes 21, 23, 40, 48, 164
   automatic 44, 55, 63, 65
   Bayesian updating 72
   bias in 6, 11
   dual-system 17n.6
   role of memory in 8–9
   role of perception in 42, 44
   unconscious, tacit 45, 119
   see also cognitive activity
Cohen, Stewart 152, 155
constitutive aims; *see* aim of belief
constitutivism about epistemic normativity 73n.6, 124–5, 134–5
constructivists methodology 13–14, 56, 184
contextualism, *see* epistemic contextualism
Craig, E. J. 12–14, 56, 113, 184–5

Davidson, Donald 83, 87
deliberation, *see* inquiry
deontological dimensions of epistemic normativity; *see* epistemic normativity
DeRose, Keith 154–5, 167
descriptivism, *see* nondescriptivism
dialectical intuitions problem, *see* contextualism

dispositions to believe 53n.23
dispositional belief 46, 64
doxastic agency:
   belief-formation as primary exercise of *see* belief-formation
   belief-system maintenance as primary exercise of, *see* belief-system maintenance
   Cartesian view of, *see* Cartesian tradition
   first-personal vs. third-personal approaches to 16, 66
   first-personal-plural and second-personal approaches to 71
   individualistic accounts of 120, 186
   performance view of, *see* performance normativity
   active state view of, *see* active states
doxastic freedom, *see* freedom
dual system views, *see* cognitive agency

empirical conditions of subjectivity 5, 55–6, 68, 72, 81
enérgeiai vs. *kinēsis* 36n.8, 58–9, 74n.13
enduring acts, beliefs as 60–1
etiology of belief, *see* belief-formation
epistemic anarchy 141–2; *see also* freedom
epistemic atomism 59
epistemic community 69–72, 120–1, 149, 186
   commitments to members of 4, 9, 102, 111–13, 121
   connection to political community 95–7, 126–31, 137
   distributed credit within 1–2, 142
   importance of testimonial sharing for 72, 129, 133
   participation in 11, 97, 135–6, 163–4
   free-riders in 128–30, 136
   Hobbesian conception of 126–30; *see also* social basis for epistemic normativity
   joint projects in 140
   nonhuman animals as part of 9, 124–5, 128, 132, 135–6
   reciprocal recognition in 126–8, 137
   role of instruction in 112–14
   Rousseauian conception of 130–5; *see also* social basis for epistemic normativity
   young children as part of 68–9, 112, 124–5, 128, 132, 135–6
epistemic contextualism 151–8, 162, 164–6, 182–3
   dialectical intuitions problem for 154
   ad hoc semantics problem for 156
epistemic domination 141–2; *see also* freedom
epistemic expressivism; *see* expressivism

epistemic normativity principle 101–2, 105, 109, 113
epistemic norms
   bio-functional accounts of 12–13, 95, 112
   categoricity of 1–2, 5–6, 10–11, 43–4, 103–10, 123–5, 137–40, 172, 185
   evidentialist vs. reliabilist versions of 120–1, 164
   as based in individual interests 122–7, 129, 137–8, 172
   reasonableness and reliability as 120–6, 128–30, 134–7, 140
   truth as constitutive, *see* aim of belief
   truth as evaluative, *see* aim of belief
epistemic normativity:
   axiological questions about 2–7, 9, 23, 31, 42, 72, 112–14, 149–50, 184–5
   deontological questions about 2–7, 23, 31–2, 34, 58–9, 70, 97, 102–4, 112, 185
   deflationary view of 7, 34, 107
epistemic responsibility; *see* responsibility
essential function, appeal to, *see* value of knowledge
ethical speaker-relativism 156–61
evidentialism, *see* epistemic norms
expressivism 12
   cognitive and noncognitive attitudes distinction in 150, 165–6
   ethical 150–1, 158–61
   epistemic 161–6, 176–83

Feldman, Richard 50n.3, 50n.5, 103–4, 109–10
forgotten evidence 41, 45, 47; *see also* belief-formation
Frege-Geach problem 165, 172–3
free riders, *see* epistemic community
freedom 51n.7, 117n.18, 139–43
   anarchy as a form of, doxastic 141–2
   socio-political 126–7, 131

genealogical method viii, 184–5
Gettier cases 23, 52n.21
Gibbard, Alan 159, 165–6
Greco, John 43–9
Goldman, Alvin 48, 144n.15

here-and-now aspects of normative evaluation 31–2, 38, 45–6, 58
Hieronymi, Pamela 56–9
Hobbes, Thomas 121, 126–31, 137–8, *see also* social basis for epistemic normativity
hypothetical normative force, *see* epistemic norms

ideal of truth, *see* aim of belief
ideals:
    epistemic, *see* aim of belief
    moral 104–5, 110
implicit reasoning, *see* cognitive processes
improved evidence, *see* barn façade case
inferentialism 173–83; *see also* descriptivism vs. nondescriptivism
inquiry 8–9, 72, 112, 114, 181
    as agential 38–40, 58–9
    as performance 39–43
    in belief-formation 39–43, 65, 91
    in belief-system maintenance 149
    norms of 72, 112, 114, 163
instruction 112–14; *see also* epistemic community
instrumental value, *see* value of knowledge
interdependence, *see* epistemic community
internalism:
    about motivation 180–1
    about justification 14, 164
International Klein Blue 46–7
introspection 1, 77n.33
invariantism 151, 158
involuntarism about belief, *see* doxastic agency
is-ought divide 11–12, 15

joint action, *see* epistemic community

kinēsis, see *enérgeiai* vs. *kinēsis*
knowledge economy 114, 163–4
knowledge-first epistemology 123–4
Kornblith, Hilary 103–5, 110

linguistic intuitions 30, 152–3, 156–7, 161
linguistic rules 106–10, 173–4
live motionless statues, *see* performance normativity
Lockie, Robert 40

manifest image of reality 15–16; *see also* Sellars
McCormick, Miriam Schleifer 51n.7
McHugh, Conor 51n.7, 76n.31, 94–5
memory, *see* cognitive processes
Meno 16n.1, 114
motive vs. goal 90–1
Meylan, Anne 40
Moran, Richard 56–7, 67
mutual recognition, *see* epistemic community

naturalism, *see* philosophical naturalism
nature of performances, *see* performance normativity
no rewards principle 101–2, 104–5, 109–10, 113
nondescriptivism 11–12, 150, 158–9, 161, 172–3, 176, 181–3

nonhuman animals as knowers, *see* epistemic community
nonstative verb categories 25, 27, 29

object naturalism, *see* philosophical naturalism
occurrences, *see* nonstative verb categories
occurrentism about belief 64
ought-implies-can 102, 105, 108, 111
ought-to-do, *see* action norms

Peirce, Charles S. 61, 173–6
perception 1, 23–4, 42, 44–5, 67; *see also* cognitive processes
performance, belief as 22–32, 34; *see also* virtue epistemology; state view of belief; performance normativity
performance normativity 21–2, 32, 38, 43, 58
    live motionless statues as illustration of 31–2, 48
    applied to sustaining beliefs 48–9
    see also Sosa; virtue epistemology
philosophical naturalism 3, 7, 15–16
    object naturalism
    role in motivating nondescriptivism 172
    subject naturalism 4, 12–13
Plantinga, Alvin 17n.5, 104
practical syllogism 91–3
preservationism about memory 48
processes, *see* nonstative verb categories

Quine, W. V. 7, 81–2

rationalizing explanations 46, 67, 135–6
reasons-responsiveness 21, 64, 69, 140–1
reflective equilibrium 14
relativism, *see* contextualism
reliabilism:
    process 48
    virtue 38–9
    see also epistemic norms
representationalism, *see* descriptivism
responsibility 50, 117n.18, 118n.21, 139–43
    epistemic 53n.25, 76n.31
role 'ought's 103–5
Rorty, Richard 83, 87–8, 92, 183–4
Rosenberg, Jay 82–95, 143n.3, 173–4
Rousseau, Jean-Jacques 130–7, *see also* social basis for epistemic normativity
rules of action, *see* action norms
rules of criticism, *see* state norms

Sellars, Wilfrid 14–16, 56, 105–13, 150, 173–5, 184–5
scientific conception of reality, *see* philosophical naturalism

self-determination, belief as act of 56–61
skeptical argument schema 151
skill, *see* performance normativity
social basis for epistemic normativity 11, 95, 113, 139–40, 149
   Hobbesian account of 126–30
   Rousseauian account of 130–9
Sosa, Ernest 21–4, 27–8, 30–4, 44, 48, 52n.21
space of reasons 14, 56, 113, 171n.32, 175, 185
   as evaluative stance, *see* knowledge attributions
stereoscopic vision 15–16
subject naturalism; *see* philosophical naturalism
success, *see* performance normativity
sustaining processes 41–2, 48–9, 132

testimony 8–9, 35n.4, 112
   role in epistemic community 119, 127–8, 133, *see also* epistemic community
telic vs. atelic 53n.29, 61–2, 67, 76n.25; *see also* aim of belief
theories of meaning 4, 187
truth as aim of belief, *see* aim of belief

unimodal perception, *see* cognitive processes

value of knowledge 31, 65, 98, 155, 172, 184
   as deriving from the essential function of belief 125
   as instrumental 122–3
   as grounded in social relations 114, 128, 134
   as objective 123–4
   as related to its stability 31, 34, 98, 114
   pragmatist approach to explaining 184
   see also axiological dimensions of epistemic normativity
Vendler–Kenny typology 25–6
verbal aspect, *see* aspectual classification of verb phrases
view from nowhere, *see* philosophical naturalism
virtue epistemology 21–4, 28, 31–2, 43–9, 65–6
   skillful belief according to, *see* performance normativity
   successful belief according to, *see* performance normativity
voluntarism about belief, *see* doxastic agency

Williams, Bernard 17n.5, 63, 70, 115n.1
Williams, Michael 173–4

young children as knowers, *see* epistemic community

The manufacturer's authorised representative in the EU for product safety is
Oxford University Press España S.A. of el Parque Empresarial San Fernando de
Henares, Avenida de Castilla, 2 – 28830 Madrid (www.oup.es/en or product.
safety@oup.com). OUP España S.A. also acts as importer into Spain of products
made by the manufacturer.

www.ingramcontent.com/pod-product-compliance
Ingram Content Group UK Ltd.
Pitfield, Milton Keynes, MK11 3LW, UK
UKHW020926230426
470302UK00019B/140